WHO'S IN CHARGE HERE?

WHO'S IN CHARGE HERE?

The Tangled Web of School Governance and Policy

NOEL EPSTEIN
Editor

EDUCATION COMMISSION OF THE STATES
Denver

BROOKINGS INSTITUTION PRESS
Washington, D.C.

Copyright © 2004
EDUCATION COMMISSION OF THE STATES

The Library of Congress has cataloged the hardcover edition as follows:
Who's in charge here? : the tangled web of school governance and policy / Noel Epstein, editor.
   p.   cm.
Includes index.
ISBN 0-8157-2472-1 (cloth : alk. paper)
  1. School boards—United States. 2. Education and state—United States. I. Epstein, Noel. II.
Title.
LB2831.W53 2004
379.1'531—dc22   2004016556
          ISBN-13: 978-0-8157-2471-1(pbk : alk. paper)
          ISBN-10: 0-8157-2471-3

First paperback edition August 2006

2 4 6 8 9 7 5 3 1

The paper used in this publication meets minimum requirements of the American
National Standard for Information Sciences—Permanence of Paper for Printed
Library Materials: ANSI Z39.48-1992.

Typeset in Minion

Composition by Circle Graphics
Columbia, Maryland

Printed by R. R. Donnelley
Harrisonburg, Virginia

Contents

Foreword

The primary role of the Education Commission of the States (ECS) is to assist state policymakers and others in improving K–12 and higher education in the states and in the nation. The publication of this book, making the work accessible to a wide readership, contributes to our efforts to accomplish that goal.

For some time now ECS has focused attention on the governance of education. In doing so, it has joined many other individuals and organizations searching for the best possible structure to meet the needs of high-quality public education. Indeed, our great concern about policy issues surrounding student achievement, the quality of teaching, testing, and the expanding role of schools in our society—all of which are considered here—may best be addressed by improvements in the way we manage education.

Who's in Charge Here? encompasses the clear thinking of some of the finest minds in the field of education and reflects ECS's continuing interest in these important topics. We are proud to have assisted in the development of the individual chapters and to have supported their publication.

TED SANDERS
President, Education Commission of the States
Denver
June 2004

Acknowledgments

The works in this volume would not have been possible without the generous financial support of the William and Flora Hewlett Foundation, the Atlantic Philanthropies, and the Joyce Foundation. At the Education Commission of the States, Ted Sanders, president, and Todd Ziebarth, who managed the project, provided critical guidance and support. Finally, many thanks also go to Strobe Talbott, president of the Brookings Institution, and to Robert Faherty, director of the Brookings Institution Press, and members of his talented team: Christopher Kelaher, Janet Walker, Theresa Walker, Tanjam Jacobson, Susan Woollen, Carlotta Ribar, and Julia Petrakis.

Who's in Charge Here?

1

Introduction:
Who Should Be in Charge of Our Schools?

NOEL EPSTEIN

I t is only common sense that institutions need to have someone in charge, someone who sets goals and strategies and is accountable for results. In business and finance it is the chief executive officer; in the military, the generals and admirals. If one were to sketch an organizational chart of the American elementary and secondary education systems, however, one would discover that there is no such line of responsibility. Instead one would find something closer to a spider's web that has grown increasingly tangled in recent years—a web in which it is difficult, if not impossible, to figure out whether anyone is in charge. This is arguably the most fundamental flaw confronting our schools, with implications for all else that happens (or does not happen) in American public education.

Although Americans rank education as one of their highest priorities, they have little understanding of this central issue, of how this system of tangled authority came to be or what might be done about it. Few are aware, for example, that the nation long ago created a separate government for education, consisting chiefly of state and local education boards and superintendents, or that this was supposed to shield schools from interference by mayors, governors, or other political figures. Nor is it widely appreciated that a transformation—a "revolution," some say[1]—is occurring in this arrangement as the general government reasserts its authority over schools. Governors and state legislators began the process in the 1970s and 1980s with the advent of state academic standards and tests, state takeovers of failing schools, and other policies. Then some mayors began wresting control of struggling local school systems. Now the president and Congress have greatly expanded their reach into U.S. classrooms with the No Child Left Behind Act of 2001 (NCLB), requiring, among other things, annual reading and math tests for all pupils in grades 3 through 8, tougher yardsticks to measure whether they are making sufficient progress, and penalties for schools that persistently fall short.

In light of this, it is not surprising that even knowledgeable observers sometimes scratch their heads over the difficulty of assigning responsibility in the education system. During the 2000 presidential race, for example, when dramatic increases in Washington's role in education were being proposed, one longtime education policymaker said: "Just who is really accountable, and for what? It is confusing enough today with people not being certain if the buck stops with the local school board, the local superintendent, the state legislature, the governor, the state board, the mayor or, in many states, the city/county council."[2]

The organizational chart actually is even more complex than that, not only because of the crisscrossing lines needed to connect a multitude of education programs across government levels, but also because others have an important voice in school affairs. Federal and state courts, for example, obviously have a large say, shaping issues ranging from desegregation to equitable school financing to the treatment of disabled students and language minorities. Outside agencies—various federal and state departments as well as local health groups, community-based organizations, social workers, and others—are engaged in school-based programs aimed at drug and alcohol abuse, school killings, sexually transmitted diseases, and other health and social issues. Education management organizations have emerged to run both traditional public schools and quasi-independent public charter schools, which are part of the broader school choice spectrum that ranges from home schooling to market-based mechanisms like vouchers for private school tuition. (Indeed, some advocates contend that vouchers are needed precisely because our messy democratic governance system makes it impossible for public schools to set and pursue sensible goals.)[3]

As if this were not enough, determining education accountability is further complicated by the fact that the public has scarcely any idea of who holds key education positions. Ted Sanders, president of the Education Commission of the States, was at various times the chief state school officer of Nevada, Illinois, and Ohio. If you ask him how many people in those states ever knew who he was, he replies, "Do you mean other than my wife and children?"[4] As a rule, state boards of education are even less visible to the citizenry, if that is possible, and the public has little interest in local school board elections, with turnouts typically of no more than 15 percent of eligible voters.[5]

Policymakers versus Practitioners

Despite all of the uncertainty about who is charge, however, some things are quite clear about U.S. school governance There is no doubt, for example, that the dominant trend has been to centralize power over education in state and federal hands. While local officials still have important management roles, the erosion of the American tradition of local school control increasingly means that they are implementing other people's goals and priorities.

It also is evident, as Stanford University's Michael Kirst notes in "Turning Points" (chapter 2 of this volume), that shifting school governance is a backdoor way of shifting school policy. Specifically, as trust has dwindled in local school systems' ability to raise student achievement, state and federal officials generally have embraced what are called standards-based reforms—aligning curriculums, teacher standards, and exams with specific academic goals and increasing testing to hold schools accountable—as well school choice programs.

Finally, a central consequence of the shifts in governance is a growing gap between those who make policy and those responsible for results. For example, governors, together with state legislators, have been primary forces in school policy for a generation, and many have won praise for initiatives to raise student achievement. One would be hard pressed, however, to find governors who are blamed when academic weakness continues in the face of their policies. The same holds for presidents. George W. Bush's education plan, for example, was central to his 2000 election victory, and passage of NCLB, which is driving school policy throughout the country, represented his first success in Congress. Yet there is little chance of the president being blamed if students' test scores do not rise appreciably as a result.

Granted, NCLB is being criticized on other grounds—particularly federal meddling and insufficient funding—even by Bush's fellow Republicans. In early 2004, for example, the GOP-controlled Virginia House adopted a resolution, 98 to 1, assailing NCLB requirements as "the most sweeping intrusions into state and local control of education in the history of the United States" and arguing that they would cost Virginia hefty sums.[6] In Utah, the Republican-controlled House adopted a bill refusing to implement NCLB "except where there is adequate federal funding." That approach was modeled on an initiative in Vermont under which several local school districts had already refused NCLB funds, as have several other districts in Connecticut. As of February 2004, about a dozen states were rebelling against the law.[7] Even with these attacks, as well as those by Democratic critics, however, the Bush education program is not expected to play the kind of central role in the 2004 presidential race that it did in 2000.

In short, despite decades of proposed solutions by governors and presidents—including governors like Bill Clinton and George W. Bush who rose to the presidency with important help from education issues—criticism of the schools persists and blame goes to others. With this kind of arrangement, advancing new plans for education might seem like a politician's vision of heaven: it triggers applause, helps to win elections, and carries relatively little risk if conditions show no notable improvement. In fairness, though, that misses the mark. Not only are many political figures genuine in their education concerns and strategies, but, with rare exceptions, they have no direct control over what happens to their policies. The president is not responsible for operating public schools, and governors generally do not control those who implement the policies that they and state legislators fashion. State education departments are run by chief state school officers, who report, as a rule, to state boards of education, not to governors, just as local superintendents in most cases report to separately elected boards of education, not to mayors or county executives. That is how it works when you have two governments.

Winds of Change

Some moves are afoot to correct this situation, to put political figures fully in charge—a step that some of us consider long overdue. The main reasons for having a separate education government, after all, long ago ceased to exist. While a measure of cronyism in school spending may continue no matter who is in charge, jobs for principals and teachers are not going to become prizes of the political spoils system again, as they commonly were at the turn of the twentieth century. Similarly, the old notion that education should be "above politics" is sheer nonsense. Political leaders obviously are deeply involved in—indeed, are dominating—education policies. They just are not accountable for the results (though they consider accountability good for everyone else).

This is beginning to change. In fall 2003, for example, voters in New Mexico approved a constitutional amendment to put the general government back in charge, shifting school control from the state board of education to Governor Bill Richardson.[8] Similarly, in early 2004 Illinois governor Rod Blagojevich caused a stir by proposing to strip authority over the schools from that state's board and put it directly under his control.[9] These steps at the state level come amid local-level transfers of direct school control from boards of education to mayors in a handful of cities, including Boston, Chicago, Cleveland, New York, Detroit, and Harrisburg, Pennsylvania, and efforts by the mayor of the District of Columbia to join the group.[10] In fact, mayors in general are becoming more involved in education, and the public already seems to be holding them accountable. According to the U.S. Conference of Mayors, education has become "a pivotal issue in reelection" even when mayors do not directly control the schools.[11] Perhaps this will encourage more mayors to reach for the school reins, at least in cities in which school dissatisfaction runs high and such control is feasible (though public support for more mayoral takeovers in general currently is low).[12]

Gubernatorial or mayoral control certainly is not a cure-all for education; there are no magic bullets. Some such efforts may well yield poor results, as was long the case when Baltimore's mayor held power over that city's schools.[13] The point is that such direct political control would provide much greater visibility and accountability for academic results, as well as helping with other important challenges, particularly the management of multiplying before-school and after-school programs, school-based health clinics, early childhood initiatives and battles against teen pregnancy, student suicides, and other social ills. State and local boards of education and superintendents simply do not have the cross-agency authority that is needed to coordinate these and other programs for children and youth.

Nor is it a simple matter to hold mayors, governors, or presidents accountable. Though new education policies might be enacted and implemented in a single term of office, for example, they cannot be evaluated in so brief a period; at reelection time, it is not possible to say whether the program at hand is effective or not. Because of this time lag, it would be valuable, at the state and local levels, for any school board that loses control over education not just to become an advisory body but also to issue annual report cards that grade progress under the governor, mayor, or county executives. At the federal level, a similar task might be assigned to an agency like the Government Accountability Office. Such report cards are, after all, essentially what NCLB requires of schools across the nation. It seems only reasonable to apply the idea to the political figures who are shaping U.S. education policy.

One Cannot Rely on the Constitution

While making more prominent political figures accountable for school performance at the federal, state, and local levels would, in my view, be an important step, it would not alter the balance of power over education among levels of government. That was the main issue that prompted the essays in this volume. In particular, the striking increase in the federal role engineered by the Bush administration gave rise to the idea of trying to clarify the responsibilities of all parties in education and of basing the work on the Tenth Amendment to the Constitution, which is cited almost ritually in the education community as evidence that states are in charge of schools. The thought was to prepare papers that would lead, for the first time, to Tenth Amendment guidelines for U.S. school governance.

However, in the scholarly spirit of following the evidence wherever it might lead, one paper swiftly put that idea to rest: "The Tenth Amendment and Other Paper Tigers," by James Ryan of the University of Virginia Law School (chapter 3 in this volume). Among other things, this persuasive work on the porous legal boundaries of school governance makes clear that contrary to common belief the Constitution does not simply leave authority over education to the states or restrain federal power over schools.

True, the Tenth Amendment says that "powers not delegated to the United States, nor prohibited by it to the states, are reserved to the states respectively, or to the people." Since the Constitution is silent on education, the states would seem to be in charge. But that is misleading, Ryan observes, because it overlooks Congress's constitutional power to spend for the general welfare—and to tie conditions to that spending. He states, in fact, that "the Tenth Amendment is no match for Congress's spending powers," that so long as states accept federal education funds, "Congress can do pretty much as it pleases with education, even establish a national curriculum and a national exam, without running afoul of the Constitution."

Some doubtless would like to curtail such congressional power over education, but Ryan warns them to be careful of what they wish for, because the result would not simply be corresponding gains for state or local authorities. An important consequence, he says, would be greater power for federal courts, which would end up making more school decisions than they already do.

If the Constitution cannot be relied on to determine who should be in charge, perhaps history or public opinion might help. Kirst's "Turning Points" (chapter 2) provides an enlightening survey of the historical road that America has traveled, from its original deep distrust of central education authority to today's growing centralization. What does the tale suggest to him? Among other things, he says, if one is concerned about democracy and accountability, "it is local school districts, with all their imperfections, that seem the superior governance choice." But he sees little chance of reversing today's centralizing trend. Nor does he think that much light will be shed on the matter by public opinion, which appears confused about the issue. On the one hand, Kirst notes, the public clings to the belief that local school boards have the most power to improve schools. On the other hand, comfortable majorities support the creation of a national curriculum and nationally standardized tests, which would, of course, drain still more power from already weakened local school systems as well as from state policymakers.

So, is there another principle that might guide education governance? Paul T. Hill of the University of Washington believes that there is. In chapter 4, "Recovering from an Accident," he notes that policymakers must start with a convoluted system that nobody of sound mind would deliberately have created. Standards-based reforms, he adds, have, with few exceptions, simply imposed new requirements atop old ones. What we need to do, he says, is stop reasoning from the Tenth Amendment and substitute other principles—specifically, "subsidiarity" and comparative advantage—to guide school governance. Subsidiarity, an idea little known to Americans but much discussed in the European Community, seeks to have decisions made as closely as possible to the citizen, turning to higher levels only when they can be shown to be more effective. Under this concept, Hill suggests, instead of fretting about constitutional powers, one should ask, "Where is what best done?" After examining the advantages and disadvantages of families, schools, districts, the states, and Washington, Hill suggests focusing on a site-based approach like charter schools, which he has long supported and which he believes can best fulfill the promise of standards-based reforms.

Asking Different Questions

In the spirit of this volume—which is designed not to provide ready-made solutions but to stimulate important debates—others have different answers. Indeed, perhaps more important, they address different questions.

Does the Growing Centralization of Power Rest on a Solid Foundation or on Sand?

Larry Cuban, professor emeritus at Stanford University and a former school superintendent and teacher, takes on that question in chapter 5, "A Solution That Lost Its Problem," and he sees a foundation of sand. Cuban notes that growing state and federal centralization has been driven by business-inspired apprehensions about economic competition, reflected at the federal level in the influential 1983 report *A Nation at Risk*, which mainly grew out of worries that "the Japanese were coming." Today, in light of what subsequently happened to Japan's economy, that fear obviously looks foolish. The United States is still the world's predominant economy and, according to the World Economic Forum, its second most competitive one, after that of Finland ("Thankfully, nobody is warning that the Finns are coming," Cuban says). The evidence is clear, Cuban remarks, that the state of our economy does not depend on student test scores or on U.S. gains or losses in international test comparisons, and that centralizing school power is a mistake that historically has not accomplished much. We need to remember, he says, that schools are far more than employment boot camps and that the only people in education who can improve what students actually learn are those in local school systems.

Are Fears about Federal Control over Education Misplaced?

Susan Fuhrman, dean of the University of Pennsylvania's Graduate School of Education, tackles that question in chapter 6—and tells us, indeed, not to worry so much about federal school dominance. While NCLB asserts a strong new federal role, she says that "historically, Washington has lacked the capacity and the political will required for full enforcement of its policies and that NCLB accountability depends entirely on state enforcement capacity, which is limited at best." So the result is likely to be "Less than Meets the Eye," an observation that has been on the mark in many respects since the chapter was first prepared in mid-2002. Fuhrman sees the American "layer-cake" governance system as inevitable and rejects any definitive sorting of responsibilities as unrealistic. She worries, however, that NCLB may not yield mean-ingful, long-term educational gains. Such improvements, she believes, require adherence to principles ranging from maximum state and local dis-cretion (without compromising program goals) to more investment in the capacities of educators and the systems that support them. Without attention to these and other needs, "policies on standards, assessment, and account-ability are likely to be both constraining, in terms of narrowing options for lower levels of government, and empty, in terms of either enforcement or the promotion of better educational practice and results."

Might an Even Larger Federal Role Be Warranted?

Linda Darling-Hammond of Stanford and Gary Sykes of Michigan State University believe that in at least one area—meeting NCLB's requirement for "highly qualified" teachers—still greater involvement by Washington is indeed required. In "A Teacher Supply Policy for Education" (chapter 7), they note that just as U.S. medical manpower programs support the train-ing and placement of doctors where there are shortages, so Washington needs to help states and districts provide well-qualified teachers for hard-to-staff schools. It is important to understand, Darling-Hammond and Sykes say, that the nation in general is oversupplied with qualified teachers—but not in the classrooms of poor, minority, and low-achieving students, where they are most needed. These shortages stem heavily from the exodus of young teachers from classrooms, with low-income schools suffering teacher turnover rates as much as 50 percent higher than more affluent ones. This problem cannot be solved, the authors argue, with "quick fix" alternate certification programs that send people from other fields into difficult schools with little training in how to teach or manage children. On the contrary, teachers from such programs—which have supporters in high places, including the U.S. Department of Education—commonly become part of the revolving-door problem that plagues disadvantaged schools and costs the nation billions of dollars a year.

When it comes to helping the needy, Darling-Hammond and Sykes, like other contributors to this volume, see important differences between NCLB's promise and its reality. Over a dozen years, that law seeks to nar-row the achievement gap between more privileged children and poor racial and ethnic minorities, the disabled, and limited-English-proficient (LEP) students. It states at the outset that it does not expect "to close the achieve-ment gap," but to reduce it to the point where all groups reach state-defined "proficient" levels on state reading and math exams.[14] This is a daunting enough goal—one that many educators, in fact, consider unrealistic for special education and LEP students—and Washington consequently eased some standards for these students.[15] But Darling-Hammond and Sykes say that it will be impossible for NCLB's goals to be attained by poor minority children, let alone by disabled and LEP students, unless they have the well-prepared teachers who are critical to student learning. A few states and urban districts have shown how to get such teachers without lowering standards with quick-fix credentialing programs. However, after reviewing all available evidence on teaching, teacher preparation, and teacher labor markets, the authors find that NCLB's goals cannot be met without a federal teacher-supply program.

In a related vein, Cuban worries that neither reforms nor resources are being targeted at the poor students who most need them. Rather, state and federal policymakers have taken a broad-brush approach aimed at all schools, including thousands of schools where students are already doing well. This approach is based, he says, on the kind of political calculus that has created resistance to school finance equalization in many states and that has spread Title I funds for the disadvantaged among virtually all school districts. "So now academic standards initially aimed at low-performing schools have been transformed to apply to all schools, seeking to hammer our . . . system into a single mold."

Has the School-Centered Choice Movement Yielded Significant Gains?

In "Multiple 'Choice' Questions" (chapter 8), Henry M. Levin of Columbia University's Teachers College uses several yardsticks to examine more than a dozen choice options and notes that alternatives to regular public schools certainly have spread. Semiautonomous public charter schools, which first appeared in 1992, multiplied to at least 2,000 in a decade. While there were just a few voucher programs for private school tuition in the 1990s, a pro-voucher Supreme Court ruling in 2002 heightened interest, and in 2004 Congress enacted a school voucher program for Washington, D.C.[16] NCLB, moreover, provides a potential foot in the door for other kinds of vouchers. Not only does it require public school choice for students whose schools fail to make sufficient academic progress for two consecutive years, but it also funds tutoring or summer classes for students whose schools fall short for three years in a row, raising the prospect that Washington might sometimes finance such services at private schools.

Choice approaches commonly assume that competition will improve the efficiency of schools, particularly in student test scores, both at choice schools and at the public schools that must vie with them. Thus far, however, the evidence for charter schools and vouchers is cloudy at best, and the school choice provisions of NCLB, Levin says, "may not be the powerful lever for reform anticipated by the act's authors." Indeed, Levin believes that despite rhetoric to the contrary, NCLB and state policies emphasizing rewards and punishments for test results are creating growing pressure for school conformity, not increased choice.

Who Should Be in Charge of the Growing Family Role of Schools?

While policymaking elites have focused for decades on academic issues, polls have shown the public to be more concerned about inadequate parental involvement in schools, student drug use, violence, gangs, and related issues. This has helped drive schools to assume responsibility for a multitude of health, social, and other programs, which I, as a former education editor for the *Washington Post,* examine in chapter 9, "The American Kibbutz?" Schools, for example, not only provide students with before-school programs, breakfast, lunch, after-school programs, after-school snacks, and sometimes dinner, but the federal government also is exploring whether to provide free school breakfast for all elementary school children, regardless of family income. Schools also have an array of other nonacademic responsibilities, from ensuring that students do not bring weapons to school, instilling ethical behavior through character education, curbing the spread of AIDS, and battling drunk driving to fighting tobacco use, tackling child obesity, making sure children are inoculated, and caring for children of teenage parents. Until recently, children in one program even occasionally spent the night at their elementary school, using sleeping bags or cots set up in the gym.

I examine how these and many related programs compare with their historic predecessors (early childhood care and education, for example, surely were not invented for today's working parents) and where they may be headed (I believe they are likely to continue growing, especially since many have acquired broad constituencies). I then look at the governance issue, at who should be in charge. This brings me back full circle, to my belief in the need to give direct school control to more mayors and governors, in part because they, not school boards or superintendents, have the cross-agency authority to coordinate these and other programs for children and youth.

Taken as a whole, this volume provides a rich collection of essays on the administrative, legal, and political complexity of governing America's schools, on the need to rethink the current tangled web of authority, and on how best to create a deliberate governance system that especially benefits children who are most in need. The issue of who should be in charge of America's schools—and the fundamental policymaking that it encompasses—is likely to occupy the nation for years to come. It is hoped that these chapters will help stimulate debate on the many important questions involved, because so much of what happens in American education will depend on the answers.

Notes

1. David T. Conley, *Who Governs Our School? Changing Roles and Responsibilities* (Teachers College Press, 2003), p. 1.

2. Christopher T. Cross, "Too Much of a Good Thing?" *Basic Education*, vol. 45, no. 2 (October 2000), pp. 1–2.

3. John E. Chubb and Terry M. Moe, *Politics, Markets and America's Schools* (Brookings, 1990), p. 2.

4. Interview with Ted Sanders, April 18, 2001.

5. Deborah Land, *Local School Boards under Review: Their Role and Effectiveness in Relation to Students' Academic Achievement* (Baltimore: Center for Research on the Education of Students Placed at Risk, January 2002), p. 7.

6. Jo Becker and Rosalind S. Helderman, "Va. Seeks to Leave Bush Law Behind: Republicans Fight School Mandates," *Washington Post*, January 24, 2004, p. A1.

7. Sam Dillon, "Some School Districts Challenge Bush's Signature Education Law," *New York Times*, January 2, 2004, p. A1; Paul Foy, "States Challenge No Child Left Behind Act," *Associated Press* (www.washingtonpost.com/wp-dyn/articles/A49192-2004Feb17.html [February 2004]).

8. Lisa Goldstein, "Gov. Richardson Notches Latest Political Win," *Education Week*, October 22, 2003, p. 21.

9. Ray Long and Diane Rado, "Governor Lambastes State's School Board: Blagojevich Calls Agency 'Barrier to Progress,'" *Chicago Tribune*, January 16, 2004, p. 1.

10. Michael W. Kirst, *Mayoral Influence, New Regimes, and Public School Governance* (Philadelphia: Consortium for Policy Research in Education, May 2000); Justin Bloom, "Williams Accedes to Council in Altering School Bill," *Washington Post*, June 8, 2004, p. B1.

11. Fritz Edelstein, "Voters Seek Accountability on Education from Their Elected Public Officials," *U.S. Mayor* (www.usmayors.org/uscm/us_mayor_newspaper/documents/03_31_03/education.asp [March 2003]). See also Fritz Edelstein and J. D. LaRock, "Takeovers or Toeholds? Mayors Don't Need to Run Schools to Make Them Better," *Education Week*, October 1, 2003, p. 44.

12. As Edelstein and LaRock note, mayoral control cannot be expected to occur where school districts are larger than metropolitan areas or in cities with multiple schools districts within their boundaries. On public support for mayoral takeovers, see

Demanding Quality Public Education in Tough Economic Times: What Voters Want from Elected Officials (Washington: Public Education Network and *Education Week*, February 2003), p. 12.

13. Kirst, *Mayoral Influence, New Regimes, and Public School Governance*, pp. 8, 11.

14. Although NCLB (P.L. 107-110) begins by calling itself "An act to close the achievement gap," section 1001 states that the statute's purpose is to give all children an opportunity to "reach, at a minimum, proficiency on challenging state academic achievement standards and state academic assessments."

15. Melissa McCabe, "Teachers: Spec. Ed. Students Should Meet Own Standards," in "Count Me In: Special Education in an Era of Standards," *Education* Week, January 8, 2004, pp. 20–21; Jay Mathews, "Schools Chiefs Seek Changes in Testing Law: No Child Left Behind Law Called Too Harsh on Some," *Washington Post*, January 31, 2004, p. B1; Michael Dobbs, "'No Child' Tests for Schools Relaxed: English Learners Get Transition Time," *Washington Post*, February 20, 2004, p. 1; Lisa Goldstein, "Long-Awaited Spec. Ed. Testing Rules Issued," *Education Week*, January 7, 2004, p. 27.

16. Spencer S. Hsu and Justin Blum, "D.C. School Vouchers Win Final Approval," *Washington Post*, January 23, 2004, p. A1.

2

Turning Points:
A History of American School Governance

MICHAEL W. KIRST

W as it just because old beliefs die hard? When asked who
has the most power to improve public schools, most
respondents to a 2002 survey by the Public Education Network
and *Education Week* said local school boards.[1] The public has
been told repeatedly, after all, how much the nation reveres local
school control—by those who have been taking away much of
that control. So Americans may be forgiven if they have not yet
come to grips with the fact that local boards as well as local superintendents and individual schools have for some time been losing
influence over education programs to state and federal officials
and other interests. Indeed, some analysts view local school
boards as an endangered species.[2]

Historically, American education has been rooted in local policy, local management, and local financial control, traditions
deeply embedded in our political culture. Until recently, in fact,
the public thought officials beyond their districts had acquired
too much power over their schools. In 2000, for example, the
annual Phi Delta Kappa/Gallup education poll reported that
61 percent of Americans wanted to reduce Washington's influence

over local education programs.[3] Yet, now the No Child Left Behind Act (NCLB) has greatly expanded federal power. Gallup reported in 2002 that "57% of Americans believe the federal government's increased involvement is a good thing; 68% of Americans would go beyond the requirements of NCLB and require all 50 states to use the same nationally standardized test to measure student achievement. Although not suggested by NCLB, 66% would go so far as to have a national curriculum."[4]

The country, which is struggling through another turning point in the history of education governance, clearly is having difficulty in deciding which way to go. Does it want more centralized state and federal control, with even less discretion for local policymakers and teachers? Does it want little or no state or local voice in what is taught or tested, as would be the case with a national curriculum and national exams, both of which the public has long supported in Gallup polls?[5] Does the nation want to scrap much of its democratically governed public school system and substitute a market-based system of school vouchers? Or do Americans want their local school boards and local educators to regain lost powers? These are some of the major governance issues confronting U.S. schools, and the answers will tell a great deal about how Americans wish to educate their children. Changing how schools are governed, after all, long has been a backdoor way of changing broad policies and priorities for education.

At the moment, it appears likely that traditional local governance structures will be overwhelmed by the trend toward increased nonlocal power over schools. Several factors point in this direction, including, among others,

—a loss of confidence by higher authorities in local decisionmakers, a phenomenon that began well before the 1983 publication of *A Nation at Risk* and its fears (some would say seriously mistaken fears)[6] about U.S. economic competitiveness;

—the intense economic rivalry among states, in which governors use education, as they use tax breaks and other lures, to help attract businesses and jobs;

—changes in school funding patterns to enhance equity and limit local property tax spending; and

—the tendency of federal and state standards-based reform to centralize far more authority than it decentralizes.

The challenge today is to rethink the institutional choices Americans have been making—to analyze the schools' purposes, examine the likely effects of governance shifts on those goals, and decide who can best serve students. Federal or state officials, for example, often play crucial roles in the areas of civil rights and school finance; local politics typically precludes consensus on policies that significantly redistribute resources. But the appropriate balance of control over curriculum, instruction, and assessment policies—the pivotal issues in today's school reforms—is much less clear.

Some states and school districts, for example, have been centralizing these functions for more than twenty years, and yet student achievement has barely budged. The deadline for the Clinton administration's Goals 2000 came and went with the nation nowhere near to fulfilling any of the education aspirations set by the Bush White House and U.S. governors a decade before. Is there reason to believe that more state and federal centralization now will yield notable academic gains and achieve such goals? To address these and other questions, it is helpful to understand earlier turning points in the history of U.S. school governance and to see how the evolution of the system has resulted in today's complex and fragmented structure, in which it appears that everybody—and therefore nobody—is in charge.

The Importance of Distrust

At the heart of the questioning of institutional control is distrust of those who hold power, and in the loss of confidence in local school authorities, America has come full cycle on this matter. In the early days of the republic, Americans distrusted distant government and wanted important decisions made close to home, especially regarding education. Thus the U.S. Constitution made no mention of schools, leaving control of education to the states, and states then delegated a great deal of power to local school districts. While states always have been able to abolish school districts or take over their management—a power rarely exercised until recent years—the doctrine of local control of public schools has occupied a special place in American political ideology.

Evidence of distrust can be found today not only in declining confidence in local education officials but also in the reassertion of authority over school policy by governors, presidents, and mayors. Although few Americans realize it, the nation has long maintained one government for schools—composed mainly of local and state boards of education and superintendents—and another for everything else. While the education government was strengthened particularly by school reforms adopted at the turn of the twentieth century, the two-government tradition dates back to 1826, when Massachusetts created a separate school committee divorced from the general government, a practice that spread nationally.[7]

In early agricultural America, of course, schooling was a very different affair from at present. Formal education for young people was by no means a universally shared goal. On the contrary, at the founding of the republic, when the principal purpose of education was religious training, there were many reasons to oppose the establishment of public schools. Echoes of these arguments are heard today among advocates of education vouchers or tuition tax credits, some of whom want public funding for private schools in the belief that the school should be an extension of the home, where children encounter only values espoused by like-minded families.

The public school as we know it did not emerge until the 1840s with the advent of the common school movement. Determined to protect and improve what the founding generation had created, the supporters of the common school had broad social purposes, from molding morals and fostering cultural unity to teaching citizenship responsibilities, spreading prosperity, and ending poverty. These schools were to be vehicles for realizing a millennial vision of a righteous republic.[8]

As advocated by Horace Mann in Massachusetts, Henry Barnard in Connecticut, and John Pierce in Michigan, among others, common schools were imbued with egalitarian and majoritarian values. Designed to produce literate, numerate, and moral citizens from children of all classes, sects, and ethnic groups, they were to be "the great equalizer," in Mann's phrase. In general, the people who built and supervised the schools were not education professionals, and young, untrained teachers instructed the pupils. Although theoretically nonsectarian and nonpartisan, the schools had a conservative and Protestant bent. This reflected the worldview of their promoters, Victorian opinion shapers who were largely of British American origin, bourgeois, and evangelical Protestant.[9] Nonetheless, most citizens (with the exception of Roman Catholics) found the teachings of the common schools inoffensive.[10]

The Protestant republican ideology embodied in the schools was vividly expressed by the *McGuffey Readers,* first published in 1836 and used by some 200 million schoolchildren from 1900 to 1940 (though their use began to fade in the 1920s). The readers, which included selections from British and American literature, as well as lessons in science, farming, history, and biography, were frankly moralistic. In story after story, good children were rewarded soon after their good deeds (and tangibly, with items like silver coins), while bad ones were punished with equal celerity. Honesty and industry were the values most promoted, followed closely by courage, kindness, obedience, and courtesy. The *McGuffey Readers* supported the temperance movement but were silent about efforts to abolish slavery and establish trade unions.[11]

By the time of the Civil War, the common school had become the main-stream of education in the United States, thriving in hundreds of thousands of school districts from Maine to Oregon, financed largely by public taxes and controlled by local trustees. Creating this system was an undertaking of immense magnitude—arguably the greatest institution-building success in American history—though the resulting structure was not uniform. Southern states developed county school districts, while the Northeast organized around small towns. Southwestern and western school districts grew by annexation; hence San Jose, California, today has nineteen separate school districts within its city limits and San Antonio, Texas, has twenty. Common school reformers also created education agencies at the state level, but these generally were bare-bones units with scant power. As late as 1890, the median size of state departments of education was two persons, including the state superintendent. (Today the California State Department of Education has about 1,400 employees.)

As for the federal government, it had no direct involvement in any of this. Washington had long given rhetorical support to education and had made a national commitment early on to use land sales to finance schools, formalized in the Northwest Ordinance of 1787. But it was not until after the Civil War, in 1867, that even a low-level Bureau of Education was created and given the modest responsibilities of collecting education data and disseminating information about school organization and teaching methods.

Taking Education "Out of Politics"

At the turn of the twentieth century (1890–1910), schools were placed under stronger control of local education governments, the result of reforms that followed disclosures of widespread municipal corruption in schools, as in city offices. Muckrakers exposed textbook publishers and contractors who allied themselves with corrupt school trustees for common boodle in the common school. The spoils system frequently determined who won or lost teaching jobs. Reformers concerned about such practices gathered information from across the country. Their reports indicted every region of the nation.

A superintendent in one of the Eastern states writes: "Nearly all the teachers in our schools get their positions by political 'pull.' If they secure a place and are not backed by political influence, they are likely to be turned out. Our drawing teacher recently lost her position for this reason." One writes from the South: "Most places depend on politics. The lowest motives are frequently used to influence ends." A faint wail comes from the far West: "Positions are secured and held by the lowest principles of corrupt politicians." "Politicians wage a war of extermination against all teachers who are not their vassals," comes from the Rocky Mountains.

In Boston, the teachership is still a spoil of office. It is more difficult, at the present time, for a Catholic than for a Protestant young woman to get a place, but, nevertheless, some Catholics secure appointments, for "trading" may always be done, while each side has a wholesome fear of the other assailing it in the open board. A member said one day, in my hearing: "I must have my quota of teachers."[12]

The corruption was reinforced with a vengeance in the final decade of the nineteenth century, when local control came to mean a decentralized school committee system rooted in ward politics, which provided extensive opportunities for undue influence as waves of new urban immigrants sought influence and jobs in the schools. In 1905, for example, Philadelphia had forty-three elected district school boards, with 559 members. Little wonder that even though consolidation of school districts began in 1900, the nation still had more than 195,000 in 1917.

Reformers contended that, among other things, board members elected by wards advanced their own parochial and special interests at the expense of the school district as a whole.[13] What was needed to counter this, they believed, was election at large or citywide, without subdistrict electoral boundaries. A good school system was good for all, not just for one part of the community.

Reformers also charged that the executive authority of the larger school boards was splintered because they worked through so many subcommittees. The 1905 Cincinnati school board, for example, had seventy-four subcommittees, while Chicago had seventy-nine. No topic, down to the purchase of doorknobs, was too trivial for some subcommittee to consider. The basic prerequisite for better management was thought to be centralization of power in a chief executive to whom the selection board would delegate considerable authority. The school superintendent would be controlled, but only on broad policies, by a board respectful of his professional expertise. Only under such a system could a superintendent make large-scale improvements and be held accountable.

By 1910 a conventional educational wisdom had evolved among the "school folk" and the leading business and professional men who had spearheaded these Progressive Era reforms. They sought to use state legislatures and departments of education to standardize public education and consolidate one-room schools into larger township or regional schools. Essentially, they aimed to "take education out of politics"—often meaning taking it away from decentralized control by certain lay people—and to turn "political" issues into matters for administrative discretion by professional educators. In some cases small groups of patricians secured new charters from state legislatures and thereby reorganized urban schools without any popular vote. The watchwords of reform were efficiency, expertise, professionalism, centralization, and nonpolitical control. Taken together, reformers thought, these ideals would inspire the "one best system."[14]

The most attractive models for this new governance structure were the industrial bureaucracies rapidly emerging during this era. The centralized power of the school superintendent, comparable to that of the plant manager, was intended to overcome the tangles and inefficiencies of school board subcommittees. The industrial model also appealed to the reformers' social class and status. The financial and professional leaders who deplored the politics and inefficiency of the decentralized ward system did so in part because it empowered members of the lower and lower-middle classes, many of whom were recent immigrants. Reformers wanted "not simply to replace bad men with good; they proposed to change the occupational and class origins of the decisionmakers."[15]

That is indeed what happened: a classic 1927 study by George Counts showed that an urban elite of professionals and big businessmen dominated the new centralized boards of education. After reforms were adopted in St. Louis in 1897, for instance, the share of professionals on the school board jumped from 4.8 percent to 58.3 percent, and the proportion of big businessmen climbed from 9 percent to 25 percent. By contrast, the proportion of small businessmen dropped from 47.6 percent to 16.7 percent, and wage earners from 28.6 percent to zero. The new professional and managerial board members delegated many formal powers to school professionals, giving educators the leeway to shape schools to meet the needs of the new industrial society, at least as defined by one segment of that society: chiefly prosperous, native-born, Anglo-Saxon Protestants.[16]

While the common school movement established a fairly uniform system of education, another nationalizing force—professionalism—was of greater consequence in this regard over a longer period. The growth of professional standards for administration, teaching, curriculum, testing, and other elements essential to the system began drawing it together in the final decades of the nineteenth century. Before this process emerged, the fabric of American schools was a ragged plaid. Experience drawn from the testing of a

jumble of ideas—transmitted through new professional journals and training for the emergent profession—did more than the common school to
instill uniformity in U.S. education.

Some prominent concerns of that time would be familiar to Americans
today. There were worries about global competition and worker training,
which prompted Washington to enact the 1917 Smith-Hughes Act for vocational education, the first federal program of categorical aid for elementary and secondary schools. There were concerns about schools where
children were taught in German or Polish rather than in English, and about
the need for educators to provide health and social services for poor pupils,
particularly in immigrant communities. There were worries about student
achievement, triggered in part by the dismal performance of World War I
recruits on newly created IQ tests and in part by complaints from such business groups as the National Association of Manufacturers in the 1920s that
many high school graduates were incompetent at basic math and at expressing themselves in English.

Nonetheless, the period from 1920 to 1950 was a "golden era" for school
superintendents, who had wide discretion to deal with these problems (and
others that emerged during the Great Depression and World War II) and
had no teachers unions to worry about. Whatever the problems, the federal government and the states were content to let most decisions rest with
local education authorities.

After World War II, the curriculum adapted, as did the society, to economic expansion and peacetime social change, particularly the postwar
baby boom.[17] School enrollments climbed, as did the percentage of students
graduating from high school. The egalitarianism of the army encouraged
egalitarianism in the schools, as it did in previously elitist institutions—
private colleges and universities—as thousands of ex-soldiers enrolled with
the help of the federal GI Bill. However, the turn-of-the-century triumph of
the doctrine of efficiency achieved through professionalism and centralization had attenuated the ties between school leaders and their constituents. Parent participation had little effect on school policymaking. Until
the 1950s, for example, Baltimore held its school board meetings in a room
that could seat only twenty-five people. As the leading citizens' "interest
group," the PTA (parent-teacher association) considered its prime function to be providing support for professional administrators.

The weakened link between education leaders and constituents had been
acceptable in the pre–World War II decades, when schooling made fewer
claims on community financial resources and when education professionals
benefited from their own publicity about education success in order to

preserve control.[18] It continued to be acceptable in the two decades after the war, when the emphasis was on the rush to obtain education for all through the expansion of school systems and bureaucracies alongside continued district consolidation.[19] But school politics and governance were about to change, and in more than one direction. The efficiency of the centralized local administration was starting to lose its aura, and new waves of both egalitarianism and elitism were to trigger new turning points for education governance.

Washington and the Quest for Equity

It was during the 1950s that confidence in local school boards and administrators began to weaken. In 1954 the Supreme Court's *Brown* decision outlawing statutory school segregation called attention to the disgraceful failure of Southern school systems to educate black students. The next year Rudolph Flesch's best-selling *Why Johnny Can't Read* bemoaned what it saw as a national literacy crisis stemming from a decline in the use of phonics to teach reading, an issue that dates back to Horace Mann (who was closer to the whole-language school) and that is debated again today. In 1957, after Moscow launched *Sputnik,* an angry chorus complained that the Soviet education system was surpassing our own. Such cold war fears galvanized a more aggressive federal role in education, embodied in the 1957 National Defense Education Act, which sought to improve math, science, and foreign-language learning (not that different from goals adopted in 1984 to deal with what was then believed to be a Japanese economic threat).[20]

The decline of confidence set in motion by the *Brown* decision accelerated during the 1960s and 1970s in the quest to remedy unequal educational opportunities tolerated by state and local policymakers. The centerpiece of that quest was President Lyndon B. Johnson's 1965 Elementary and Secondary Education Act (ESEA), which would transform Washington's role in education.

Over the course of a century, between 1862 and 1963, Congress had considered unrestricted general aid to schools thirty-six times and had rejected it thirty-six times. Opponents had long argued successfully that because the Tenth Amendment to the Constitution left control of schools to the states, Washington had no constitutionally defensible role in education. Although by 1930 the Supreme Court supported a less restricted federal role, Washington's school programs after World War II were still modest. In 1950, the U.S. Office of Education (USOE) was transferred from the Department of the Interior to what became the Department of Health, Education, and Welfare. It had a staff of 300 to spend $40 million (compared with the $20 billion the Department of Education disburses today for the No Child Left Behind Act and the $50 billion it spends overall). Focusing on such matters as mathematics, libraries, and school buses, USOE appointed specialists and consultants who identified primarily with the National Education Association (NEA). Federal grant programs operated in deference to the priorities and judgments of local and state education agencies. The USOE regarded state administrators as colleagues who should have the maximum decisionmaking discretion permitted by federal laws.[21]

In 1963, the year of President John F. Kennedy's assassination, the Department of Defense and the Veterans Administration spent more on education programs than the Office of Education and the National Science Foundation combined. But that was to change after President Johnson's landslide election victory in 1964, when Democrats also won substantial majorities in both houses of Congress. Johnson made ESEA central to his antipoverty and Great Society programs. Rather than pursuing the unrestricted general aid that Kennedy had sought in vain, Johnson tied education money to special needs categories (schools with low-income and low-achieving pupils) that existed in every congressional district, spreading the funds far and wide and thus winning lawmakers' hearts and minds. Johnson also began the federal role of stimulating innovation and experiments with new types of schools and teaching methods.

Amid growing racial and class strains, including big-city race riots, ESEA steadily expanded, and programs for other neglected groups—children with disabilities, minority-language students, and others—were added, often as a result of court rulings. Federal courts in the 1970s led the way not only in the fight against segregation but also in establishing the right of disabled children to an appropriate free education, in requiring extra help for limited-English-speaking students, and in combating sex discrimination, as measured by school expenditures and curricular opportunities. Federal courts, for example, ordered high schools to stop tracking women into sex-stereotyped training to become secretaries, waitresses, or nurses. Those rulings were a stimulus for Title IX of the Civil Rights Act, which is best known for expanding women's opportunities in intercollegiate sports but in fact prohibits sex discrimination in funding at all levels of education.

The mid-1970s also was the peak expansion period for new state court regulations on local schools, indicating that local schools could not be trusted to guarantee student rights or due process. This trend expanded through state education codes and through lawsuits increasingly directed at local authorities.[22]

While this era brought a dramatic increase in federal activity in education, the basic mode of delivering federal services remained the same. This specified funding route sought bigger and bolder categorical and demonstration programs. The delivery system highlighted the need for more precise federal regulations to guide local projects. Today's overlapping and complex categorical aids, which restrict spending to specified programs and purposes, evolved as a mode of federal action on which a number of otherwise competing education interests could agree. This collection of categoricals, which dominated national education politics from 1965 to the election of President Ronald Reagan in 1980, was not the result of any rational plan for federal intervention but rather the outcome of political bargaining and coalition formation.

The national movements behind such programs, moreover, often spawned new local interest groups on such issues as civil rights, women's roles, special education, students' rights, and ethnic self-determination. Hence, atop Washington regulations, these new forces began agitating locally for reforms. They sought black history and bilingual education programs. They challenged the use of IQ tests for pupil placement and tracking. They pressed for revised student suspension policies and for community control of school boards. Indeed, big-city "decentralizers" in the 1970s sought to revive something resembling the old ward boards of education that had been abolished at the turn of the century. They ended up winning partial decentralization through subdistrict board elections, with tighter oversight of superintendents. All these efforts further eroded the power of local school authorities—and there was more to come.

When Teachers Organize for Pay and Politics

In the 1950s, teachers found themselves cut off from school boards and the public. Increasingly, business managers, administrative assistants, subject-matter coordinators, and department heads were telling them how to conduct their classrooms. With the postwar baby boom, however, came extraordinary growth in education spending, in teachers' ranks, and in pressure to give teachers a greater voice. Between 1949 and 1970, the share of the gross national product devoted to education more than doubled, from about 3.5 percent to 8 percent. Where the nation had provided only $2 billion in 1940, it spent $50 billion in 1970 and more than $100 billion in 1980. With this massive injection of funds, the teacher workforce grew from just over 1 million in 1940 to nearly 2.5 million in 1971. By the mid-1970s the country had substantially more teachers than autoworkers, steelworkers, teamsters, or doctors.

It was also during the 1950s that the teachers' perception of their "proper professional role" began to change. Once viewed as submissive, they now began to form unions, to engage in collective bargaining, and—despite laws in many states barring strikes by public employees—to walk picket lines. Indeed, teacher walkouts escalated annually, climbing from thirty-five in the 1955–56 school year to 114 in 1967–68 and to 131 in 1969–70. By 1980 the teacher drive for collective bargaining had spread to most regions, except the Southeast and the mountain states, resulting in a significant reduction in the administrative dominance of local school governance.[23]

The outcome of collective bargaining is a written central office contract covering wages, hours, and employment conditions for a specific length of time. What happens to administrators' authority, particularly that of principals, when such contracts filter down through the loosely coupled school system? One major study found that some provisions tightly limit the principal's freedom of action, while others get redefined to fit the requirements at the particular school.[24] Principals who have high standards and expect much of teachers earn tolerance and even respect in interpreting the contract; for teachers, a good school is more important than union membership, close contract observance, or control of schools. As one administrator observed, "Teachers like to be part of a winning team." While the effects of central office contracts vary widely by district and school, they nonetheless generally restrain the power of school boards and superintendents and force principals to react to centralized personnel policies.

Because teachers unions negotiate districtwide accords, they also tend to be wary of school-based management (SBM), another force that has reduced the authority of local school boards and superintendents. Indeed, the basic assumption of SBM, which has evolved into today's charter school movement, is that schools would do better if only they were not under the thumb of boards, superintendents, and central offices; if power were decentralized to the school level. Although the concept has spread in various forms to numerous states and school districts, full-blown SBM has eluded most policymakers. Education reform has been characterized as "tinkering towards utopia," and SBM keeps inching forward, while state and federal mandates for academic standards, aligned curriculums, and tests are having far larger centralizing effects.

Teachers organized not only to gain strong local contracts but also to obtain preferred policies through state and national political processes.[25]

This led the NEA in 1976 to endorse a presidential candidate for the first time—the Democrats' Jimmy Carter—and to spend $3 million in support of federal candidates that year. The nation may have been fond of the Progressive myth that it could "keep education out of politics," but it clearly could not keep politics out of education.

Because Congress was closely divided throughout his term (1976–80), Carter could not expand the federal role much, as the NEA would have wished. Rather, he chiefly embellished and refined existing equity-driven programs while federal regulation and enforcement continued to expand, as they had under his Republican predecessors. It was President Richard M. Nixon, for example, who successfully pressed for large sums for school desegregation. It was President Gerald R. Ford who issued the Title IX regulations that still stir controversy today.

Similarly, from the Nixon presidency through the Carter years, there was bipartisan support for aggressive enforcement of the ESEA requirement that Title I funds supplement, not supplant, local resources for disadvantaged children. Republicans did periodically attempt to decategorize programs by creating block grants to states and districts, but those efforts were defeated by the Democrats who held majorities in both houses of Congress, as well as by the interest groups that benefited from categorical programs.

What Carter did achieve was the creation, in 1979, of a cabinet-level Department of Education, which the NEA had greatly desired and was justified partly on the ground that it would consolidate scattered education programs in one accountable department. A number of groups, however, wary of seeing their programs distorted by a department they presumed would be dominated by professional educators, successfully lobbied to keep them separate. As a result, the school lunch program is still housed in the Department of Agriculture, and the National Science Foundation still provides research and demonstration grants for secondary school science. Similarly, Head Start is part of the Department of Health and Human Services, even though it is designed to help preschool children in their transition to kindergarten.

Reagan tried but failed to reorient federal education policy. He proposed a tuition tax credit for parents with children in private schools, an idea pushed by some conservative lawmakers for decades but never before endorsed by the White House. While a Democratic Congress defeated the tuition tax credit plan, the Reagan endorsement did help keep federal aid for parents of private school students on the national agenda. Indeed, as part of his big tax cuts in 2001, President George W. Bush succeeded in enacting tax-free saving accounts that can be used for private school tuition. The

Reagan administration also attempted to scale back federal education activity in general—indeed, it initially wanted to dismantle the Department of Education—and equity-driven education programs in particular, urging flexible block grants for the states instead. Equity concerns, however, remained Washington's principal thrust in education—though the emphasis already had begun to change elsewhere in the nation.

The Rise of the States and Academic Concerns

Among the important effects of greater federal involvement in education was the dramatic expansion of state education agencies, and thus of the capacity of state education agencies and boards of education to intervene in local school affairs. Starting in 1965, Washington began funding additional state staff members to enforce local ESEA implementation and compliance. Thirty years later, in 1995, the GAO (now the Government Accountability Office) found that Washington had become the largest funder of several state agencies, in some cases footing 70 percent of their budgets. Many states, moreover, mirrored the federal thrust by creating their own categorical aids for groups neglected or underrepresented in local politics. Thus by 2002 California had 124 state programs in addition to the federal programs for poor, disabled, limited-English-speaking, and other children.

Atop the expansion of state agencies came other developments that moved school power to state capitals. The most important was a rapidly spreading state school finance movement, based on state court rulings that local property tax bases were inherently unequal. Another, albeit inadvertent, development was a consequence of California's Proposition 13; by cutting local property taxes, that 1978 measure shifted most school funding and power to Sacramento. As a result of such developments, states became the largest source of school financing nationwide: in 1930 states provided only 17.3 percent of school funding; in the early 1970s, about 40 percent; and by the late 1990s, their portion had climbed to 48 percent, exceeding the 45 percent local share.[26]

With mushrooming school spending and enlarged education agencies, states increasingly asserted the control over local schools that was theirs by law but that they had so far exercised only modestly. During the nineteenth century, supporters of local schools had successfully resisted state control, and for the early part of the twentieth century, states concentrated on minimum standards for rural schools; big-city school systems were thought not to need state intervention. States mainly focused on such matters as enforcing minimum standards for teachers and facilities, requiring a few courses, and dispensing federal aid. But in the 1970s, local education authorities came to be seen as the problem—and states as the solution. Indeed, despite Washington's greatly enlarged role, perhaps the most striking change in U.S. education governance in the last forty years has been the growth of centralized state control and the ascendance of governors over school policy in most states. Organizations of local administrators, teachers, and school board members dominated state policy agendas no longer.

The ascendancy of governors often has brought them into conflict with chief state school officers, usually called the state superintendent or state commissioner of education. These officials, after all, long have been accustomed to being administrative bosses of the state education government, providing some insulation between it and the general state government. This is especially true of elected chiefs, but appointees also view themselves as working for the state board of education, not the governor, just as local superintendents overwhelmingly work for local school boards, not mayors.

As governors have grown more active in education, however, they have sought more direct control, whether by repealing the election of superintendents and commissioners or overseeing the state boards that appointed them. Since they rarely are members of the governor's cabinet, however, these officials still tend to view themselves as quasi-independent voices for education, following some of their own policies unless governors appoint them or exert heavy pressure on state boards of education. In only fourteen states, however, are chief state school officers still elected today, down from thirty-three in 1930. Governors now appoint all state board members in twenty-five states and some members in fourteen states.[27]

The growth of gubernatorial influence had its origins in state economic development strategies that used improved schools to help attract businesses and jobs. Southern governors with uncertain economies and historically weak school systems led the way in the 1970s, and others soon followed. While Washington was expanding equity programs, governors and state legislators were impressed by arguments that local school officials had permitted academic standards to decline. Surely businesses would look favorably on state education systems that produced well-trained workers and good schools for employees' families by requiring a more demanding curriculum, stricter requirements for teachers, minimum competency tests for high school graduation, and other such measures. In state plant-siting competitions lay the seeds of U.S. education's new focus.

The growth of state and gubernatorial influence accelerated in the 1980s as a result of the 1980–82 recession and fear of increasing global competition, especially from Japan. That worry triggered a series of highly critical private and public studies, most notably *A Nation at Risk,* which assailed schools for producing "a rising tide of mediocrity" that threatened nothing less than "our very future as a nation and a people." Education suddenly became a leading electoral issue. Governors across the country proposed major reform packages, which, in the mid-1980s, began including higher standards for student learning. Then, as now, states differed in how strenuously they asserted control of education, ranging from the highly aggressive, such as California and Florida, to the more decentralized, such as Vermont and Iowa. The growing assertion of state control over education, moreover, prompted local reactions by decentralizers, with the idea of charter schools—essentially, much more independent public schools—beginning to gain attention in 1987–88. The main governance thrust, however, remained more state control, as reflected, for example, in state curriculum initiatives.[28]

Until the 1980s, most states left curriculum decisions largely to local discretion, satisfied to specify a few required courses and issue advisory curricular frameworks for local consideration. States did respond to influential curricular lobbies, another force that impinges on the discretion of local school authorities. The most vigorous curricular lobbying often came from proponents of relatively newer subject areas such as vocational education, physical education, and home economics. Such subjects, introduced amid great controversy after 1920, had to rely on state laws to gain a secure place in the curriculum. Hence teachers of these subjects used state NEA affiliates to lobby state lawmakers, supported by manufacturers of the hardware, such as sports equipment and home appliances, which was required for the classes. Teachers of driver's education are a more recent lobby, but they have been so effective that almost all states now mandate that subject.

By contract, teachers of such "standard" courses as English, math, and science—subjects that did not require political power to ensure inclusion in the curriculum—have been more poorly organized at the state level. Academic subjects therefore were less frequently mandated by state law, sometimes with curious results. Until quite recently, for example, many states required high school students to take only one year of science or math but four years of physical education. That sort of anomaly was swiftly put to an end starting in 1983–84. In those two years alone, thirty-four states established high school graduation requirements in standard academic subjects. They were determined to focus schools on academics much as in post-*Sputnik* days, but this time for economic reasons.[29]

Unfortunately, despite these and many other state reforms of the 1980s— financial incentives for teachers, more student tests required for promotion or graduation, longer school days—there was little improvement in student performance. The growing impatience of business leaders, public officials, and others led to the birth of the more comprehensive standards-based reform movement, with the overarching aims of helping students master more challenging academic content and increasing the emphasis on its application. As the standards-based reform bandwagon began to roll, business executives, governors, education policymakers, subject-matter specialists, even the White House jumped aboard.

Increasing Federal Centralization

In 1989, shortly after his election, amid continued economic concern and frustration at the snail's pace of education progress, President George H. W. Bush invited the nation's governors to an education "summit" in Charlottesville, Virginia. With great fanfare, participants agreed that what America needed was standards or goals at the national level, issuing six such standards to start with. Clearly, the states could not be trusted to produce the desired education gains, either. So, in 1990 the White House and the National Governors Association (NGA) declared that by 2000 the nation would meet such goals as ensuring that all children began school ready to learn and that American students were first in the world in math and science achievement.

The rest of the Bush years included support for more specific national student standards and assessments, but those ideas died in ideological crossfire that ultimately doomed the Bush education legislation. President Bill Clinton, however, whose political rise owed much to his efforts on education and who had played a prominent role at Charlottesville, picked up the torch and in 1994 won enactment of Goals 2000, a measure that reinforced three key state education reforms then spreading across the nation:

1. The creation of challenging academic standards defining what all students should know and be able to do in each subject area. By 2001, forty-six states had accomplished this in most academic subjects, a remarkable shift in the historic state role.

2. The alignment of policies—testing, teacher certification, professional development, and accountability programs—to state curricular standards. All states but Iowa had statewide student achievement tests in 2002, and most were addressing the other systemic components.

3. The restructuring of the governance system, ostensibly to delegate to schools and districts responsibility for developing specific instructional

approaches that meet the academic standards for which states hold them accountable. The 1994 reauthorization of the Elementary and Secondary Education Act, called the Improving America's Schools Act, also linked categorical programs such as Title I and bilingual education to standards developed under Goals 2000 and required schools to make progress, as defined by the states, annually toward meeting those standards.

Goals 2000 legislation certainly encouraged the rapid spread of standards-based state and local policies, but it is impossible to isolate and assess its distincive contribution.[30] State-level funding under Goals 2000 added flexible state money for the development of tests and standards, as well as for systemic initiatives that state categoricals rarely permit. But 90 percent of Goals 2000 appropriations, which never exceeded $400 million, went to local school districts, and the law's effectiveness is questionable.

The Clinton administration proposed to supplement Goals 2000 with a voluntary national test in 1995. Although this initiative would have been a logical successor to Goals 2000, the fourth grade reading and eighth grade math exams were blocked by a rare congressional coalition of conservative Republicans, African Americans, and Hispanics. The Republicans were wary of excessive federal control, while the minority Democrats worried that low-income students would not have the opportunity to learn the content of the test.

In his second term, Clinton changed his priorities from standards and testing to the reduction of class sizes and the construction of schools, issues that moved Washington closer to providing general aid for education. At the end of 2000, as the Clinton presidency drew to a close the nation still had not advanced very far toward the goals set for that year by the first President Bush and the governors. With little attention, the 2000 goals faded away. Thus since the 1970s, when states first zeroed in on academic concerns, relatively little progress had been made in U.S. student achievement, though governance had become much more centralized and much money had been expended. In the years since the 1983 release of *A Nation at Risk,* for example, federal funding for elementary and secondary education had more than tripled.

None of this, however, discouraged the new president. On the contrary, George W. Bush, another former governor from the South whose political popularity rested heavily on education initiatives, had made education central to his White House victory. Once in office, he pressed hard for his No Child Left Behind Act, the latest reauthorization of the ESEA, and signed it into law in January 2002. Thus, Republican presidents had done an about-face, going from Reagan's desire to dismantle the U.S. Department of Education to Bush's dramatic expansion of Washington's power over education.

While NCLB generally extends the approach of the Improving America's Schools Act, it compels states to comply with numerous stricter assessment, accountability, and performance requirements. States must test all students in grades 3 through 8 each year in several subjects, starting with reading and math, and then adding science. They must develop "adequate yearly progress" objectives that result in all students becoming "proficient" in core subjects within twelve years. They must participate biennially in a version of the National Assessment of Educational Progress (NAEP) for states, to check on the rigor of their standards and assessments. They must find "highly qualified" teachers for every classroom, and for Title I schools, prepared paraprofessionals who know more about classroom instruction techniques. They must break down student assessments by poverty, race, ethnicity, disability, and English proficiency to determine progress in closing education gaps among student subgroups. They must issue public school "report cards," with basic aggregate and disaggregated information on assessment, graduation, teacher qualifications, and the identification of low-performing schools.

These mandates require, among other things, unprecedented gathering, analysis, and reporting of data by state education agencies. A recent report by the Education Commission of the States noted that only fifteen states had the required testing programs and "most states do not have the infrastructure to support the level of data collection, disaggregation and reporting that the new law requires."[31] Congress recognized the burden of developing new assessments by including $380 million for test development. At current rates of spending, Congress will have appropriated $1.5 billion over five years to help states develop and implement new assessment tools. More money will be provided in each subsequent year.

Local Authorities Beseiged and the Turn to Mayors

It should be abundantly clear from this discussion that over four decades many forces have been squeezing the authority of local school boards and superintendents into a smaller and smaller space. From the top, local discretion in education has been eroded by the growing power of the states, the federal government, and the courts. Greater influence also has accrued to business elites and other private interests, professional "reformers" (organizations such as the Ford or Gates foundations), interstate organizations (such as the NGA), and nationally oriented groups (such as the Council for Exceptional Children). From the bottom, superintendents and local boards have been hemmed in by teachers' collective bargaining, pressures from local offshoots of national social movements, and the growth of charter schools and related decentralizing forces. The decline in the student population during the 1970s and the spread of resistance to increased school taxes further constrained local initiative and options.

The general public may think that school boards still have the most power to improve schools, but the reality is that boards have been greatly weakened. Indeed, if one projects current trends for twenty or more years, the likelihood of minimal local discretion becomes quite striking, and with it the threat of declining voter and taxpayer support for local public schools that cannot respond to many of their grievances. Little wonder, then, that in 1980 Assistant Secretary of Education Chester E. Finn called the school board a "dinosaur left over from the agrarian past" and that Albert Shanker, the late president of the American Federation of Teachers, recommended a major overhaul modeled on hospital boards, which meet less than once a month.

This does not mean that local authorities are helpless. Rather, they have much less control over their agendas and policies than in the past. Superintendents and administrative staffs frequently are reactive, trying to juggle diverse and changing coalitions across different issues and levels of government. They must deal, for example, with a small army of administrative specialists in remedial reading, bilingual education, child nutrition, and other areas, who are paid by federal or state categorical programs and insulated from the superintendent's influence. Indeed, the specialists' allegiance often is to the higher levels of education governance rather than to the local community. Similarly, superintendents must address policy items on local board agendas that are generated by external forces or are reactions to proposals from teacher organizations and other local interest groups, including parents organized to support equity-driven programs. As Paul Hill of the Center on Reinventing Public Education at the University of Washington has noted,

> Federal programs have deliberately put schools under new political pressures. On the assumption that past neglect of disadvantaged students was caused by local politics, in which their parents had few allies and little influence, federal programs tried to change the balance of local political forces. All large federal programs were expressly organized

around constituency groups, helped parent groups organize, and gave parents official roles in school decisionmaking. Some gave parents new access to judicial remedies on the assumption that the ability to threaten litigation would increase their influence on schools. Most tried to colonize state and local education agencies with individuals paid to advocate for compliance with federal program rules. As a result, teachers are sometimes forced to treat students differently, depending on their links to organized external groups that have been set up and empowered by government actions.[32]

If concerns have arisen about the effects of categorical programs on teacher practices, they have multiplied as a result of state and federal curriculum mandates. For example, new state requirements specifying the grade level at which particular math concepts must be taught can conflict with the autonomy that enhances teacher response and professionalism. Teachers unions, as well as a vocal minority of parents, are troubled by the proliferation of state tests and may form coalitions on the issue. At the district level, the increasing centralization of instructional policy forces the curriculum function into the central office (whose growing control of information gives it more authority over other issues as well, at least in urban school systems), with a consequent loss of discretion at the school.

Not surprisingly, some observers believe that besieged local authorities are sorely in need of help—or of replacement. In the past decade, big-city mayors increasingly have asserted authority over education, some becoming modestly involved, a handful taking over their school systems entirely.[33] Given the extent to which the reforms of the Progressive Era were in reaction to Tammany Hall–type political corruption, this is another ironic return to the past. The Progressives assumed that a professional education bureaucracy, headed by a board-appointed superintendent, would guarantee efficiency, accountability, and neutrality. Critics, however, would argue that professional bureaucracy often leads to the very inefficiency—and to political power without accountability—that these reformers sought to eradicate. Some dysfunctional city education systems, for example, not only have suffered from corruption themselves but also have been unable to provide even adequate school facilities; Cleveland and Detroit were cases in point, before their mayors injected themselves into the schools. Theodore Lowi of Cornell University characterizes school systems as "New Machines," explaining that they "are machines because they are relatively irresponsible structures of power. That is, each agency shapes important public policies, yet the leadership of each is relatively self-perpetuating and not readily subject to the control of any higher authority."[34]

Just as state economic competition prompted governors to assert more control over education policy, so economic concerns were the principal driver of city hall's involvement. Indeed, because of the growing belief among business leaders and others that the improvement of deeply troubled city schools is critical to urban economic development, mayors no longer can avoid education-related issues. Mayors also may be better able to integrate other children's services—health, housing, police, arts and recreation programs—with schools. Moreover, they have financial incentives to become more involved. As James Cibulka, dean of the college of education at the University of Kentucky, notes, "Increasingly tight city budgets also place pressure on mayors to keep taxes down. Schools consume a large portion of that tax dollar, and in some cities the mayor has little direct control over decisions made by urban school officials." Thus there are economic, social, and budgetary reasons for mayors to seek greater school control.

Such mayors as Richard Daley in Chicago, Thomas Menino in Boston, and Michael Bloomberg in New York have mustered support at both city and state levels for their efforts to assert more control over education. In part, this is because of the belief that highly visible mayors are more likely than relatively unknown school board members to be held accountable by voters for public school performance. In part, some city and state politicians also have political motives for shifting control over education from an elected board that they cannot direct to a mayor over whom they may have some influence.

There are limits, however, to the spread of mayoral involvement. Many cities, for example, are not contiguous with school districts. As noted above, cities such as Phoenix, San Diego, and San Antonio have many school districts within their borders, and southern cities are part of county school districts. A decline in teacher strikes, moreover, has removed one crucial trigger for mayoral takeover. Nonetheless, more mayoral efforts to control city schools seem likely. This would complete the cycle of putting politics firmly back into education, with presidents, governors, and mayors (as well as Congress, state legislatures, city and county councils, local and state school boards, teachers, and many others) spinning an extensive political web around the public schools.

It is this political web that has led some to effectively seek an end to democratically controlled schools and to substitute market-based alternatives, a view that began receiving increased attention after John E. Chubb and Terry M. Moe's *Politics, Markets, and America's Schools* was published in

1990. In that book they contended that "the specific kinds of democratic institutions by which American education has been governed for the last half century appear to be incompatible with effective schooling."[35] Chubb and Moe viewed school autonomy as a vital determinant of pupil performance, essentially arguing that it was severely restricted because the political web surrounding schools was so complex, fragmented, and incoherent. In place of the gridlock they saw, they called for a version of school choice that included federal, state, and local disengagement from laws and regulations as key instruments of control. Students would receive scholarships that they could use to attend any public or private school that met minimal state standards.

Who Should Be in Charge of Schools?

On who should be in charge of schools, the nation faces another kind of choice, picking a path through the present turning point in education governance. Do Americans want more or less centralization? Do they prefer greater control by Washington, the states, or local school districts? Should politicians, educators, or the marketplace rule schools? These are not easy questions and there are no easy answers, only, as William Clune of the University of Wisconsin has noted, "least worst" choices among imperfect institutions. One must choose those who are trusted the most (or distrusted the least) to achieve and who have the capacity to accomplish the nation's highest goals, understanding all the while that no matter how these choices are made, their effects will be uncertain and continually subject to political change.

Governance and Student Achievement

Consider the goal of improving student achievement. Although this is not uppermost in the public's mind, U.S. elites have put it at the top of the education policy and governance agendas, increasingly taking key teaching and testing decisions away from low-performing local school systems. Those decisions first moved to state capitols. When it was felt that states could not be relied upon to meet achievement goals either, more decision-making moved to Washington, most recently with NCLB.

That law's implementation, however, will depend on strengthening federal-state partnerships and increasing state education agencies' capacity to monitor and manage progress and reform. Are Washington and the states likely to succeed? In a survey of fifty states, Margaret Goertz of the University of Pennsylvania prepared a matrix of instruments that states use to influence local academic standards and overcome local resistance to state-imposed curriculums. She distinguished between *performance standards,* which measure an individual's performance through tested achievement observations; *program standards,* which include curricular requirements, program specifications, and other state mandates affecting time in school, class size, and staffing; and *behavior standards,* which include attendance requirements, disciplinary codes, homework, and the like. Her study demonstrated dramatic increases in state specification and influence for all three types of standards from 1983 to 2001.[36]

While the scope of state activity is wide, however, the effectiveness of state influence on local practice often has been questioned. Some think it is quite potent, while others see a "loose coupling" between state policy and local schools that leads to symbolic compliance at the local level. Still others believe that worries about federal dominance of education are greatly exaggerated precisely because NCLB is unlikely to be implemented as intended.[37]

Then there is the question of student test motivation. The tests that stir up the most controversy are the high-stakes tests used for promotion or graduation. But none of the exams required by NCLB—neither the annual tests in grades 3 through 8 nor the biennial NAEP samplings—carry direct rewards or punishments for students, only for persistently failing schools and their staffs. It is reasonable to wonder to what extent students will be motivated to strive to raise their scores on these tests.

There is similar reason to wonder how much importance the 88 percent of eighth grade students hoping to attend a postsecondary institution will attach to state tests, beyond passing the minimum number of exams needed to graduate. Higher education authorities, after all, generally pay no heed to state exams. Forty-nine states, all but Iowa, now have statewide K–12 content and testing standards in most academic subjects. Almost all, however, have ignored the lack of coherence in content and assessment—the veritable Babel—between K–12 and higher education standards.[38]

In light of all this, will the nation's big bet on centralized, standards-based reform pay off and yield the significant gains (at least as measured by state tests or the NAEP) that have eluded the U.S. students in recent decades? Unfortunately, nobody can say with any confidence. The same question, of course, should be asked of other governance arrangements. Can public charter schools or market-based vouchers, for example, be expected to yield significant gains in student learning? The evidence so far is, at best, ambiguous.[39] Are mayoral takeovers likely to lead to improved classroom performance? There have been slight to moderate test score gains for elementary school students under mayoral regimes in Boston and Chicago, for example, though no gains for secondary students.[40] But mayors are just beginning to understand how to connect their control of schools to improving classroom instruction.

Citizen Influence and the Accountability of Policymakers

Another important goal one might consider is which level of school governance promotes the most democracy (other than market-based initiatives, which, of course, reject democratic governance). Is local school district control more democratic than federal or state control? Will citizens hold policymakers equally accountable at the federal, state, and local levels?

In general, citizens, for a variety of reasons, have more opportunity to affect policy in their local districts than they do at the federal or state levels. Local policymakers serve fewer constituents than state or federal officials and are much closer to citizens psychologically, as well as geographically. (Indeed, local officials understand better than anyone else their community's zone of school policy tolerance.) It is difficult for most citizens to get to the state capital or to Washington. Local school board elections provide a much more direct means to influence local education policy than election of a state legislator, who represents many local school districts on a far wider variety of issues. In the thousands of small school districts in the nation, a significant portion of community residents personally know at least one school board member. Local media provide better information and can capture the attention of citizens more effectively than reports from distant state capitals.

This is by no means to suggest that local school politics approaches the democratic ideal. While the Institute for Educational Leadership found strong public backing for the idea of local school boards as buffers against state and professional administrator control, for example, the individuals do not necessarily support their own local boards and know little about the role of school boards in general. Importantly, moreover, rarely do more than 10 to 15 percent of eligible voters turn out for the school board elections in which about 95,000 board members are chosen for three- or four-year terms on a staggered basis. As columnist Neal Peirce has observed: "If the school boards' popular constituency misperceives their role and doesn't care enough to exercise its franchise in their selection, how fully or forcefully will the boards *ever* be able to function?"[41]

That is an important question, one that must be addressed by anyone interested in strengthening the American school board tradition and local control over education in general. It also should be remembered, however, that the public barely holds state and federal officials responsible for educational results. Although officials at all levels will no doubt claim credit if U.S. schools are seen to improve, for example, it is difficult to think of any president, governor, state legislator, or member of Congress who has lost an election because of educational failures. Yet these officials increasingly have been driving education policy in recent decades, with modest results to show. On the other hand, while local school board members, as well as superintendents, principals, and teachers, have less and less say over education, the public still holds them accountable for school results. In terms of democracy and accountability, then, it is local school districts, with all their imperfections, that would appear to be the superior governance choice.

Notes

1. Mary-Ellen Phelps Deily, "Boards, Parents Seen as Powerful," *Education Week,* June 5, 2002, p. 5.

2. Deborah Land, *Local School Boards under Review: Their Role and Effectiveness in Relation to Students' Academic Achievement* (Baltimore: Center for Research on the Education of Students Placed at Risk, January 2002), p. 15.

3. Lowell C. Rose and Alec M. Gallup, "The 32nd Annual Phi Delta Kappa/Gallup Poll of the Public's Attitudes toward the Public Schools," *Phi Delta Kappan,* September 2000, p. 55.

4. Lowell C. Rose and Alec M. Gallup, "The 34th Annual Phi Delta Kappa/Gallup Poll of the Public's Attitudes toward the Public Schools," *Phi Delta Kappan,* September 2002, p. 42.

5. Ibid., p. 53. See also Michael Newman, "American Public Ready for National Curriculum, Achievement Standards, Annual Gallup Poll Finds," *Education Week,* September 6, 1989, p. 11.

6. See, for example, Larry Cuban, "A Solution That Lost Its Problem," in this volume.

7. David B. Tyack, *The One Best System* (Harvard University Press, 1974).

8. David B. Tyack and Elisabeth Hansot, *Managers of Virtue: Public School Leadership in America, 1820–1980* (Basic Books, 1982).

9. Ibid.

10. While Roman Catholics constituted a considerable exception, even by the late nineteenth century they made up only 10 percent of the population.

11. Lawrence A. Cremin, *The Transformation of the School* (Vintage Books, 1964).

12. David B. Tyack, "Needed: The Reform of a Reform," in National School Boards Association, *New Dimensions of School Board Leadership* (Evanston, Ill., 1969), p. 61.

13. Tyack, *The One Best System*.

14. Ibid.

15. Tyack, "Needed," p. 61.

16. George Counts, *School and Society in Chicago* (Harcourt Brace, 1928).

17. Dianne Ravitch, *Left Back* (Simon and Schuster, 2001).

18. David B. Tyack, Robert Lowe, and Elisabeth Hansot, *Public Schools in Hard Times: The Great Depression and Recent Years* (Harvard University Press, 1984).

19. From 130,000 school districts in 1930, the number had declined to 89,000 by 1948, compared with fewer than 15,000 today.

20. Dianne Ravitch, *The Troubled Crusade: American Education 1945–1980* (Basic Books, 1983).

21. Frederick M. Wirt and Michael W. Kirst, *The Political Web of American Schools* (Little, Brown, 1972).

22. Frederick M. Wirt and Michael W. Kirst, *Schools in Conflict* (Berkeley, Calif.: McCutchan Publishing, 1982).

23. Anthony M. Cresswell, Michael J. Murphy, and Charles T. Kerchner, *Teachers, Unions, and Collective Bargaining in Public Education* (Berkeley, Calif.: McCutchan Publishing, 1980).

24. Susan M. Johnson, *Teacher Unions in Schools* (Temple University Press, 1984).

25. Lorraine M. McDonnell and Anthony Pascal, *Teacher Unions and Education Reform* (Santa Monica, Calif.: RAND, 1987).

26. James W. Guthrie, Walter I. Garms, and Lawrence C. Pierce, *School Finance and Education Policy: Enhancing Educational Efficiency, Equality, and Choice* (Prentice-Hall, 1988).

27. Education Commission of the States, *Models of State Education Governance* (Denver, 2002).

28. Frederick M. Wirt and Michael W. Kirst, *The Political Dynamics of American Education* (Richmond, Calif.: McCutchan, 2001), pp. 209–54.

29. Michael Kirst and Robin L. Bird, "The Politics of Developing and Sustaining Mathematics and Science Curriculum Content Standards," in Paul Thurston and James Ward, eds., *Advances in Educational Administration*, vol. 5 (Greenwich, Conn.: JAI Press, 1997), pp. 107–32.

30. See the contributions to Dianne Ravitch, ed., *Brookings Papers on Education Policy* 2000 (Brookings, 2000).

31. Education Commission of the States, *No State Left Behind: The Challenges and Opportunities of ESEA 2001* (Denver, 2002).

32. Paul T. Hill, "The Federal Role in Education," in Ravitch, *Brookings Papers on Education Policy 2000*, p. 19.

33. James G. Cibulka and William Lowe Boyd, eds., *A Race against Time: The Crisis in Urban Schooling* (Westport, Conn.: Praeger, 2003), pp. 63–166.

34. Theodore Lowi, *The End of Liberalism* (Norton, 1979), p. 145.

35. John E. Chubb and Terry M. Moe, *Politics, Markets, and America's Schools* (Brookings, 1990), p. 2.

36. Margaret E. Goertz, *Assessment and Accountability Systems: 50 State Profiles* (Philadelphia: Consortium for Policy Research in Education, 2001).

37. See, for example, Susan Fuhrman's "Less than Meets the Eye" in this volume.

38. Andrea Venezia, Michael Kirst, and Anthony L. Antonio, *Betraying the College Dream: How Disconnected K–12 and Postsecondary Education Systems Undermine Student Aspirations* (Palo Alto, Calif.: Stanford Institute for Higher Education Research, 2003).

39. Brian P. Gill and others, *Rhetoric versus Reality: What We Know and What We Need to Know about Vouchers and Charter Schools* (Santa Monica, Calif.: RAND Corporation, 2001).

40. Michael Kirst, *Mayoral Influence, New Regimes, and Public School Governance* (Philadelphia: Consortium for Policy Research in Education, 2002).

41. In Lila Carol and others, *School Boards: Improving Grass Roots Leadership* (Washington: Institute for Educational Leadership, 1986), p. iv.

3

The Tenth Amendment and Other Paper Tigers: The Legal Boundaries of Education Governance

JAMES E. RYAN

American education governance provides fertile ground for myths and misunderstandings. Consider, for example, the belief that the U.S. Constitution leaves states in charge of our schools. The Tenth Amendment to the Constitution declares that "powers not delegated to the United States by the Constitution, nor prohibited by it to the states, are reserved to the states respectively, or to the people." Since the Constitution makes no mention of education, federal involvement in this arena must be quite limited, right?

Tell that to the state education officials required to do Washington's bidding today under the No Child Left Behind Act (NCLB). The fact is that the Tenth Amendment is no match for Congress's spending powers, which allow Washington to attach numerous regulatory strings to spending programs. So long as states accept federal funding, Congress can do pretty much as it pleases with education—even establish a national curriculum and a national exam—without running afoul of the Constitution.

I would like to thank Dick Howard, Peter Schuck, and Noel Epstein for helpful comments and Sarah Baker for excellent research assistance.

Some may bemoan this fact and yearn for a day when Congress's power over education will be restricted. These critics should beware of what they wish for. Curtailing Congress's power over schools would not simply shift that authority back to state or local governments, as they presumably imagine. Rather, a good portion of that power would go to the federal courts.

The misapprehensions about education governance filter all the way down to the school district level, where Americans are supposed to enjoy "local control" of public schools, another cherished belief that is, if not a myth, a striking exaggeration. State and federal officials have been taking more and more control away from local school districts for several decades. More fundamentally, state constitutions grant legal authority over education almost exclusively to state legislatures, which are largely free to retain that authority or delegate it to localities as they see fit. By contrast, local school board members, superintendents, principals, and teachers—those held most accountable by the public for results in education—have little to no constitutional authority or responsibility over education.

Misconceptions such as these should be given a decent burial, especially at a time when education authority is undergoing significant change. What is needed in their place is a clearheaded examination of the genuine and shifting legal boundaries of American education governance, a prerequisite for any consideration of who should be responsible for U.S. school policies and performance.

At bottom, these legal boundaries are determined by federal and state constitutional law, which in turn establish limits on federal and state authority. There are, to be sure, myriad statutory rules, administrative regulations, and court decisions that define with bewildering specificity the overlapping roles and responsibilities of the various players in public education, from the federal Department of Education to state boards of education, state departments of education, local school boards, superintendents, and teachers. This complex web of authority and responsibility, however, rests on a relatively simple structure. If one understands this basic structure and its mechanics, one can understand the fundamental legal boundaries of education governance.

Described functionally and at its most basic, this structure consists of two complementary rules. First, because of its spending power, the federal government has almost unfettered discretion to direct the education policies of the states. Second, the states, because of their constitutional status vis-à-vis political subdivisions, have even more authority over local school districts. To be sure, neither Washington nor the states need exercise the powers they possess or control all facets of education. Federal and state governments can and have devolved or delegated authority to states and localities, respectively. Nonetheless, the legal rules that serve as the foundation for education governance effectively allow Washington and the states to decide how much they wish to delegate and how much they wish to control. This, in turn, renders the legal boundaries of education governance remarkably porous.[1]

Indeed, it is helpful to recognize that almost none of the legal boundaries of education governance is hard and fast. That is, there are no state or federal constitutional rules that apportion clear and inviolable spheres of responsibility for education among local, state, and federal governments. Instead, the foundational legal rules render the boundaries a matter of politics and policy choices. It is perhaps little wonder, then, that responsibility for education has varied over time and across states and localities.

At one time, for example, Washington's role in public schools was negligible. Now the federal government is driving education policy through NCLB. At the state level, some states have sought to disperse power to individual schools, while others have sought to consolidate and centralize authority. These variations have occurred and continue to occur because the legal rules defining responsibility for education allow them to.[2]

This chapter explains how these rules operate and considers whether they should be altered. It consists of three parts. The first describes Washington's constitutional ability to dictate the education policies of states and localities. Because Congress's power to attach conditions to federal spending is quite broad, Congress's ability to induce states to follow federal directives regarding education is equally broad. The second part examines the similarly strong ability of states to control the education policies of localities. The third part considers the possibility and advisability of strengthening the existing limits on either federal or state authority.

Federal Power to Set Education Policy

The federal government's role in setting education policy has grown dramatically in the past forty years. Washington now funds more than sixty education programs. The two largest are Title I of the Elementary and Secondary Education Act (ESEA), which is intended to provide resources to disadvantaged students, and the Individuals with Disabilities Education Act (IDEA), designed to assist disabled students. All major federal programs, including Title I and IDEA, provide money to states and localities, and the money comes with strings that, over the years, have formed a tangled web of rules and regulations enveloping public schools.[3]

There is little indication that federal involvement will recede any time soon. Indeed, the signs point in the opposite direction. Consider the No Child Left Behind Act of 2002, which is the most recent reauthorization of the federal Elementary and Secondary Education Act. It imposes unprecedented requirements on the states and localities that it funds, including obligations to develop academic standards, hire "highly qualified" teachers for all core subjects within the next few years, test all students annually in grades 3 through 8, and "reconstitute" persistently failing schools.

In addition, NCLB inflicts a slew of reporting requirements on state and local education agencies and contains literally hundreds of specific directives that states and localities must follow. IDEA, which establishes broad substantive and procedural protections for disabled students, is similarly intrusive, requiring states and localities not only to follow a detailed federal statutory scheme but also to spend hefty sums of their own to fund the program.[4]

At first glance, this federal intrusion in education policy might seem puzzling and even unconstitutional. After all, as anyone with even passing knowledge of the Constitution knows, the federal government is one of limited powers. The Tenth Amendment says as much. The Constitution does not explicitly grant the federal government power to regulate education. How, then, can Washington exert so much control over education policy? The answer lies in the Constitution's Spending Clause. This clause grants Congress the power to tax and spend to "provide for the common defense and general welfare of the United States."[5] As interpreted by the Supreme Court, this clause grants vast powers to Congress. To understand and appreciate the remarkable scope of the Spending Clause, one first must understand some of the basic mechanics of federalism and the Supreme Court's decisions on the issue.

What Congress Can Do Directly

For the bulk of the twentieth century, the most important source of federal authority was the Commerce Clause, which grants Congress the ability to regulate interstate commerce. Before the New Deal, the Supreme Court policed the boundaries of federal authority by occasionally striking down federal legislation that, in the justices' opinion, purported to but did not actually regulate interstate commerce.[6]

In the late 1930s and early 1940s, however, the Court all but abandoned its efforts to restrict congressional authority pursuant to this clause. Recognizing that in an integrated economy even purely local activities could

affect interstate commerce, the Court essentially indicated its willingness
to allow Congress to regulate anything and everything. Thus, the Court
upheld federal restrictions on how much wheat a local farmer could grow
for his own consumption; it upheld minimum wage laws; and it approved
civil rights laws that prohibited discrimination in restaurants and hotels—
all on the ground that these restrictions protected the flow of interstate
commerce.[7] By the early 1960s, it was generally understood that Congress's
authority to regulate private behavior was practically limitless.[8]

A similar expansion occurred more recently regarding Congress's ability to regulate state and local governments. Despite the fact that the Court
was willing to allow Congress almost unlimited power to regulate private
behavior, until 1985 the Court sought to protect certain core functions of
the states from federal interference. The Court relied on the Tenth Amendment to limit Washington's ability to interfere with "integral" or "traditional" state activities.[9]

Although the Tenth Amendment seems merely to state the truism that
all that is not delegated to Congress is reserved to the states, the Court
found in this amendment a core principle of state sovereignty. This principle required that the federal government not intrude in areas traditionally controlled by the state. The Court never explicitly defined what
constituted a traditional or integral state function, so it was never entirely
clear how broadly the protection extended. But given that states and localities traditionally controlled education, this interpretation of the Tenth
Amendment arguably meant that Congress could not make education
policy.

In 1985, however, the Supreme Court abandoned its efforts to protect
state sovereignty through the Tenth Amendment. It did so on the ground
that defining traditional or integral state functions is impossible and
"inevitably invites an unelected federal judiciary to make decisions about
which state policies it favors and which ones it dislikes." The court rejected,
"as unsound in principle and unworkable in practice, a rule of state immunity from federal regulation that turns on a judicial appraisal of whether a
particular government function is 'traditional' or 'integral.' "[10]

The Court's Commerce Clause jurisprudence, taken together with its
Tenth Amendment jurisprudence, meant that after 1985 there were no real
constitutional checks on congressional authority to regulate either private
activities or those of state and local governments. In practical terms, states
and localities that sought to prevent congressional regulation, in the field
of education or elsewhere, would have to rely on the political process rather
than the courts for protection.

In 1995, however, the Court in *United States* v. *Lopez* struck down federal legislation on the ground that it exceeded congressional authority under the Commerce Clause.[11] This decision stunned students of the Court, as it was the first time in more than half a century that it had ruled in such a manner. More important, the decision came in a case involving public schools. The Court struck down the Gun Free School Zones Act on the ground that the act did not regulate economic or commercial activity. In so doing, the Court emphasized that education was an area in which states "historically have been sovereign" and suggested that public schools might simply be beyond the scope of Congress's regulatory authority.

The Court's shot across the bow in *Lopez* was followed in 2000 by another volley. In *United States* v. *Morrison,* the Court struck down a portion of the Violence Against Women Act, again on the ground that because it sought to regulate noneconomic activities, it exceeded Congress's authority under the Commerce Clause.[12]

At the same time as the Court began enforcing limits on Congress's power under the Commerce Clause, it also began to resurrect a principle of state sovereignty, relying at least nominally on the Tenth Amendment to do so. In two cases decided in the 1990s the Court established what has come to be known as the anticommandeering principle. This prohibits Congress from directly requiring state legislatures or executives—or their local counterparts—to enact, administer, or enforce federal programs.

In *New York* v. *United States,* the Court struck down a federal law that required states to either "take title" to radioactive waste within their borders or enact legislation that would handle the disposal of such waste.[13] In *Printz* v. *United States,* the Court struck down a provision of the popular Brady Handgun Violence Prevention Act that required state and local law enforcement officers to conduct background checks on prospective handgun purchasers.[14] In both instances, the Court found that Congress had exceeded its authority by attempting to commandeer the legislative or executive processes of the states, which the court held were crucial aspects of state sovereignty and immune from congressional control. More important, these limits apply even when Congress is properly regulating an activity under the Commerce Clause. The anticommandeering rule, in other words, does not prevent Congress from regulating the underlying activity; rather, it restricts the *means* by which Congress may regulate.

Taken together, the newfound limits on Congress's Commerce Clause authority and the anticommandeering principle impose substantial restrictions on Congress's ability to set education policy directly. To the extent that education is not considered by the Court to be an economic activity and is deemed an area over which states are sovereign, Congress may lack any *direct* power to regulate education. Even if regulating education, or some aspects of it, is within Congress's Commerce Clause authority, the anticommandeering principle prohibits Congress from ordering state and local governments to enact or administer federal programs. This presumably would bar Washington from, say, ordering states to ensure that all public schools administer standardized tests in grades 3 through 8, to hire "highly qualified" teachers, or to reconstitute persistently failing public schools. It also would render unconstitutional any attempt by Congress to order states and localities to provide disabled students with the extensive protections found in IDEA.

To be sure, Congress still retains the ability to enforce antidiscrimination rules that are grounded in the Constitution. Under Section 5 of the Fourteenth Amendment, Congress is granted authority to enforce the protections guaranteed by that amendment, including the right of equal protection. This means that Congress can enact legislation to protect minorities from discrimination in education and elsewhere. But under the Supreme Court's current interpretation of Section 5 authority, Congress cannot grant minorities much *more* protection than the Constitution itself requires.[15]

What this means, as a practical matter, is that federal authority under Section 5 is not especially extensive or especially important in the field of education policy. Pursuant to its Section 5 power, Congress can ensure, for example, that students of color are not intentionally discriminated against. But it cannot offer much protection to other students, including the poor and disabled, who do not receive heightened protection under the Equal Protection Clause. Thus, neither of the two major federal education programs—Title I for poor students or IDEA for disabled students—could be justified as a legitimate exercise of Congress's Section 5 powers.[16] Both programs were enacted pursuant to Congress's spending powers, and it is only pursuant to those powers that the programs can be justified.

What Congress Can Do Indirectly

Once one recognizes that there are substantial limits to Congress's power to regulate public schools directly, it becomes possible to appreciate the importance of the Spending Clause. Through the magic of this clause, Congress can accomplish indirectly what it cannot require directly. The expansive scope of Congress's authority under the Spending Clause is especially important in the field of education, for the simple reason that most federal education programs have been enacted pursuant to this power. It is also important because states that receive money may be in a poor position to turn down federal funds, which means that Congress may be able to regulate public education through the Spending Clause just as effectively as it could were it able to regulate schools directly. What is true for education is true for a host of other fields of regulation, which has prompted many observers to question whether and when the Court might revisit its current approach to the Spending Clause.[17]

Since the Spending Clause grants Congress the authority to tax and spend for the "general welfare," the scope of authority granted by this clause turns on the definition of general welfare, which is not provided in the clause or anywhere else. Two obvious possibilities were apparent almost immediately after the Constitution was ratified and were urged by two of the most influential founding fathers, James Madison and Alexander Hamilton.

First, one could interpret the clause to require that spending for the general welfare be restricted to spending that carries out one of Congress's enumerated powers. This position, Madison urged, would essentially prevent Congress from using its spending powers to pursue objectives beyond those encompassed by Congress's enumerated powers; it would, in other words, preclude Congress from using the Spending Clause to accomplish indirectly what it could not accomplish directly. The alternative view, pressed by Hamilton, was that Congress could use its spending authority to pursue goals beyond those encompassed by its other enumerated powers, provided that the spending advanced the general welfare of the United States, an obviously capacious concept and thus a weak to nonexistent limitation.[18]

Hamilton's view won out in 1936. In *United States* v. *Butler* the Court rejected Madison's view and held that the "power of Congress to authorize expenditure of public moneys for public purposes is not limited by the direct grants of legislative power found in the Constitution."[19] As a consequence, Congress can attach conditions to federal funds that require recipients to perform acts or administer regulations that Congress could not directly command. The intuitive, if overly simplistic, notion underlying this approach is that federal spending programs operate much like any other contract: in return for federal funds, states or localities agree to comply with federally imposed conditions.

As the Court explained in a more recent decision, at least in theory "the residents of the state retain the ultimate decision as to whether or not the state will comply. If a state's citizens view federal policy as sufficiently contrary to local interests, they may elect to decline a federal grant."[20] The difficulty with this view, of course, is that states, as a practical matter, may not have much of an option to decline federal funds.

The Supreme Court has recognized this potential problem, but it has yet to do much about it. To be sure, the Court has acknowledged that Congress's power under the Spending Clause must be somewhat limited, given the vast financial resources of the federal government. Otherwise, Congress could "render academic the Constitution's other grants and limits of federal authority."[21] The court also has established five limitations, or requirements, on the exercise of the federal spending power, all of them fairly weak.[22]

The most basic requirement is that the spending power must be used in pursuit of the general welfare. This requirement stems directly from the language of the clause, but it does not offer much in the way of a restriction. As the Court instructed in 1987 in *South Dakota* v. *Dole,* which remains its most recent and thorough pronouncement on the scope of the Spending Clause, "courts should defer substantially to the judgment of Congress" when considering whether a particular expenditure is designed to advance the general welfare. Indeed, the Court suggested that the level of deference is such that the general welfare requirement may not be "a judicially enforceable restriction at all."[23]

A second requirement is equally vapid, though for different reasons. Congress cannot, through conditional funding, induce states to engage in otherwise unconstitutional behavior.[24] It could not, for example, offer states funding provided they inflict cruel and unusual punishment on prisoners or discriminate against racial minorities. This requirement, unlike the first, surely would be enforced by courts were Congress to contravene it. But Congress is not typically in the business of using its conditional spending power to induce states to violate the Constitution, so it is not a particularly difficult requirement to meet.

The third requirement is that any conditions placed on federal funds must be stated unambiguously, so that states can decide whether to accept funds knowingly and fully aware of the consequences.[25] This requirement has a bit more bite than the first two and has been used by the Supreme Court and lower courts to invalidate attempts to enforce ambiguous conditions by withdrawing federal funds.[26] The Court of Appeals for the Fourth Circuit, for example, invalidated an attempt by the U.S. secretary of education to withdraw federal funds from Virginia because of the commonwealth's policy of expelling disabled students for disruptive behavior not associated with a student's disability. Because it did not read IDEA as conditioning funding on the continued provision of education services to disabled students regardless of misconduct, the court ruled that it was improper to withdraw funds because of Virginia's disciplinary policy.[27] Despite occasional reliance by courts on this requirement, however, it obviously does not impose much of a substantive limit on congressional authority or prevent Congress from overreaching. It simply requires Congress to speak clearly when attaching conditions to funding.

The final two requirements could potentially impose serious restrictions on Congress's authority to attach funding conditions, but they have not been enforced with much zeal. One demands that conditions on federal funding must be germane; in the Court's words, the conditions must not be "unrelated to the federal interest in national projects or programs."[28] At first blush, this seems like a serious requirement. The Court, however, has indicated that the federal interest can be stated at a high level of generality and that the relationship between the conditions and the spending can be fairly tenuous and still survive constitutional review.

In *South Dakota* v. *Dole,* for example, the Court upheld a federal program that conditioned money for highways on an agreement by recipient states to raise their minimum drinking age to twenty-one. The Court held that this condition was related to the federal interest in "safe interstate travel," which it concluded was one of the "main purposes for which highway funds are expended."[29] Notice that it described the federal interest in highway spending at a fairly abstract and general level. This in turn made it much easier for the condition on that spending to be relevant to the interest, for the simple reason that the more broadly and abstractly the federal interest is described, the more conditions will relate to that interest.

In addition, notice that the relationship between raising the drinking age and increasing the safety of interstate travel is plausible, but it obviously is not perfect. Indeed, Justice Sandra Day O'Connor dissented from the majority's decision in *Dole* because she thought the relationship should have to be tighter to uphold a condition on federal funds.[30] The majority of the Court has yet to agree with this argument, however; in a recent opinion (authored, ironically, by O'Connor) it reiterated that there need only be "*some* relationship" between the conditions and the purposes of the federal spending.[31]

Finally, the Court has stated that the financial inducement offered by Congress must not be "so coercive as to pass the point at which pressure turns into compulsion."[32] Like the germaneness requirement, the coercion limitation seems at first glance to place a serious restriction on Congress's spending power. After all, while states remain free in theory to refuse federal funds, there will always be a great deal of pressure on them to accept the funding, since the alternatives will be either to use state funds (and perhaps increase state taxes) or to forgo the program. At the same time, however, divining the line between pressure, which is permitted, and compulsion, which is forbidden, will never be an easy task. As the Court observed as long ago as 1937, and repeated again in its 1987 *Dole* decision, motive or temptation should not be confused with coercion: "to hold that motive or temptation is equivalent to coercion is to plunge the law in endless difficulties. The outcome of such a doctrine is the acceptance of a philosophical determinism by which choice becomes impossible."[33]

Perhaps because of these difficulties, the Court has never found a conditional spending program to be unconstitutionally coercive, nor has it offered much guidance as to how this determination should be made. It has simply hinted that this determination should turn on the amount of money at stake. The hint appears in *Dole*, where the Court rejected the contention that the highway program at issue was coercive. It concluded that this argument was "more rhetoric than fact," because states would lose only 5 percent of their federal highway funds if they did not raise the minimum drinking age to twenty-one. This "relatively mild encouragement" meant that enactment of the minimum drinking age remained "the prerogative of the state not merely in theory but in fact."[34]

Obviously, the Court's statements raise more questions than they answer, leaving one to wonder just where the point of coercion is to be found. Does it turn on whether a state will lose a greater percentage of federal funds if it fails to meet the condition? The overall amount of money at stake? The percentage of funding for a state-federal program that comes from Washington? Such questions have yet to be answered by the Court.

Lower courts, meanwhile, have been quite reluctant to find undue coercion in federal spending programs. Almost all courts addressing the coercion issue have ruled against the states. A number have recognized the difficulty of discerning the difference between an offer that states "cannot refuse and merely a hard choice," and some have questioned whether any "sovereign state which is always free to increase its tax revenues [could] ever be coerced by the withholding of federal funds."[35]

The only court to buck this trend has been the Court of Appeals for the Fourth Circuit. In its 1997 IDEA decision, the court found that the act's language was ambiguous on the issue of discipline and thus could not prevent Virginia from expelling students for misbehavior unrelated to their disabilities. It also held that this condition was coercive, insofar as Virginia would lose *all* of its federal funding under the IDEA program if it refused to rescind its disciplinary policy. The court thus concluded that the federal government went too far in using its financial might to impose federal education policy on the states.[36]

The problem with this analysis, and with the coercion inquiry in general, is apparent from the fact that the court chose to focus on the percentage of federal funds that Virginia would lose rather than the relative percentage of funding that Virginia received from the federal government to educate disabled students. Federal funding constituted only 5 percent of the funds necessary to educate disabled students in Virginia.[37] If this were the basis of analysis—and there is little reason, in principle, for it not to be—it would be much harder to conclude that Virginia was unconstitutionally compelled to accept federal money and abandon its disciplinary policy. Looking at the percentage of funding that comes from Washington for a state-federal program does not have to be *the* benchmark, of course, but that really is the point. The benchmark chosen—whether total dollars, percentage of federal funds at stake, or percentage of funds for a state-federal program that come from Washington, to name three—will affect the coercion determination, but there is no incontrovertible way to select the benchmark.

In sum, given the general reluctance of courts to find unconstitutional coercion in conditional spending programs, notwithstanding the Fourth Circuit's aberrational decision, Washington has wide latitude to affect education policy by attaching conditions to its funding. So long as the conditions are stated clearly and relate in some way to the purpose of the spending program, states effectively have but two options: walk away from the funding or comply with the conditions.

Such conditions, it bears emphasizing, can place severe burdens on states and localities and can intrude considerably on state and local decision-making in the realm of education policy, as demonstrated by NCLB. Its funding conditions, coupled with its extensive reporting requirements, have the potential to dictate everything from hiring decisions to curriculum to whether a school even remains a traditional public school or is turned into a charter school. Many, if not all, of these conditions would be deemed unconstitutional if imposed upon the states in the form of direct federal regulation or directives. Yet because they have been imposed pursuant to Congress's spending power, these conditions are legally valid.

At least at the moment, then, the only real limits on federal power over education policy are political. These limits are either self-imposed by Washington or established by those state leaders who make a political decision to decline federal funding. Self-imposed limits are obvious in NCLB. Even though the act was, ironically, the brainchild of a Republican president, some Republicans in Congress remain wary of nationalizing education policy, and the act contains provisions designed to protect state autonomy. It does not, for example, establish a national curriculum, a national set of academic standards, or a single testing system, and it does not dictate how states should assess whether their schools are failing. Congress presumably refrained from such impositions precisely out of respect for the tradition of state and local control over education, despite the fact that it could have imposed such requirements without running afoul of its spending power.

Notwithstanding the restraint that Congress has exercised, it is clear that federal involvement and control are on an upward trajectory. Telling proof of this point is found in the intriguing history of a single word, "specific," which first made its way into federal education legislation in 1994 and was repeated in the No Child Left Behind Act.[38] Prior to 1994, the federal government promised that its ESEA legislation could not be read to mandate, direct, or control a state or locality's curriculum or program of instruction.[39] In 1994, and again in 2001, the federal government modified this prohibition by indicating that the legislation could not be read to mandate control over a school's "specific" instructional content, standards, or curriculum.[40] This may seem like a minor modification at first glance, but it captures quite well a significant policy shift in recent federal legislation, one marked by increased federal control over state and local education policy.

Just how far the federal role advances may turn on the willingness of state leaders to continue dancing to the tune paid for by the federal piper. In the past, state leaders have usually capitulated to federal demands, despite initial grumbling and despite serious reservations.[41] Southern state leaders in the 1960s and 1970s, for example, ultimately abided by fairly aggressive desegregation plans at least in part to avoid losing federal funds.[42] Similarly, states have established and enforced generous programs to educate the disabled to avoid losing federal funding, despite the fact that these funds represent only a small fraction of the cost of maintaining these programs. More recently, all states but one (Iowa) ultimately accepted federal funding under the Goals 2000 Act, which was designed to encourage states to establish rigorous academic standards.

There is some sign, however, that NCLB might be asking too much in return for federal money. At least one governor and several legislatures have proposed turning down federal funding because they do not wish to follow all the federal requirements, especially those involving testing and accountability. They also believe that the act costs more money than the federal government provides to administer it.[43] Frank Keating, Oklahoma's Republican governor, predicted that a number of states might opt out of the federal program due to opposition to its testing requirements—opposition fueled, at least in part, by objections from teachers and parents who dislike the act's heavy emphasis on standardized testing.[44]

Whether any states follow through with such threats remains to be seen. It may be that Washington is at or near the apex of its ability to cajole states into following federal policy. As federal intrusion increases, especially requiring states to spend significant sums of their own, the possibility that states might balk increases accordingly. It may indeed be that there are hard and fast political limits on federal power that state leaders, by refusing to accept federal money, are willing to enforce. Whether such limits exist, however, begs the question of whether there should be stronger constitutional limits on federal power, a question that I address below. For the moment, however, it is important to complete the picture of education governance by considering state power over local school districts.

State Power to Set Education Policy

The constitutional rules governing state power over education are in some ways even simpler than those governing federal power. All fifty state constitutions guarantee a right to public education and place the responsibility, as well as the authority, for providing that education in the hands of state governments. State legislatures, as a result, have plenary authority to make laws regarding education.[45]

Although there are some variations, these constitutions in the main provide little detail as to how a state's system of education should be organized and governed. About half require the creation of a state board of education and/or the appointment or election of a state superintendent. Eleven require, either explicitly or implicitly, some local governance for public schools; the rest are silent as to local participation. None of the constitutions specifies in much detail the powers to be exercised by state or local boards or superintendents.[46]

State legislatures traditionally have delegated much of their authority over education to various state-level agencies, as well as to local school districts. It is through the latter delegations that the tradition of "local control" of schools has remained alive, even if it has been greatly weakened in recent decades. The key point, however, is that these delegations of power are not constitutionally compelled and the recipients have no independent sources of legal power.

In addition, states generally remain free to restructure education governance as they wish. For example, they can create, abolish, consolidate, or reorganize local school districts, usually without the consent of local citizens. Most states also can decide how local school board members are selected, as well as what powers they can exercise.[47] Indeed, most states could abolish local school boards and take direct control of a school district, as a number of them have done in the last decade.[48]

The central constitutional question concerning the state legislature's authority over education policy is thus the opposite of that concerning Congress's power. With Congress, the question is whether the federal government is authorized to act in a particular field of education—in other words, is it exercising *too much* power? With state legislatures, the central question is whether they have delegated too much authority to state or local agencies—in other words, are they exercising *too little* power?

State constitutions vest in state legislatures the power to enact legislation. Courts have derived from these vesting clauses a limitation on the legislatures' ability to delegate authority. In effect, courts have reasoned that state legislatures alone can legislate on behalf of the state and that they cannot give away this authority. The resulting "nondelegation doctrine" limits the extent to which state legislatures can delegate authority horizontally, to other state agencies, or vertically, to local districts.[49] Although this doctrine has on occasion been used by state courts to curtail delegations in some contexts, the limits on the legislatures' ability to delegate authority over education are fairly weak.

Two general constitutional rules are relevant here. The first pertains to legislative delegations to state administrative agencies: it bars the legislature from conferring upon administrative agencies "unrestricted authority to make fundamental policy decisions."[50] Legislatures therefore must provide adequate standards to guide and restrain the delegated functions. Such standards ensure the legislature is not delegating legislative authority but instead is granting authority to administer a legislative program or execute a legislative directive. Over the past several decades, state courts generally have become more permissive of legislative delegations of power, perhaps in recognition of the increased complexity of governmental business in general, and education in particular.[51] Thus fairly broad guidelines that are consistent with a legislative plan usually are sufficient to safeguard a delegation from constitutional attack.

The second general rule pertains to legislative delegations to political subdivisions in general, and school districts in particular. It is widely accepted that state legislatures may more freely delegate authority over local affairs to municipal corporations and other political subdivisions of the state. Hence, such delegations need not contain the same sort of guidelines as attend delegations of authority to state agencies. Although this rule is most typically applied to delegations of authority to general municipal governments, it also has been used by some courts to justify delegations of authority to school districts and their boards, on the theory that school districts are quasi-municipal corporations.[52]

Other courts view school districts not as quasi-municipal corporations but as state agencies, in which case the nominally more restrictive nondelegation rules presumably would apply.[53] Whichever way they are viewed, however, the important point is that state legislatures can grant school districts a good deal of power and discretion.

Absolute state authority over education, combined with loose restrictions on the delegation of power and a tradition of local control, have led in nearly all states to a complex set of legal and administrative relationships among state and local policymakers.[54] Although there are fifty different systems of education, which makes generalization somewhat hazardous, they have enough in common that it is possible to give a sense of the current governing structures in most states.

Forty-eight states have established some type of state board of education, which is usually charged with exercising general control over the elementary and secondary schools in the state and with implementing legislative mandates. Board members are appointed in some states and elected in others. In addition, all fifty states have designated a chief state school officer, usually known as the state superintendent of public instruction or the commissioner of education. In some states, this officer is elected; in others, he or she is appointed by the governor or the state board of education. Generally, the chief officer is charged with general supervision of the schools, and often with adjudicating controversies over education.

The superintendent also organizes and directs the state department of education, which consists of education specialists who provide information and consultation to state and local school boards. State departments also collect information from school districts to determine whether legislative enactments and state board policies are being implemented, and they conduct research in an effort to improve educational practice within the state.[55]

Although education is legally controlled by the states, in almost all cases it is administered locally. Every state except Hawaii has created local school districts, which in turn are governed by local school boards, most of which are elected. Almost all school districts are independent of general local governments, even when the district and municipal boundaries are coextensive.[56] Most local school boards have been granted the authority to raise revenue, usually through property taxes.

Typically, local school boards are also responsible for overseeing school operations, although the powers of school boards have varied over time and from state to state. The basic legal rule, however, has remained constant: local boards possess only those powers granted by state law, as well as other powers necessary to achieve the purposes of their express powers. Local boards cannot delegate their decisionmaking authority to other agencies, associations, or individuals, including local superintendents, principals, teachers, or teachers associations.

Indeed, school district employees, such as superintendents, principals, and teachers, technically are authorized only to perform "ministerial duties"; that is, they are empowered to carry out the local school board's decisions.[57] Thus, at the end of this long and complicated chain, those who have the closest and most persistent contact with students have the least legal authority and responsibility over education.

Neither the elaborate state administrative structure nor the authority exercised by different entities is fixed by constitutional law. Both are matters of state policy and generally are governed by state statute. As a result, both have been altered over time, and states have divided education authority in different ways. Most recently, there have been two divergent and somewhat contradictory trends in state education governance.

On the one hand, there has been a movement toward greater centralization and increased involvement by states in areas traditionally left to local control. This has been due primarily to three factors. First, school finance reform, often provoked by the courts, has increased the state share of education funding in many states. With increased state funding has come increased state control over the distribution of resources, as well as increased involvement in academic decisions.

Second, and more important, states have become actively and aggressively involved in school improvement. A principal impetus for this was the 1983 report *A Nation At Risk*, which predicted in dramatic terms that the United States might lose its status as an industrial and economic leader unless it improved its schools. In response, states began, with the encouragement of the federal government, to establish content and performance standards and create accountability systems to ensure that students, teachers and schools met those standards.

By January 1999, forty-nine states had established standards in some subject areas and forty-eight had created assessments or tests for their students. The creation of state standards and assessments effectively means that states are playing a larger role in shaping the curriculum.[58] States have also increased control by raising high school graduation requirements, setting higher teacher certification or minimum competency requirements, extending the school day and the school year, and even imposing minimum homework requirements.[59]

Finally, the continued existence of abysmal urban schools has led to legislation granting states the power either to intervene directly in cases of "academic bankruptcy" or to shift control over urban school systems from locally elected boards to mayors. Twenty-four states have enacted legislation allowing state education officials to intervene and eventually take over persistently failing school districts.[60] New Jersey's law, perhaps the best known and a model for others, lets state officials take complete control of a district and dismiss school board members and school administrators.[61] A number of states also have enacted legislation that transfers the power to select school board members and superintendents in failing urban school systems from the local electorate to city mayors.[62] The mayors of Detroit, Chicago, Boston, and most recently New York have all acquired this power and now exert significant control over local schools.[63]

On the other hand, there has been a movement, sometimes within the same states, to decentralize control over local schools. Some states have repealed state regulations or directives. In the last decade, for example, South Carolina has eliminated almost 100 state statutes governing education and more than 500 rules governing K–12 education. Similarly, Michigan has removed 205 sections from its education code, Texas has reduced the number of state directives by one third, and South Dakota has purged hundreds of rules and close to 100 state education statutes.[64]

In addition to deregulation, a number of states support what is known as site-based management. In these states, some decisionmaking responsibility has been taken away from local school boards and given to schools and their advisory boards, which usually comprise some combination of teachers, parents, and administrators.[65] Schools and their advisory boards typically are granted the authority to make decisions on issues ranging from hiring principals and other administrators to developing an annual budget to fashioning school improvement plans.[66] Chicago's experiment with site-based management was perhaps the best known and most closely studied. It was also quite short-lived, at least in its most expansive form. Seven years after the experiment began, the Illinois Legislature passed the Chicago School Reform Amendatory Act, which recentralized authority in the mayor, although it did not eliminate the local school councils entirely.[67]

Other decentralizing forces include charter schools, which are found in thirty-six states and the District of Columbia, and a smaller number of voucher programs, which operate in three states.[68] Charter schools are a cross between public and private schools. Although they are publicly funded, tuition-free, and nonsectarian, they are exempted from various state rules and regulations regarding such issues as the hiring of teachers, curriculum, calendar, and the length of the school day. The basic idea is to grant these schools greater flexibility in exchange for greater accountability; like the private schools that participate in voucher programs in Cleveland, Milwaukee, and Florida, charter schools have a certain degree of autonomy from the state. To be sure, they are not completely free to select their own goals, but they nonetheless represent a movement away from centralized control toward more localized, school-based control.[69] At the same time, charter schools face stiffer accountability demands, at least in theory, and they can be closed if they do not meet the performance goals established in their charters.

These cross-cutting trends in education governance illustrate the degree of flexibility that states have in structuring public school systems. None of the changes noted, neither those increasing state control nor those dispersing it, raises serious constitutional questions about state authority.[70] Because states have absolute authority over education, *increases* in state control will rarely, if ever, run afoul of state constitutions. By contrast, the *delegation* of state control could raise constitutional questions, but these would be only as serious as the application of the nondelegation doctrine by that state's courts. Given that most state courts do not police delegations of power in the field of education very aggressively, states effectively have nearly as much freedom to devolve power to localities as they do to concentrate it at the state level.

Both the federal and state governments thus possess great power to influence education policy, as well as great discretion over how much control they exert over local schools. There is a popular belief that public schools are locally controlled. As a legal matter, this has always been something of a myth. Local control exists only insofar as states are willing to delegate authority, and even then localities can control only what a state lets them control. As a practical matter, it is becoming more difficult to identify many, if any, areas over which local school boards retain exclusive or significant control. Local boards, like local schools, are being pushed and prodded by federal and state directives, so much so that some commentators describe local boards as essentially holding entities for state and federal policies.[71]

To be sure, some states have repealed state statutes and regulations and others have granted more authority to schools themselves, but even they maintain statewide standards and assessments, which drive curricular and instructional decisionmaking at the local level. By requiring states to develop such standards and assessments, NCLB ensures that states will continue to play a dominant role in local education policy. Along with IDEA, NCLB also ensures that the federal government will exert significant influence over state and local decisionmaking.

Many have questioned, with good reason, whether the current structure of education governance is the most effective.[72] Should the federal government play such a strong role in setting education policy? Should its role be even stronger? Should states be setting standards or simply encouraging best practices among diverse local districts? Should schools be controlled by locally elected boards that are independent of general municipal governments or mayors and their advisers? These and other policy questions are fascinating, difficult, and addressed by others in this volume. My task is to concentrate on the legal issues involved, and the last issue that must be addressed is whether the legal boundaries of educational governance should be made clearer and firmer.

Altering the Balance of Power

Before addressing whether it would be wise, in theory, to rein in Congress's spending power, it should be recognized that the Supreme Court might take such a step before too long. Recall that the Court in the past decade has issued decisions designed to curtail Congress's power. In addition to its Commerce Clause decisions and its anticommandeering rules, the Court has also limited Congress's ability to enforce the Fourteenth Amendment and to abrogate the sovereign immunity of states.[73]

The Court appears to be spinning a judicial web around Congress, designed to limit federal authority to regulate private individuals and interfere with state and local decisionmaking. But although these decisions have been important symbolically, at the moment this web is fairly weak. The reason is that Congress's power under the Spending Clause has yet to be significantly curtailed. Congress can thus avoid many of the limits established by the Court by simply attaching conditions on federal spending programs, and thereby accomplish indirectly what it cannot accomplish directly.

Many commentators contend that all the Court's efforts so far will have been largely for naught unless it does something to limit Congress's spending power. As Lynn A. Baker, a leading authority on the Spending Clause and a strong proponent of the restriction of federal spending power, has stated:

> The greatest threat to state autonomy is, and has long been, Congress's spending power. No matter how narrowly the court might read Congress's

powers under the Commerce Clause and Section 5 of the 14th Amendment, and no matter how absolute a prohibition the Court might impose
on Congress's "commandeering" of state and local officials, the states will
be at the mercy of Congress so long as there are no meaningful limits on
its spending power.[74]

It makes little sense, so Baker and others suggest, for the Court to establish
formalistic limits on Congress's powers while at the same time permitting
Congress to circumvent these limitations with conditional funding. A number of constitutional law scholars, for just this reason, predict that restricting Congress's spending power will be next on the Court's federalism
agenda.[75]

These predictions are plausible, as the Spending Clause currently stands
as a gaping loophole in the Court's federalism jurisprudence. Predicting
what the Supreme Court will do is a risky exercise. It is nonetheless a useful exercise in this instance, because it offers an opportunity to consider two
important questions. First, would any general restrictions on Congress's
spending power likely affect Washington's specific ability to influence education policy? To answer that question, one needs to consider the likely
means by which the Court might restrict the spending power. Second,
would limiting Congress's spending power *increase* the power of federal
courts to set education policy, and if so, would this be a change for the better? Put differently, if restricting federal spending power means granting
federal courts more discretion to set education policy, should we support
such restrictions?

Revisiting the Spending Power

There are a number of possible means by which the Court might restrict the
federal spending power. Recall that the Court has established five criteria
that govern the use of the spending power:

1. Spending must be for the "general welfare."
2. Spending conditions must not require recipients to engage in unconstitutional behavior.
3. Spending conditions must be stated unambiguously.
4. Spending conditions must be related to the purpose of the spending.
5. Financial inducements of federal spending programs must not be
coercive.

The first three of these do not seem good candidates to accomplish the task of limiting Congress's spending power.

The first criterion *could* be used to accomplish a fairly radical reworking of Congress's spending power. The Court could decide that "general welfare" should be reinterpreted in accordance with Madison's view, which would let Congress spend money only to further its other enumerated powers. Such a reinterpretation would effectively prevent Congress from attempting to achieve indirectly what it could not directly accomplish. Were the court to pursue this avenue, Congress's ability to influence education policy would be drastically limited, since it has little to no ability to determine education policy directly. Congress would retain the ability to enforce antidiscrimination rules that are themselves constitutionally based, since it would retain authority to enforce the Fourteenth Amendment's Equal Protection Clause. But it would be difficult under such a reinterpretation to justify either Title I or IDEA, neither of which is constitutionally compelled or within Congress's other enumerated powers.

It is unlikely the Court would take such a radical step. Such a sweeping ruling would affect countless federal spending programs. It also would require the Court to abandon an interpretation of the Spending Clause articulated in the 1936 case of *United States* v. *Butler* and followed ever since. None of the sitting justices has suggested *Butler* should be revisited. On the contrary, the four who presumably are most interested in further restricting Congress's spending powers—Chief Justice William H. Rehnquist and Justices Anthony M. Kennedy, Antonin Scalia, and Clarence Thomas—recently cited the *Butler* rule without objection. Dissenting in a 1999 decision, Kennedy, whose opinion was joined by Rehnquist, Scalia, and Thomas, began by quoting the basic *Butler* rule—that Congress's spending power "is not limited by the direct grants of legislative power found in the Constitution"—and did not question its wisdom or validity, accepting it as settled law.[76]

Kennedy did suggest that the Court should more strictly enforce the requirement that any condition placed on funding must be stated unambiguously, the third of the five criteria listed above.[77] It is certainly possible that the Court will police this requirement more aggressively on a case-by-case basis. But this would not accomplish much in terms of restricting Congress's substantive powers under the Spending Clause, and its actual impact on spending programs would be occasional rather than systematic. Its impact on federal education legislation would likely be minimal, given that most of the conditions on federal money for education are fairly clear and specific.

The second criterion, which prohibits Congress from requiring that recipients of federal funds violate the Constitution, hardly matters, as Congress is not in the business of mandating that funding recipients violate the Constitution. There is nothing, in any event, that the Court could do to strengthen this requirement, so it can safely be put to the side.

The Court could, however, strengthen the final two requirements. It could require that funding conditions be more closely related to the purpose of the funding, and it could establish standards that make it easier for courts to conclude that spending programs are coercive. Of these two possibilities, only the latter would likely have a significant effect on federal education legislation. This is because conditions placed on federal education funds are quite closely related to the purposes of the funding.

For example, the conditions attached to Title I money, though intrusive, certainly are related to its goal of improving the educational opportunities afforded to poorer students. Requiring states to establish challenging standards for all students and to devise accountability mechanisms to ensure the standards are accomplished may be a controversial step for any government, especially the federal government, to take. But it would be hard to conclude that these requirements are not closely related to the purpose of Title I. Similarly, IDEA requires states to create an elaborate scheme of procedural and substantive protections for disabled students in exchange for federal funding. Again, the wisdom and equity of those requirements, and especially the amount of money that states and localities must pay to fulfill them, certainly can be questioned. But the close relationship between those requirements and IDEA's purpose—to ensure that disabled students receive an adequate and appropriate education—can scarcely be questioned.

Thus, even if the Court were to require a closer relationship between conditions on federal funds and the purposes for which they are used, this would not likely affect current education legislation. To be sure, some specific provisions in federal education legislation that stray quite far from the purpose of the federal funding might be struck down, but the core elements of programs like Title I and IDEA would not be at risk.

A quicker trigger on finding coercion, however, could indeed call federal education legislation into question. From one perspective, it would seem to make sense for a court interested in curtailing Congress's spending power to focus on the requirement that the federal government actually leave states a choice as to whether to accept federal money and the conditions attached to it. After all, the practical inability of states to decline federal money is at the heart of almost all complaints about conditional spending. Were states able to turn down federal funds easily, most problems associated with conditional spending would effectively disappear, as states presumably would be in a sufficiently strong position to bargain for whatever terms suited them and walk away from deals they did not like. In theory, then, it seems right to focus on the coercive nature of conditional spending programs.

The difficulty is translating theory into a workable test. Every federal dollar attached to a condition is designed to induce states to fulfill that condition. Yet given that states have the ability to raise their own revenues, there is simply no easy way to discern permissible inducement from impermissible compulsion. Indeed, it is precisely for this reason that some courts have declined to undertake this task, observing that "[t]he courts are not suited for evaluating whether the states are faced . . . with an offer they cannot refuse or merely a hard choice."[78] It may be for the same reason that the Supreme Court has never relied on this theory to strike down a funding condition.[79]

Were the Court nonetheless to develop standards for determining coercion, one thing is clear: those standards would necessarily leave a good deal of discretion to courts, letting them decide for any particular case whether the offer of federal money constituted compulsion or presented a hard choice. Similarly, in any attempt to tighten up the germaneness requirement, courts would likely retain plenty of discretion to determine, on a case-by-case basis, whether conditions attached to federal money were sufficiently related to the purpose of the program to satisfy whatever new test might be created. The two most plausible avenues for restricting Congress's powers, therefore, would likely enhance the influence of federal courts. With this in mind, one can tackle the final question: whether the Court *should* limit Congress's spending powers and perhaps thereby establish stricter boundaries on congressional authority over education policy.

To answer this, one must envision alternatives to the current system, which essentially leaves the issue of federal spending power to the political process. The most important point to recognize is that judicial limits on state and federal power are not likely to be self-enforcing. The most likely alternative to the current approach would be a system where courts take a more active role in policing the boundaries of federal power. Courts would thus have to decide, on a case-by-case basis, whether a federal program goes too far, either because it runs afoul of a stricter germaneness requirement or because it constitutes undue coercion. Given the unlikelihood that clear standards would guide such determinations, granting this power to courts raises the distinct possibility that unelected judges would make their decisions on the basis of whether they like or dislike specific federal policies.[80]

Whether one thinks this would be an improvement over the current approach may turn on one's view of the proper role of courts in setting education policy. Federal courts, as many have observed, have played an important role in establishing certain education policies and in controlling certain aspects of public schooling. The Supreme Court and lower courts have required and actively monitored school desegregation, including fairly extensive busing programs. Federal courts have actively policed religious exercises in the schools and have generally banished them from public school classrooms or ceremonial events. The Supreme Court and lower courts have been active in adjudicating the rights of disabled students, both before and after passage of IDEA. State courts have been equally active, especially in the field of school finance.[81]

Several of the Supreme Court's decisions, such as *Brown* v. *Board of Education,* have been justly celebrated.[82] At the same time, however, many have questioned whether federal courts should exercise significant control over the operation of public schools. Indeed, the conservative members of the current Supreme Court have suggested that federal courts should soon end desegregation decrees and return school systems to the control of state and local officials.[83] The irony of recent efforts to restrict federal legislative power is that they have been spearheaded by conservative justices and endorsed by political conservatives. Yet, these are the same individuals and groups that tend to oppose the active involvement of federal courts in education policy, on the ground that accountable policymakers, rather than unelected judges, should determine the goals, rules, and regulations governing public schools.

To curtail *Congress's* power over education policy, however, would require giving more power to federal *courts* to determine education policy. Granted, the role of federal courts would not be as extensive as was necessary in setting out and monitoring extensive school desegregation plans. But there can be little doubt that federal courts would influence, if not determine, significant elements of education policy were they to police more actively the boundaries of federal spending powers.

None of this is to suggest that there is no role for courts to play in the world of education. Nor is it to suggest that court involvement in this arena has caused more harm than good. But one must recognize that there are costs to increasing court involvement in education policy, as elsewhere. Given the lack of objective benchmarks to establish the "proper" amount of federal control over education, the primary cost is that individual judges and justices may impose their own policy preferences when setting the boundaries between state and federal control.[84] For those who generally distrust the political process in this instance—who do not believe that states can protect their own interests against federal encroachment—this might be an acceptable price to pay. After all, the same dangers attend the judicial enforcement of individual rights and liberties, but few would argue that courts should not protect free speech or equal protection rights, for example, simply because vague constitutional standards allow room for judicial discretion.

Whether the political process *can* be trusted to determine the boundaries of federal power over education and other issues is a question that has been debated in the legal academy for at least fifty years.[85] It will not be resolved soon, and certainly not here. It seems fair to say, however, that there is less reason in the abstract to distrust the political process when it comes to states' rights than when it comes to the rights of disfavored individuals or groups, if only because the former have a great deal more political muscle than the latter.

The onus is therefore on those who encourage federal courts to restrict Congress's power to demonstrate both that the federal government has overstepped its proper bounds and that federal courts are better suited to establish the proper limits of federal education authority. Because there is as yet no convincing demonstration of either point, increased court involvement here seems unwarranted. Federal representatives and officials will not always respect state autonomy. But if one really values state autonomy, one should focus less on creating new judicial tests to limit federal authority and more on using the political process to ensure that Congress respects state and local power over education policy.[86]

Reconceiving State Authority over Education

Pursuant to most state constitutions, at least as interpreted by courts, states have absolute authority over education but also a good deal of freedom to delegate authority to local school districts. Those interested in altering the balance of power over education between states and localities have at least two divergent options to explore. On the one hand, they could urge courts to restrict the ability of states to delegate authority to local districts and ensure that states retain control over the policies and operation of local schools. On the other hand, they might seek amendments to state constitutions (generally much easier to obtain than amendments to the federal Constitution) that grant more decisionmaking authority to local districts.

Restricting the states' power to delegate authority seems unwise for many of the same reasons that restricting federal spending authority seems unwise. Such a move would plunge state courts into the depths of education policy and governance, with little guarantee that they would have a comparative advantage over state legislatures in determining the appropriate amount of local discretion. Some delegation of authority to local districts seems both inevitable and wise, given the complexity of running public schools and the diverse settings and circumstances in which those schools operate.

It is highly unlikely that a state court would be in a better position than the state legislature to figure out whether local districts have been granted too much decisionmaking authority. In addition, given that most states have centralized authority over education policy during the past decade, there currently seems little reason to fear they will give away too much authority if not checked by state courts.

Perhaps, then, the real danger is that local districts do not have *enough* authority over their local schools and that a move to grant local school districts more constitutional power should be supported. Such proposals have been offered by commentators and some state legislators, who argue that local school districts should be afforded a version of the "home-rule" power that many state constitutions grant to general municipal governments.[87] Home rule for school districts would allow them greater room to set local education policy and to govern their schools.

The difficulty with home rule proposals is that not all school districts can be trusted with this authority. Some districts require more state oversight and involvement than others. Were home rule authority guaranteed in state constitutions, state legislatures and executives might be hampered in efforts to intervene in or take over failing districts. To the extent that home rule authority were granted to local school boards, moreover, state legislatures would be unable to shift control from school boards to mayors when school boards seem to be failing. Protecting and even enhancing local autonomy over schools might be wise in many cases, but it seems unwise to relinquish control over *all* districts, since some are dysfunctional and others may become so.

A better course would seem to be to allow states to use their broad discretion to delegate authority to those districts that have demonstrated their competence, while maintaining stronger control over districts in need of assistance. Again, there may be reason to disagree with particular instances of state authority, but occasional disagreements and mistakes seem a worthwhile price to pay for a governance system that can respond to diverse local needs and abilities.

Conclusion

The legal boundaries of education governance are drawn in political arenas and they vary over time and place. Political arenas, of course, can be
brutish and messy places. Even when representatives are attempting to act in
the best interests of the public, compromises must be made and deals must
be struck if legislation is to be enacted. The influence of special interest
groups makes the process even more complicated and unseemly.

By contrast, adjudication, at least at the appellate level, appears quite
principled and neat. The route by which judicial decisions are reached is
shrouded in secrecy for the most part, and the public sees only the end
result: an opinion that usually appears (especially to the lay public)
grounded in defensible reason and logic. It is only natural, then, that those
dissatisfied with the way the boundaries of legal governance have been
drawn by the political process might be attracted to the judicial forum.
Increasing the involvement of federal or state courts, however, carries its
own price, and it is quite dear: the loss of the ability of state and federal
representatives, accountable to the public in a way that the judiciary is not,
to make decisions on behalf of their constituents.

In the field of public education, which is designed in part to prepare
students to participate in democratic governance, relinquishing public control over the boundaries of education may simply be too high a price to
pay for the seemingly neat and principled results that could be obtained
through the judiciary. Others may argue convincingly that the current system of education governance is in need of repair and revision, and there
are many who have offered thoughtful and attractive ways to improve the
system.[88] Even if repairs are needed, one ought to hesitate before contracting out such repairs to the judiciary and look first to the admittedly messy
and often less-than-satisfying machinery of democratic politics.

Notes

1. On Congress's spending power, see, for example, Lynn A. Baker, "Conditional
Federal Spending after *Lopez*," 95 *Columbia Law Review* (1995), p. 1911. On the authority of state governments over school districts, see, for example, Roald F. Campbell and
others, *The Organization and Control of American Schools*, 6th ed. (Prentice-Hall, 1990),
pp. 85–87.

2. For a discussion of the changing role of the federal government, see, for example,
Paul T. Hill, "Getting It Right the Eighth Time: Reinventing the Federal Role," in Marci

Kanstoroom and Chester E. Finn Jr., eds., *New Directions: Federal Education Policy in the Twenty-First Century* (Washington: Thomas B. Fordham Foundation, 1999), pp. 147–54. On state efforts to devolve and consolidate authority over education policy and local schools, see, for example, *Governing America's Schools: Changing the Rules,* report of the National Commission on Governing America's Schools (Denver: Education Commission of the States, 1999), p. 9, and Robert C. Johnston and Jessica L. Sandham, "States Increasingly Flexing Their Policy Muscle," *Education Week,* April 14, 1999, p. 19.

3. On the growth of federal programs, as well as the requirements they impose upon the states, see Hill, "Getting It Right the Eighth Time," pp. 148–54, and Charles F. Faber, "Is Local Control of the Schools Still a Viable Option?" 14 *Harvard Journal of Law & Public Policy* (1991), pp. 447, 452–56.

4. The earliest version of IDEA was enacted in 1975 as the Education of the Handicapped Act. The name of the statute was changed to IDEA in 1991, when amendments were made and additional protections provided. See *Cedar Rapids Community School District* v. *Garrett F.,* 526 U.S. 66 (1999), p. 68.

5. U.S. Constitution, Article I, Section 8, Clause 1.

6. See Geoffrey R. Stone and others, *Constitutional Law,* 4th ed. (New York: Aspen Publishers, 2001), pp. 160–75.

7. See, respectively, *Wickard* v. *Filburn,* 317 U.S. 111 (1942); *United States* v. *Darby,* 312 U.S. 100 (1941); and *Heart of Atlanta Motel, Inc.* v. *United States,* 379 U.S. 241 (1964), *Katzenbach* v. *McClung,* 379 U.S. 294 (1964).

8. See Stone and others, *Constitutional Law,* pp. 175–85. As one federal judge colorfully described the state of the law after 1960: "I wonder why anyone would make the mistake of calling it the Commerce Clause instead of the 'Hey, you-can-do-whatever-you-feel-like Clause.'" Alex Kozinski, "Introduction to Volume Nineteen," 19 *Harvard Journal of Law & Public Policy* (1995), pp. 1, 5.

9. See *National League of Cities* v. *Usery,* 426 U.S. 833 (1976) (holding that the Tenth Amendment prohibited Congress from interfering with "integral" or "traditional" state activities, without defining what those activities were).

10. *Garcia* v. *San Antonio Metropolitan Transit Authority,* 469 U.S. 528 (1985), p. 546 (overruling *National League of Cities* v. *Usery*).

11. *United States* v. *Lopez,* 514 U.S. 549 (1995).

12. *United States* v. *Morrison,* 529 U.S. 598 (2000).

13. *New York* v. *United States,* 505 U.S. 144 (1992).

14. *Printz* v. *United States,* 521 U.S. 898 (1997).

15. See *City of Boerne* v. *Flores,* 521 U.S. 507 (1997); *United States* v. *Morrison,* 529 U.S. 598; *Board of Trustees of the University of Alabama* v. *Garrett,* 531 U.S. 356 (2001).

16. Section 5 of the Fourteenth Amendment likely would allow Congress to require states to ensure the disabled access to public education. It is plausible to infer from other Court decisions that disabled students have a constitutional right, protected by the Equal Protection Clause, to attend public schools and perhaps even to receive a minimally adequate education. See *San Antonio Independent School District* v. *Rodriguez,* 411 U.S. 1 (1973); *Plyler* v. *Doe,* 457 U.S. 202 (1982); *Papasan* v. *Allain,* 478 U.S. 265 (1986) ("As *Rodriguez* and *Plyler* indicate, this court has not yet definitively settled the

question . . . whether a minimally adequate education is a fundamental right . . . "). It is much less plausible to suppose that disabled students have the constitutional right to all of the substantive and procedural protections specified in the IDEA; if they do not, Congress presumably lacks the power under Section 5 of the Fourteenth Amendment to order states to provide those protections.

17. See, for example, Baker, "Conditional Federal Spending after *Lopez*"; Celestine Richards McConville, "Federal Funding Conditions: Bursting through the Dole Loopholes," 4 *Chapman Law Review* (2001), pp. 163, 165.

18. For a discussion of Madison's and Hamilton's views of the proper scope of the Spending Clause, see, for example, McConville, p. 168.

19. 297 U.S. 1 (1936): 65. Ironically, after stating this view of the Spending Clause, the Court nonetheless struck down the federal act in question under the Tenth Amendment, because it regulated agriculture, which the Court held was beyond the reach of Congress's power. Id. at 68. The court thus endorsed Hamilton's view but seemed to apply Madison's, making this "one of the few truly ridiculous opinions delivered in two centuries of Supreme Court jurisprudence." David E. Engdahl, "The Spending Power," 44 *Duke Law Journal* (1994): pp. 1, 36. The endorsement of Hamilton's view has been repeated in later opinions; the application of Madison's view has not.

20. *New York* v. *United States*, p. 168.

21. Ibid., p. 167.

22. The court discusses all five of these limitations in *South Dakota* v. *Dole*, 483 U.S. 203, pp. 207–08 and note 2, and pp. 210–11 (1987).

23. Ibid., pp. 207–08 and note 2.

24. Ibid., pp. 210–11.

25. Ibid., p. 207.

26. See, for example, *Pennhurst State School and Hospital* v. *Halderman*, 451 U.S. 1 (1981); *Virginia Department of Education* v. *Riley*, 106 F.3d (1997), p. 559.

27. *Virginia Department of Education* v. *Riley*, 106 F.3d, pp. 561–69.

28. *South Dakota* v. *Dole*, p. 207 (internal quotation omitted).

29. Ibid., p. 208.

30. See ibid., pp. 212–18 (O'Connor dissenting).

31. *New York* v. *United States*, p. 167 (emphasis added).

32. *South Dakota* v. *Dole*, p. 211.

33. Ibid., pp. 211–12 [quoting *Steward Machine Co.* v. *Davis*, 301 U.S. 548 (1937), pp. 589–90].

34. Ibid. See McConville, "Federal Funding Conditions: Bursting through the Dole Loopholes," pp. 180–81 and note 4 (discussing and quoting decisions).

35. See McConville, pp. 180–81 and note 4 (discussing and quoting decisions). *Virginia Department of Education* v. *Riley*, pp. 569–72.

36. *Virginia Department of Education* v. *Riley*, pp. 569–72.

37. Ibid., p. 570.

38. My thanks to Noel Epstein for bringing this issue to my attention, as well as for tracking down the story behind the insertion of the term into recent federal education legislation.

39. See 20 U.S.C., Sec. 1232A.

40. See Improving America's Schools Act of 1994, Section 14512, codified at 20 U.S.C., Sec. 6514; No Child Left Behind Act, Section 1905, codified at 20 U.S.C., Sec. 6301.

41. The one glaring exception is important: many states did not comply with the requirements of the Improving America's Schools Act, which was the precursor to the No Child Left Behind Act. See, for example, Michael Cohen, *Implementing Title I Standards, Assessments and Accountability: Lessons from the Past, Challenges for the Future,* paper prepared for a Thomas B. Fordham Foundation conference on the No Child Left Behind Act (February 13, 2002). The federal government may face similar problems in enforcing the No Child Left Behind Act, since Cohen suggests that given the federal government's track record in the past, "no one believes that it will ultimately withhold funds from state or local districts." Ibid., pp. 9–10.

42. See, for example, Michael J. Klarman, "Brown, Racial Change and the Civil Rights Movement," 80 *Virginia Law Review* (1994), p. 7.

43. See David S. Broder, "GOP Solicitation Lurks in Letter from 'Census,' " *Washington Post,* May 5, 2002, p. A6; David J. Hitt, "Debate Grows on True Costs of School Law," *Education Week,* February 4, 2004, p. 1.

44. See David S. Broder and Dan Balz, "Bush Agenda Concerns Governors over U.S. Role," *Washington Post,* August 7, 2001, p. A2.

45. Martha M. McCarthy and Nelda H. Cambron-McCabe, *Public School Law: Teacher and Student Rights,* 3rd ed. (Newton, Mass.: Allyn and Bacon, 1992), pp. 2–7.

46. The figures in this paragraph come from *State Constitutions and Public Education Governance* (Denver: Education Commission of the States, 2000).

47. McCarthy and Cambron-McCabe, *Public School Law: Teacher and Student Rights,* pp. 2–7, and Edmund E. Reutter Jr., *The Law of Public Education,* 4th ed. (Westbury, N.Y.: Foundation Press, 1994), pp. 104, 154.

48. See Aaron Saiger, "Disestablishing Local School Districts as a Remedy for Educational Inadequacy," *Columbia Law Review,* vol. 99, no. 7 (November 1999), pp. 1830, 1848–52.

49. For a discussion of the nondelegation doctrine, see Clayton P. Gillette and Lynn A. Baker, *Local Government Law,* 2nd ed. (New York: Aspen Publishers, 1999), pp. 775–90.

50. Reutter, *The Law of Public Education,* p. 106 (internal quotation omitted).

51. See ibid., p. 116; Campbell and others, *The Organization and Control of American Schools,* p. 89.

52. See Reutter, *The Law of Public Education,* p. 119.

53. See McCarthy and Cambron-McCabe, *Public School Law: Teacher and Student Rights,* pp. 2–7.

54. Hawaii is a partial exception, because it is the only state that does not have any local school districts. See Saiger, "Disestablishing Local School Districts as a Remedy for Educational Inadequacy," p. 1846, note 80. The District of Columbia is also a single district with a single board of education.

55. For an overview of the organization and governance of state and local education, see, for example, McCarthy and Cambron-McCabe, *Public School Law: Teacher and Student Rights,* pp. 2–7.

56. See Campbell and others, *The Organization and Control of American Schools,* p. 113.

57. See McCarthy and Cambron-McCabe, *Public School Law: Teacher and Student Rights,* pp. 2–7.

58. See *Governing America's Schools,* p. 9, and Johnston and Sandham, "States Increasingly Flexing Their Policy Muscle."

59. See Richard Briffault, "The Role of Local Control in School Finance Reform," 24 *Connecticut Law Review* (1992), pp. 773, 781; Faber, "Is Local Control of the Schools Still a Viable Option?" pp. 449–52.

60. See Education Commission of the States, *State Takeovers and Reconstitutions,* p. 1.

61. See Faber, "Is Local Control of the Schools Still a Viable Option?" p. 451, and Saiger, "Disestablishing Local School Districts as a Remedy for Educational Inadequacy," p. 1848.

62. See Saiger, "Disestablishing Local School Districts as a Remedy for Educational Inadequacy," p. 1849 and note 92.

63. See, for example, Debra Viadero, "Big City Mayors' Control of Schools Yields Mixed Results," *Education Week,* September 11, 2002, p. 8; Elizabeth Benjamin, "Control of State Schools at Issue," *Albany Times Union,* March 15, 2002, p. B2.

64. See *Governing America's Schools,* p. 9; Johnston and Sandham, "States Increasingly Flexing Their Policy Muscle."

65. See *Governing America's Schools,* p. 10.

66. See Mark G. Yudof and others, *Educational Policy and the Law,* 4th ed. (Belmont, Calif.: Wadsworth Publishing, 2001), pp. 890–91.

67. See ibid., p. 895.

68. The information in this paragraph comes from James E. Ryan and Michael Heise, "The Political Economy of School Choice," 111 *Yale Law Journal* (2002), pp. 2043, 2073–85.

69. For further discussion of charter schools and voucher programs, see Ryan and Heise, pp. 2073–85.

70. Tyll Van Geel, *The Courts and American Education Law* (Amherst, N.Y.: Prometheus Books, 1987), p. 70. Van Geel observed that the enormous changes in policy and governance at the state level, many of which have resulted in centralizing authority, have "all taken place without the necessity of a change in legal doctrine because state legislatures have plenary authority over education. These changes have occurred with few doubting that the legal authority existed to make the changes."

71. See, for example, Hill, "Getting It Right the Eighth Time," pp. 147, 155.

72. See, for example, Hill, "Getting It Right the Eighth Time"; Faber, "Is Local Control of the Schools Still a Viable Option?"

73. The cases limiting Congress's ability to enforce the Fourteenth Amendment are *City of Boerne* v. *Flores,* 521 U.S. 507 (1997); *Morrison,* 529 U.S. 598; and *Garrett,* 531 U.S. 356. Cases limiting the ability of Congress to abrogate state sovereign immunity include *Seminole Tribe of Florida* v. *Florida,* 517 U.S. 44 (1996); *College Savings Bank* v. *Florida Prepaid Postsecondary Education Expense Board,* 527 U.S. 666 (1999).

74. Lynn A. Baker, "The Spending Power and the Federalist Revival," 4 *Chapman Law Review* (2001), pp. 195–96.

75. See, for example, McConville, "Federal Funding Conditions: Bursting through the Dole Loopholes," p. 165; Baker, "Conditional Federal Spending after *Lopez*," p. 1916; Ronald J. Krotoszynski Jr., "Listening to the 'Sounds of Sovereignty' but Missing the Beat: Does the New Federalism Really Matter?" 32 *Indiana Law Review* (1998), pp. 11, 15–16.

76. *Davis* v. *Monroe County Board of Education*, 526 U.S. 629 (1999), pp. 654–55 (Kennedy dissenting).

77. Ibid., p. 655 (Kennedy dissenting).

78. *Oklahoma* v. *Schweiker*, 655 F.2d 401 (1981, D.C. Circuit), p. 414.

79. See Erwin Chemerinsky, "Protecting the Spending Power," 4 *Chapman Law Review* (2001), p. 89, 102.

80. *Garcia* v. *San Antonio Metropolitan Transit Authority*, p. 546 (recognizing that any rule of state immunity that turns on whether the state is performing a "traditional" or "integral" function "inevitably invites an unelected federal judiciary to make decisions about which state policies it favors and which ones it dislikes").

81. For a general discussion of all of these cases, see, for example, Yudof and others, *Educational Policy and the Law*.

82. 374 U.S. 483 (1954).

83. See, for example, *Board of Education of Oklahoma City Public Schools* v. *Dowell*, 498 U.S. 237 (1991), pp. 247–48; *Freeman* v. *Pitts*, 503 U.S. 467 (1992), p. 490; *Missouri* v. *Jenkins*, 515 U.S. 70 (1995), p. 99.

84. Judith Resnik, "Categorical Federalism: Jurisdiction, Gender and the Globe," 111 *Yale Law Journal* (2001), pp. 619, 630–56 (demonstrating the malleability of categories used in Commerce Clause jurisprudence to demarcate federal and state spheres of authority).

85. See, for example, Larry D. Kramer, "Putting the Politics Back into the Political Safeguards of Federalism," 100 *Columbia Law Review* (2000), p. 215; Herbert Wechsler, "The Political Safeguards of Federalism: The Role of the States in the Composition and Selection of the National Government," 54 *Columbia Law Review* (1954), p. 543.

86. See Earl M. Maltz, "Sovereignty, Autonomy and Conditional Spending," 4 *Chapman Law Review* (2001), pp. 107, 116.

87. See, for example, Charles W. Goldner, "Home Rule School Districts: An Opportunity for Meaningful Reform or Simple Window Dressing?" 21 *Southern Illinois University Law Journal* (1997), p. 255.

88. See, for example, Hill, "Getting It Right the Eighth Time," pp. 164–68; Faber, "Is Local Control of the Schools Still a Viable Option?" pp. 472–81.

4

Recovering from an Accident: Repairing Governance with Comparative Advantage

PAUL T. HILL

The following statements can be made with confidence about how American education is run. Clearly it is an accidental system. Nobody of sound mind would have deliberately created the collection of laws, regulations, court orders, intergovernmental relationships, and contracts that goes by the name "education governance." Nobody ever thought through its costs, benefits, and unintended consequences. If someone had, this ungainly system would have been scrapped long ago. Finally, nobody claims that our governance system is optimized to support teaching and learning. If the system did work, most analysts would be applauding the current state of American education, not wringing their hands about it.

So why do we have this system, and what should we do with it?

Conflict and Confusion

At the heart of this undertaking is another simple question: Who should be responsible for a child's education? Should it be the federal government, the state, local school district, or the broader *use dots to determine class belief?*

...community? Should it be the individual school, a student's teachers, or the child's parents alone? There is, unfortunately, no simple answer. The state, for example, has a constitutional responsibility for schools, but agencies in state capitals, often hundreds of miles from some children, do not educate anyone. The same can be said for school districts, which, except in the smallest communities, are hiring and logistics agencies that operate at some remove from their pupils. Those in direct contact with children, however, are not fully responsible. Teachers are hired and paid by public agencies, which can remove or reassign the ones they think are not serving children well. Even parents are subject to actions by the government, which compels their children's attendance and commonly tells families which schools their children will attend.

Stating that "all those entities are responsible for children's education" may be true, but it can set up a train wreck. A parent might be concerned above all about preserving a child's religious identity or avoiding influences that might threaten the child's attachment to an ethnic group. States or school districts are likely to place little, if any, value on those aspects of a child's education. Their overriding concern is to ensure that children learn what they need to know to support themselves and act in their own interests in a complex society. Within localities, the most potent interest group in public education, the teachers union, often disagrees with district leaders and parents about how schools should operate, teachers' salaries, and what should happen to teachers if children do not learn enough. Thus, saying that "everyone is responsible" evades the question of the appropriate roles for different parties and how to resolve differences in perspective. If the responsible parties act on different premises, conflict and confusion ensue.

Of course, conflict and confusion are what we often have, and, as explained elsewhere in this volume, legal and constitutional analysis does little to clarify matters. The Tenth Amendment to the Constitution, for example, does not enlighten us much about how to allocate responsibility for education. That amendment may have been designed to reserve power over education and other issues to the states or to the people, but it tells us nothing about the education roles of many parties, and it neither prevents federal education mandates nor compels states to assume responsibility.[1] Indeed, although states are assigned responsibility for education by state constitutions, initially states did little about education. In the early nineteenth century, most made no provision for education in rural areas and little provision in cities. Groups of families created schools by hiring teachers and sharing responsibility for paying, housing, and feeding them. While the roots of public education in many communities can be traced back to these schools, they were, in today's terms, essentially private, funded and supervised by voluntary subscribers.

How State Involvement Grew

Unlike state constitutions, which are eighteenth- and nineteenth-century creations, most active state government oversight of education started in the twentieth century. Most states enacted compulsory attendance laws affecting children from 7 to 16 years of age long after their constitutions had accepted responsibility for K–12 education. Three states waited until after 1915 to make school attendance compulsory (Massachusetts was first, in 1852, and Alaska the last, in 1929).[2] Even then, most states deferred to local school committees and did nothing to ensure that all schools were uniform or, for that matter, that a school was available to every child.

Even after states began getting involved in education, moreover, their efforts were spotty. Until the mid-1960s, state education agencies paid more attention to vocational education than to basic K–12 schooling. Some states approved textbooks and began licensing teachers and establishing minimum standards for hours and days of instruction. Many, however, let localities make key decisions, including how much to spend on education and whether to operate racially segregated schools.

Starting in the mid-1960s, federal forces were important in increasing state regulation and oversight of schools. Title I of the Elementary and Secondary Education Act (ESEA) and other federal initiatives assigned oversight to state departments of education and provided substantial funds for state staffing. Litigation also compelled states to become active. After the U.S. Supreme Court decision in *Brown* v. *Board of Education,* when states became codefendants in segregation lawsuits, state political and administrative leaders began taking greater interest in how local districts educated their children.[3] States also became the primary defendants in school finance lawsuits. Starting in the 1960s, researchers funded by the Ford Foundation developed data showing spending disparities among school districts in states and argued that these differences violated the equal protection guarantees of the Fourteenth Amendment to the Constitution. On these grounds, courts in forty-seven states ordered changes in school finance, including reduced reliance on local property taxes and greater state assumption of funding responsibility.

As is always the case in politics, as state legislatures were forced to pay a larger share of the bills, they insisted on more control. State legislative committees on education became more active, with the volume of education-related legislation rising dramatically during the 1970s and 1980s. By the late 1960s, state legislatures had begun imitating Congress in enacting categorical programs that gave school districts money tied to certain services or groups of students. Legislatures started treating school districts as state agencies, responding to perceived problems by assigning new responsibilities to local boards. Thus the school boards' duties over time became more detailed, explicit, and intrusive.

Local School Board Authority Defined by Accretion

In most states, local school boards exist through a grant of authority from state legislatures. Courts have upheld legislatures' power to create, reorganize, and abolish local school boards, even when local residents object.[4] Moreover, legislatures can alter the mission of local boards through amendments or new statutes. For example, Texas rewrote its entire education code in 1995, changing the governance responsibilities of all players in education, including local school boards.

An inventory of six state education codes shows how legislatures have heaped more tasks on local boards, including ones that do not necessarily align with the local agency's stated mission.[5] Board members must wade through a sea of legislated responsibilities, from levying taxes and hiring the superintendent to selecting materials for sex education courses and ensuring that students dress appropriately. State codes establish school board responsibilities in these basic areas:

—School buildings and grounds—acquisition, construction, and maintenance;

—Professional and support staff—hiring, training, and supervising;

—Funding—acquiring, allocating, and accounting;

—Curriculum—developing, ensuring compliance with state requirements;

—Transportation of students;

—Attendance—enforcing mandatory attendance laws;[6]

—Dispute resolution;

—Federal and state categorical programs—implementation;

—Federal civil rights laws and court orders—compliance management and implementation; and

—Vendor contracts—entering and administering.

Given the haphazard way school board duties have been defined, confusion of mission and priorities has been almost inevitable. School boards were assigned duties from above, by legislatures that needed to offload problems to a subordinate agency and by courts that needed someone to administer their decisions. Nobody was responsible for maintaining a clear mission or for fending off assignments that would diffuse school boards' effort and attention. Like state cabinet departments, school boards were assigned a grab bag of requirements and left to do the best they could. School boards have also been assigned duties from below, as unions gained the power to bargain over teachers' hiring, assignments, and working conditions, as well as wages, and as groups—such as parents of handicapped or "gifted" children—advocated, organized, and won concessions in district policy.

Since the mid-1960s, school boards have become much more overtly political. For decades before that, board controversies were mostly nonideological, and there were few well-organized interest groups other than the parent-teacher association and the business community. After 1964, however, a great deal changed. Federal programs like Title I of ESEA encouraged formation of parent groups to advocate for the disadvantaged children who were the intended beneficiaries. Federal civil rights officials reviewed district spending and student assignment policies and investigated citizens' complaints. Families who objected to desegregation plans or other district policies also organized. School employee unions and cause groups—from religious right supporters concerned about textbooks or reading assignments to those on the left advocating unconventional lifestyles—learned that they could advance their interests by getting people elected to the school board.

The Importance of the Central Office and the Superintendent

District central offices grew dramatically after the 1960s, largely in response to federal and state categorical programs (many of which required the creation of special administrative units and provided money to pay for them) and court mandates. As school districts became legally responsible for desegregation and equity issues, there was more to administer. As districts entered increasingly complex agreements with teachers unions and created advisory groups in response to federal mandates, the demand for new central office specialists increased.

Big-city district central offices reflect past and current waves of school reform. For example, most districts once created, and many still retain,

vestiges of units for evaluation and accountability, managing decentralization and training principals to handle money, setting standards and offering
related staff training, administering district choice plans and managing
admissions lotteries, planning and managing fundraising, and coordinating
social services. These offices are in addition to new units for such things as
overseeing charter schools. Like presidents and Congresses, which try to
ensure implementation of their priorities by establishing special bureaus,
school boards and superintendents have continually reorganized and added
to central offices. Even when district reforms included cutting central office
staff, little was done to reduce the responsibilities of the central office. The
result often was gridlock, as functions once performed by defunct central
office units were neither eliminated nor reassigned.[7]

The central office is the 400-pound gorilla that everyone tries to ignore.
It is convenient to assume that the central office—associate and assistant
superintendents, technical specialists, and itinerant service providers to
schools—is a neutral civil service structure that simply helps the superintendent and school leaders do their work. Nothing could be further from
the truth. As studies of superintendents and school leaders show, big-city
central offices have their own cultures and agendas, and they consistently
distort the transmission of signals between top district leadership and the
schools.[8] Central offices control a great deal of money. In Seattle, for example, the "student-weighted funding formula" that drives school-level budgets accounts for less than half of district spending. Everything else is in
the hands of a central office unit or function.[9]

Superintendents anguish over their need to delegate implementation of
reform strategy to central office groups that often are philosophically
opposed to the superintendent's office and expect to outlast it. They observe
that central office staff members frequently have local constituencies and
patronage networks that the superintendents lack and that many run federal and state grants programs that insulate them from the superintendent's
influence.[10] Superintendents also note that many central office staff are
tenured former principals who are doing jobs (for example, human resource
management and procurement) for which they have no training. Few business and community leaders understand that, as a rule, the central office is an
independent entity that in no sense "works for" the superintendent.

The superintendency has been defined by accretion as well. Since the
1960s, superintendents have become defendants in lawsuits, implementers of
federal and state programs, responders to organized interest groups, negotiating partners for teachers unions, recipients of new mandates and instruc-
tions from school boards, and public figures leading civic coalitions that

include businesses and philanthropists. These new roles have become necessary, but they have burdened superintendents and made it difficult for them to spend time in schools and perform the "chief educator" function.

In recent years, writers like Richard Elmore have urged superintendents to focus on instructional leadership, citing the example of Anthony Alvarado.[11] Alvarado truly functioned as chief educator, as superintendent of New York City's Community School District 2 and as chancellor of instruction in San Diego. Alvarado's example has proved inspiring, leading many superintendents to think more deeply about how their work affects teaching and learning. But Alvarado's example has proved difficult to follow. As head of District 2, he led a subordinate district, for which the New York City schools chancellor handled many political and financing issues. In San Diego, Alvarado split the superintendent's job with Alan Bersin, an influential local figure who handled the politics and community relations. Similar arrangements could be possible elsewhere, but they represent a new way of handling the complexities of the superintendent's job, not a way of reducing all of its duties to instructional leadership.

In a recent study of big-city superintendents' job experiences, Fuller and others found many superintendents who have concluded that, in the words of one, "the job is undoable."[12] Though other superintendents are more optimistic, most agree that a successful superintendent now is usually one who has avoided a financial crisis or survived a tense labor negotiation, not one who has transformed a district's schools.

Heroic school board members, central office staffers, and superintendents can sometimes sweep aside the constraints that face them. However, such individuals are rare, and their tenures often are short. Alvarado, for example, recently agreed to leave San Diego after a creative but contentious period. Even his political protector, Bersin, has been forced to go slower and limit instructional change in light of community, political, and financial pressures.

New Reforms atop Old

Educators and state policymakers have long recognized that this accidental governance system is too complex. An alliance of education scholars and business leaders, for example, has suggested that the dissonant demands on school boards and schools be resolved by eliminating all requirements unrelated to student safety and civil rights and aligning spending, curriculum, testing, and teacher and student accountability requirements with specific expectations for student learning.[13]

"Alignment-based" reforms include the standards-based reforms that have been at least officially endorsed in forty-nine states. These initiatives, whose objective is to discipline the system rather than replace it, have left the political and bureaucratic structures of public education intact. Though standards certainly have entered the everyday lives of schools with many positive consequences, their implementation has largely worked within the constraints set by the system. Thus, though schools are expected to attain higher levels of performance, few control more money or have any greater freedom to adapt practice to children's needs than before standards-based reform was adopted.

Responsibility for alignment-based reforms was placed in state and local bureaucracies, which defined aligned sets of school performance standards, and tests to measure performance, but which did not eliminate any existing regulations or oversight layers. Alignment became a competing imperative, not the dominant one.

The standards-and-alignment movement prescribes a desirable end without the means or methods necessary to attain it. With few exceptions (notably Kentucky, North Carolina, and Texas), standards have simply imposed new requirements atop old ones. Even in the states where standards-based reform is most advanced, school boards' attention is still drawn to adult conflicts over jobs, money, and allocation of students to "desirable" programs.[14] That is why many educators consider the demand that all children be educated to high standards unfair: in the late 1990s many standards-based reform initiatives were remodeled to fit the system, rather than the other way around.

Sorting Roles by Comparative Advantage

If constitutional principles do not create a workable structure of relationships for education, can some other principle suggest a more productive and stable division of labor among federal, state, local, and school-level governance? Recent efforts to redesign school district governance have suggested a school-centric principle: start with what schools must do, and then distinguish capacities that must be located at the school site from those that can only come from outside. The Annenberg Design Group on Organizing, Managing, and Governing Schools adopted this premise and proposed sharp distinctions among school leaders, organizations above the school level (including but not limited to the superintendent, district central office, and local school board), and state-level agencies.[15]

Individual schools, it suggested, should control as many decisions as possible about staffing, use of time and money, and adaptation of instruction to current students' needs. For school districts it recommended the following responsibilities: providing student achievement standards clear enough to guide instructional decisions but not so prescriptive as to eliminate adaptability; creating pools of capable teachers from which schools can choose; and letting school leaders pick the options they prefer for teachers' professional development and other school improvements. The group also recommended ensuring that funds are allocated equitably, so that poor and minority students are educated in schools with the same or greater real-dollar resources as schools in more affluent neighborhoods and protecting the educational opportunities of all students by identifying failing schools promptly and swiftly creating options for children in those schools.

The Annenberg report, which also called for changes in the roles, missions, and structures of district central offices and school boards, provides a stark alternative to the reasoning from constitutional principles that has produced our current education governance problems. Its limitations are understandable: as a national task force with members from key stakeholder groups, it stopped short of demanding the major changes in collective bargaining laws and school board powers that its recommendations imply. Further, as a task force on school districts, it said little about how state and federal roles would have to change if school districts were to operate as suggested.

This chapter builds on the Annenberg recommendations by defining a principle by which all key roles in education governance can be redesigned. That principle is *subsidiarity*. This Latinate word is unfamiliar to most Americans, but it is the focus of intense discussion in Europe as national governments struggle to define and limit the powers of the central European Community government.[16] According to the Glossary of the European Community, "the subsidiarity principle is intended to ensure that decisions are taken as closely as possible to the citizen and that constant checks are made as to whether action at Community level is justified in the light of the possibilities available at national, regional or local level. Specifically, it is the principle whereby the Union does not take action (except in the areas which fall within its exclusive competence) unless it is more effective than action taken at national, regional or local level."

Subsidiarity is expressly focused on nurturing the capacities of people and institutions in local governments and even in smaller communities. The intellectual roots of subsidiarity are in the Roman Catholic Church, which has struggled for millennia over the relationship between a central authority and far-flung local congregations set in diverse cultural contexts. From a 1931 papal encyclical letter:

> Just as it is gravely wrong to take from individuals what they can accomplish by their own initiative and industry and give it to the community, so also it is an injustice and at the same time a grave evil and disturbance of right order to assign to a greater and higher association what lesser and subordinate organizations can do. For every social activity ought of its very nature to furnish help to the members of the body social, and never destroy and absorb them.[17]

Subsidiarity is a principle, not a formula: to this day the church that issued that letter struggles with how much to leave in local hands and how much to control centrally. But unlike a constitutional provision like the Tenth Amendment, subsidiarity invites principled debate and reinterpretation in light of experience.

What would our public education system look like, then, if we ignored questions about the inherent and reserved powers of different levels of government and focused instead on the question "Where is what best done?"

As the Annenberg report suggests, any analysis of comparative advantage must start at the school: that is where teaching and learning happen. The work of all other agencies is futile if the school does not work well. What does the school do? It organizes the work of adults to teach students. It adapts instruction to the evident needs and progress of the real students there. It maintains an environment in which teachers can teach and children can learn. To do those things it sets priorities on using the time and talents of both child and adult. (Schools do other things, too, but some functions, such as organizing athletic teams, are accidents of history and might not derive from schools' comparative advantage.)

For schools to perform their main functions well, other things must happen. Funds must be raised to pay teachers and buy facilities and equipment. Teachers must be trained. Someone must monitor changes in bodies of knowledge and economic processes so that the schools can teach what their students will need to know. Some will argue that individual schools can do these things by charging tuition, running apprenticeship programs for potential teachers, and the like. But it is hard to argue that individual schools can do these things more efficiently than other organizations. Governments, but not schools, can impose taxes on people who will benefit from the school's work even if they have no children enrolled. Programs to train teachers for many schools can be more efficient than cottage-industry apprenticeship programs. Groups dedicated to monitoring social and economic trends can do these jobs more efficiently than individual schools.

That some functions are best performed for many schools does not mean that government is necessarily the best provider. Some functions, such as creating a pool of teachers from whom schools can choose, might best be carried out by a private employment service or, as Kerchner, Koppich, and Weers have suggested, by a hiring hall organized by a teachers union.[18]

Statements of comparative advantage emphasize what could be, not what is. Some governments, training institutions, or organizations setting standards for student learning might do their jobs so badly that individual schools would be better off doing those tasks themselves. In fact, some schools might do their jobs so badly that parents would be better off teaching their children at home. Again, the purpose of this analysis is to identify potential comparative advantage, not to judge current capacity.

Table 4-1 provides a rough analysis of potential comparative advantage, distinguishing schools, local districts, states, and the federal government. The rest of this chapter focuses on the middle three layers in table 4-1, the school, district, and state. I have previously suggested, in *Brookings Papers on Education Policy 2000*, how to realign the federal role in light of the comparative advantage of that level of government. There I argued for redefining the federal role according to four principles: subsidizing children, not jurisdictions; strengthening schools, not cross-school or subschool programs; defining results in terms of student and school performance; and attacking emergent problems with short-term, special-purpose grants.[19]

At present, few entities in education governance are operating according to their comparative advantages. States regulate school districts but seldom judge their overall performance or act against districts with consistently low test scores or large numbers of failing schools (the federal No Child Left Behind Act of 2001 may press states to take on this function, but there is little evidence that they have the desire or the capacity to do so).[20] School districts are instruments of the state and can be dissolved and reconstituted by the state government, but this seldom happens, even to very low-performing districts. Recent state takeovers of troubled city systems in Pennsylvania, Ohio, Michigan, and California are telling exceptions. They did not arise from normal state performance oversight but from extreme political pressure or, as in Cleveland, from a court order. Even in Pennsylvania, where obligations for a state takeover were recently established in a state law, they are relevant only when district performance is extremely low for an extended period. The state still does not have the capacity—or

Table 4-1. *Potential Advantages and Disadvantages of Families, Schools, Districts, States, and the Federal Government*

Entity	What they do well	What they do poorly
Families	Support students emotionally; demand schooling appropriate to individual child's needs	Create well-ordered curriculums and apply expertise to the teaching process
Schools	Organize teaching; adapt to present needs of children; set priorities on use of child and adult time	Raise public funds; train teachers; monitor social and economic changes; judge their own performance
Districts	Tax citizens to pay for schools; set local spending levels high enough to attract good teachers; oversee school performance and save children by transforming or replacing bad schools	Resist local politics that favors some groups and schools over others; monitor social and economic changes; judge their own performance
States	Support spending in poor communities; make sure districts can get good teachers; counter local politics favoring some groups over others; monitor social and economic changes; judge districts' performance; decertify and replace school boards that tolerate large numbers of ineffective schools	Run schools that require local adaptation; resist state-level politics that favor some groups and districts over others; resist pressures to resolve problems by over-regulation; judge their own performance
Federal government	Support spending in poor communities and states; counter state politics favoring some groups over others; make national investments in capacities required by social and economic change	Run schools that require local adaptation; resist pressures to resolve problems by overregulation; judge own performance

accept the responsibility—for routinely assessing and attaching incentives to district performance.

Districts also seldom oversee schools closely. Districts, lacking strong analytic tools to assess school performance, shy away from acting decisively toward failed schools. The tradition of accountability based on compliance and propriety, rather than on performance, is extremely difficult to overcome. Though principals and teachers often appear buffeted by regulatory actions from above, their jobs do not depend on performance except in the most extreme cases. When schools are staffed according to formula and almost every teacher is the most senior person who applied for the job, districts can do little to change schools or hold them accountable.

Thus American public education governance is not based on having different institutions operate according to what they do best. In theory, all parties above the school could do things to focus the school's work and improve its performance. But few have such clearly defined missions or the resources to act according to their comparative advantages.

This chapter is not the first work to recognize the mismatch between potential comparative advantage and actual performance. As Mary Beth Celio and I argued in *Fixing Urban Schools,* several competing reform movements focus on holding schools accountable for performance rather than compliance, increasing schools' control of decisions that let instruction be tailored to current students' needs, and investing in individual schools' ability to solve problems for themselves (as opposed to having solutions mandated by school districts or state governments).[21] All of these movements seek site-based management, meaning that the school would become a real organization, not just a job site manned by bureaucrats, and that it would have considerable control over staffing, instruction, and use of time and money. These movements include

—*Standards-based reform,* which, in theory, limits states to setting standards about what students should know and be able to do and to providing aligned tests and teaching materials. Schools gain extra money to invest in instructional improvement and relief from regulations other than those protecting health, safety, and civil rights.

—*Charter school laws,* which allow independent groups of teachers and community members to operate quasi-independent schools. Charter schools must be authorized by school districts and other government agencies, and they are paid on a per capita basis for students whose parents choose to enroll them. Charter schools are free to select teachers, devise instructional methods, and decide how to use time. States and school districts may not

impose new regulations on a charter school if it fulfills the terms of its charter, which specifies instructional methods, admission practices, and learning goals for students.

—*Universal school contracting,* which would make every school a charter school and eliminate most current functions of school district central
offices except for school performance assessments. It would put all money
now spent for central offices into schools and let schools purchase the help
and other resources their leaders think they need.

—*Regulated vouchers,* which would eliminate direct public funding of
schools in favor of giving parents vouchers to be redeemed for tuition at
any school. Schools would be licensed and required to follow bias-free
admission policies and teach certain subjects, but they would determine their
own staffing and use of technology, methodology, time, and money.[22]

As Celio and I argued, these reform efforts might not be as distinct from
one another as their advocates think. All share the objective of establishing
a division of labor that locates greater freedom of action at the school level
and constrains higher levels of government, including the district, from
overregulation. They all retain roles for state and local government in
authorizing schools to receive public funds, protecting students from fraud
and abuse, creating common metrics for assessing schools, and ensuring
that all students are taught basic skills needed for whatever work they eventually pursue.

A Synthesis of Ideas about State and Local Roles

In a national study of charter school accountability, Robin Lake and I discovered that all of the basic reform theories noted share three common
ideas. They orient public education institutions other than schools to supporting roles, vest individual schools with significant freedom over staff
selection and use of time and money, and hold schools accountable for student performance. Advocates of standards-based reform, school district
decentralization, charters, contracting, and vouchers agree that schools
should be accountable for performance, not compliance, and that higher
levels of government should be constrained by law and contract from
adding requirements that draw the attention of teachers and principals
away from instruction. They also agree that district and state officials are
responsible for protecting children from schools that cannot teach them
effectively.

These reforms differ, however, on two issues. The first is how far state and local officials should be allowed to go if a school is not functioning effectively. Should they be limited to advice and assistance, or could they go so far as to close a school, assign it to a different group of professionals, or release the students to attend private schools? The second issue is how much choice families should have. School district decentralization and standards-based reform have been silent about choice. Allied reforms (chartering, contracting, and vouchers) agree that the inevitable differences among schools imply that no student should be compelled to attend a particular school.

As Lake and I looked closely at the reform ideas, however, the distinctions became blurry. As states develop standards-based reform systems, they are forced to struggle with whether remedies for failing schools should end with advice and assistance to existing schools or extend to closing schools that consistently fail to improve student outcomes and creating new options for children in those schools. The federal No Child Left Behind Act of 2001 essentially resolves the issue: states must use their standards to identify failing schools and create options for children in those schools. Moreover, states unable to judge the performance of thousands of local schools must rely on school districts to judge school performance and to determine whether to invest new resources in existing schools or to create new ones. School districts must develop the capacity to judge school performance and determine whether the most efficient way to create new options for students is to invest in existing schools, use district resources to start new schools, or rely on chartering or vouchers.

Thus, reforms that were designed independently of one another come together to support a vision of the school district as a manager of a portfolio of schools using different instructional approaches and run under varied auspices. To me, this means that the distinctions among standards, chartering, contracting, and regulated vouchers have broken down. All require districts to manage portfolios of educational options for children, and all focus the relationship between school and district on performance accountability.

Chartering and Standards: Two Sides of the Same Reform

Standards and chartering have blurred together.[23] Standards-based reform starts at the top of the system by trying to align state goals, performance measures, and actions toward schools. Chartering starts at the bottom by creating great freedom at the school level. Despite such differences, however, chartering and standards-based reform have a great deal in common. Both impose a new obligation—performance-based oversight of individual schools—on government agencies. Both try to deregulate schools so that teachers and administrators can concentrate on serving students and raising achievement. Both make individual schools directly responsible for demonstrating student learning.

Supporters of standards-based reform often see advocates of charter schools as rivals, and vice versa. Bruce Fuller, for example, casts the difference between charters and standards sharply, as between totally decentralized (charters) and strongly centralized (standards) approaches to public oversight. There are, however, a few education policy analysts, including Chester E. Finn Jr. and Diane Ravitch, who consider themselves supporters of both standards and charters.

Despite Fuller's characterization, standards-based reform is not purely a movement toward centralization. It does have an element of centralization—statewide standards for student learning in core subjects—but it also has an element of decentralization—increased school freedom to use time and resources to promote student learning. However, chartering is not a purely decentralizing reform. It relies heavily on public authorities to act decisively to cancel the charters of failed schools and to charter new schools for students whose needs are unmet.

Supporters of charter schools and standards-based reform differ on what might be called matters of taste. Charter supporters are comfortable with entrepreneurship by groups of teachers, parents, and administrators and with parent choice. Standards-based reform supporters are nervous about relying on entrepreneurship and family choice, though most are comfortable if these phenomena are limited to a fixed group of district-operated schools.

These differences in taste have fewer practical consequences than most people think. Charter schools and standards-based education are, in fact, different faces of the same reform. Both seek schools capable of problem solving, free to allocate time and money in response to students' needs. Both need school districts or other public agencies capable of competent, consistent, performance-based oversight. Both require authorizers to have some fair and explicit mechanism by which to judge school performance and to oversee schools individually, since schools face different challenges and have different performance track records.

The failure of public agencies to develop capacities for school oversight, demonstrated in Katrina Bulkley's *Education Policy Analysis Archives* article on charter school accountability, is as much a problem for standards-based reform as for charter schools.[24] Both require states and school districts to stop piling on regulations and evaluating schools on the basis of rule compliance and scandal avoidance. Neither can survive if authorities play favorites and demand less stringent performance of schools that they con-trol directly than of schools that operate with greater independence.[25] Gov-ernment's success or failure in operating fairly will determine, as Richard Elmore has written of standards-based reform, whether "we . . . get the version of standards-based reform that advocates envision, or we . . . get a corrupted and poorly thought-out evil twin."[26]

Chartering and standards-based reforms complement each other and can converge to form a new vision of accountability in public education.[27]

Why Standards Enable Chartering

Chartering is not a pure market system. Though chartering provides parental choice, it also assumes performance-based public oversight. Char-tering requires public authorities that can judge whether students are learn-ing and whether schools are fulfilling their charters. These authorities must be able to cancel a charter that is not benefiting children and to charter new schools to serve children whose schools have failed them.

Standards provide a common metric against which individual charter schools can be judged. They also enable public agencies to oversee diverse portfolios of schools: schools can differ in many ways as long as they demon-strate that students are making genuine progress toward attaining standards. State standards need not be the only basis on which schools are judged—many charter schools want to be judged on such measures as student reten-tion and graduation rates, proportion of students making normal progress toward graduation, proportion of students failing multiple courses, and graduates' performance at the next higher level of education. But standards provide the common basis on which diverse schools can be measured.

Conflict within the charter school movement has masked its dependence on standards. Some enthusiasts see charter schooling as a way to get away from all the trappings of regular public education, including the use of con-ventional student achievement tests and other performance measures. These teachers and parents—many of whom favor education approaches in which students construct knowledge through exploration rather than by learning according to a fixed schedule—dislike any form of comparative performance measurement. They feel that it takes time from learning, nar-rows the focus of instruction, and provides discouraging and inappropri-ately negative feedback to disadvantaged students.

Some charter school leaders, hoping to avoid achievement testing, prefer to rely on their ability to win a future political struggle. Some are even willing to accept new requirements, not contemplated by their charters, as a way of building up political "credits." But such efforts to avoid testing put charter schools at great risk. When charter school leaders reject any clear and universal measure of student performance, they give new life to the compliance mentality, under which a school's existence depends on avoiding conflict with persons of influence and maintaining a spotless record of following rules.

Except under a wholly unregulated voucher system, in which parental satisfaction would be the sole element of accountability, there must be some basis of public oversight.[28] Both charters and standards-based reform assume that school performance is measurable and can be fairly assessed and compared. They absolutely require some efficient measures of school performance. These need not all be based on student test performance—skills demonstrations, written products, and more "authentic" measures of student outcomes, such as performance at higher levels of education, are highly desirable. Moreover, charter school operators have every right to object to tests that are biased or poorly aligned with state standards. But it is in their interest, just as it is in the interest of supporters of standards-based reform, to suggest what common, objective measures of student performance should be used instead.

Both chartering and standards-based reform recognize the public interest in schooling—in ensuring that students learn basic skills, prepare for responsible lives as earners and citizens, and understand basic democratic values. Both require government agencies, normally local school boards, to monitor individual school performance, promote school improvement, adapt school offerings to meet emerging needs, and protect children in schools that do not work.[29]

For accountability, there is no conflict between standards and chartering. On the contrary, they reinforce each other. Standards provide a basic structure for valuing school outcomes and characterizing the performance of individual schools. Chartering creates a process whereby districts can act on information about school performance, making it clear that performance (as judged according to standards) is the basis on which the district rewards, targets intervention in, and on occasion replaces schools. Chartering enables districts to work directly on the supply of schools in their localities, creating new ones to meet emerging needs that might be dictated by demographics or technology and that may be required in areas poorly served by existing public schools.

How Chartering Can Complete Standards-Based Reform

While charter school advocates have given a great deal of thought to problems of individual school accountability, standards-based reform leaders have given it relatively little.[30] This discrepancy is understandable, because standards-based reformers began at the top of the system and have only recently gotten beyond problems of standard setting and test development. A few states—Kentucky, Texas, North Carolina, Massachusetts, and Washington—have begun to consider what it means to hold individual schools accountable for what children learn.[31] However, as states take on the problem of standards-based school accountability, they will need to draw some lessons from the experience of charter schools. These lessons focus on the environment of rules, funding, and assistance that makes it possible for individual schools to take responsibility for student performance, methods of effective oversight, and the importance of schools' being accountable to multiple entities.

LESSONS ABOUT THE ENVIRONMENT OF RULES, FUNDING, AND ASSISTANCE. Chartering creates three circumstances that promote school accountability. First, it creates performance incentives by making it clear that all adults in a school have stakes in the school's success (or failure) in educating students. Second, it creates freedom of action for schools, letting staff use time and money in ways they believe are likely to have the greatest effect on student learning. Third, it creates opportunities for private and public investments in school capacity, including teaching methods, materials, and staff training and recruitment.

Schools cannot be accountable under standards-based reform unless these three circumstances exist.[32] Even when states are clear about what they expect students to learn, schools are not accountable if teachers and administrators stand to gain or lose nothing no matter how students perform. Without performance incentives, standards-based reform is purely exhortation. Moreover, when states set standards and are determined to reward and penalize individual schools based on what they add to student learning, schools are unlikely to improve unless teachers and administrators are free to change their instructional programs to make the best possible uses of students' and teachers' time and talent. In the absence of freedom of action, standards-based reform establishes a double bind: schools must improve, but they may not change. Finally, even when states set standards, create incentives, and offer freedom of action, schools are highly unlikely to improve unless teachers and administrators learn about more effective ways of providing instruction, have the information necessary to make good choices, and can purchase the assistance and materials (including technology) necessary to give students the full benefit of improved methods. Without investment, schools with low capacity experience pressure to improve and are free to change, but they are limited by the skills and knowledge of the adults working there.

Chartering provides performance incentives, freedom of action, and investments and capacities to extreme degrees. Schools in which children do not learn can lose their charters and be forced to close. Schools are supposed to be bound only by the terms of their charters; they receive real dollars on a per pupil basis and are free to allocate them among staff, rent, materials, and other expenses. Charter schools are free to invest funds in teacher training and other instructional improvement strategies and can solicit funds and other help from private parties.

Does standards-based reform require states to go that far? What if schools were just praised or criticized for performance? What if all current rules and contracts stayed intact and schools were simply invited to ask for the waivers they want? What if schools did not control money and hiring decisions but could ask for waivers? What if schools did not control money, but a wise and benevolent central office administration made investments for them?

These are understandable questions, because the changes implied by performance accountability, freedom of action, and investments in school capacity are wrenching. They imply that school boards, central offices, and teachers unions must do their jobs differently. However, modest measures are almost certainly not sufficient. Earlier efforts to decentralize public school districts (under the site-based management banner) typically had little effect on student learning precisely because they did not go far enough. Though some schools seized the opportunities provided by district site-based management initiatives, most changed little, if at all, in part because there was no strong pressure for them to change.

As Bryk, Hill, and others reported after a study of six cities' decentralization efforts, few schools change just because they have the freedom to do so.[33] Without performance incentives, those teachers and administrators who want to change their schools are hamstrung by others who feel no need to change.

New York City's Community School District 2, when it was led by Anthony Alvarado, is sometimes offered as an example of a standards-based reform based solely on investments in teacher training. Major increases in money spent on professional development for literacy instruction were definitely keys to that district's success. Those investments, however, were combined with a massive turnover of teachers and principals who did not want to cooperate with the district's initiative. Such staff changes were possible in a community district that could easily export teachers and principals to jobs in the rest of New York City's million-student public school system. Moreover, other factors were at work in District 2. The superintendent created clear agreements between the district and individual schools, focused on improvement strategies and the scope of site-level discretion. Within these de facto charters, school site leaders had significant freedom of action. Though District 2 is not exactly a charter district, it exemplifies a reform that holds schools accountable for performance and that employs a combination of incentives, freedom of action, and investments in school capacity.

LESSONS ABOUT EFFECTIVE OVERSIGHT. Even under the best-designed standards-based reforms, few school districts and state education agencies are structured to oversee a system of performance-based accountability. Central office staff and governing officials are not accustomed to letting schools make their own decisions and mistakes, and schools and parents are not used to taking responsibility for their decisions and mistakes.

There are, however, some charter authorizers that take performance oversight seriously. Agencies specifically created to assess charter schools are greatly concerned about learning how to oversee school performance.[34] The Massachusetts State Board of Education and the Chicago district charter school office are good examples. They have created thorough charter approval processes, site visits, and renewal inspections. Many heads of chartering agencies are people with political and managerial credibility. They act to build a new agency's track record and preserve their personal reputations.

Authorizers committed to chartering think of a charter as a scarce resource, and they are unwilling to waste it on a mediocre school. They think harder about approval and monitoring—how to distinguish proposals from groups likely to be able to open and run schools from those likely to fail, how to help schools get started, and how to oversee school performance—than do conventional school boards, for whom chartering is an unfamiliar and often unwelcome task.

If school boards are to develop the capacity to oversee schools on the basis of student performance, as standards-based reform requires, they must imitate special-purpose chartering agencies in:

—Learning to negotiate performance agreements that take account of a school's unique focus and goals without sacrificing bottom-line objective measures. The accountability agreements developed by Chicago and Massachusetts are strong models. The vague "school improvement plans" now required by districts could be replaced by such concrete accountability plans.

—Training oversight boards and central office staff to monitor data and set policy direction, rather than create directives. The Charter School Development Center in Sacramento is a model.

—Learning how to make refined judgments of school progress through inspectorates and self-assessment processes, rather than letting politics alone guide decisionmaking. The new National Association of Charter School Authorizers is building a network of such knowledge. Excellent new guidebooks for charter-authorizing agencies are now available.[35]

—Drawing from the experience of chartering agencies about how to assess proposals for new schools.[36]

This knowledge could enable standards-based districts and states to become "smart buyers" when it comes time to reconstitute or provide alternatives to a failed school.

LESSONS ABOUT BALANCED ACCOUNTABILITY. Charter schools are accountable in several directions, not just one. They are accountable to authorizing agencies, parents, teachers, and private donors. As Robin Lake and I have argued elsewhere, this strengthens, rather than weakens, charter schools as educational institutions.[37] School leaders lack the time and resources to pander separately to each constituency. The only way they can manage their accountability relationships is to stick to their instructional knitting, making sure that students have the learning experiences promised and that the instructional program is effective. Thus the need to balance accountability forces school leaders to attend to their most important obligation to authorizers and parents. It also requires schools to create a climate where teachers can work effectively. Charter schools that do not balance their accountabilities by focusing on quality instruction are always in danger of losing their charters or their parental or teacher support.

The original theory of standards-based reform does not include this concept of multidirectional accountability. It assumes that other parties—families, teachers, and potential donors—will work through the oversight agency. The agency (for example, a local school board) is supposed to balance the interests of different parties and act accordingly.

However, as states try to design standards-based school accountability systems, the original theory does not stand up well. Schools that cannot have direct relationships of mutual choice with families and teachers are constrained in ways that limit their effectiveness. Schools that cannot reap the benefits of private investments cannot innovate as much as those that can accept ideas and resources from any source that has something to offer.

Enhancing Performance Accountability

Family choice of schools, reciprocal choice between teachers and schools, and schools' freedom to enter investment and assistance agreements with independent parties can enhance schools' performance accountability.

FAMILY CHOICE. Though family choice creates pressures for schools, it also increases their freedom of action. If no family is compelled to send its children to a particular school, no school needs to meet absolutely every family expectation. Schools can (and must) be clear about what methods of pedagogy they use and what services they provide. Public schools must not exclude children on the basis of race, sex, or disability status. But they can choose their own methods to deliver instruction and assess student progress. Parents who find an individual school's methods distasteful, or think they are inappropriate for their child, have no reason to choose the school. Though schools that rely on family choice are reluctant to conclude that they cannot serve a student, it is nonetheless possible for an unhappy family to leave.[38] Thus a school is not obligated to diversify its services to meet every taste, and it is able to focus on a coherent instructional program consistent with the promises made to parents.

Family choice strengthens schools in another way. It makes it possible for a school to specify the effort and attendance required for success. If these are made explicit at the time of admission, a school has leverage to demand that parents and students fulfill their ends of the bargain.[39] This is not possible in a school that families have not chosen. The fact that a school of choice has made the same promises to all parents gives it leverage in dealing with children who decide they do not want to attend, work, or behave in ways agreed to upon admission. The school owes it to other children and parents not to permit erosion of its promised climate of respect, studiousness, and decorum. At the limit, a school of choice can conclude that a student has chosen, by failing to work and behave as promised, not to be a member of the school community.

Nothing can exempt public schools from the obligation to serve students of all income levels and ethnic groups. Public schools cannot expel students who attend, try to achieve, and behave in ways that do not disrupt the education of others. However, if schools are to be held accountable for student outcomes, they must be free to uphold minimum standards of diligence for parents and students. If a school is to be truly accountable for results, it must be able to require responsible behavior from everyone, and it cannot permanently shield anyone from the consequences of his or her actions. Students must be given many chances to succeed, but that does not mean that schools struggling to meet standards should bear the burden of some students' unwillingness to attend school, do work fairly assigned, or respect the learning opportunities of others.

This will be a troubling conclusion for people who fear that schools will make arbitrary use of the freedom provided by family choice. Indeed, government authorizers must ensure that schools make and keep their promises about equitable student admission and retention policies. But consider the alternative: schools that have no leverage to require student effort (and family support for effort and attendance) and cannot protect their instructional climates against serious disruption cannot realistically be held responsible for whether students learn. If higher authorities deprive schools of the authority to maintain a climate conducive to learning, they cannot realistically hold teachers and principals accountable for student learning.

RECIPROCAL TEACHER-SCHOOL CHOICE. Teacher-school choice also promotes school performance accountability. Schools that have to attract teachers need to make promises about working conditions and the quality and diligence of colleagues. A school that keeps its promises becomes attractive to teachers. Such schools are far more able to deliver on their promises to parents and government authorizers than schools that have no choice about whom they employ.

To a degree, teacher choice makes schools into competitors. Schools that mismanage the hiring of teachers or do not sustain a good professional climate will lose teachers and find it hard to deliver on their promises to parents. In situations where good teachers are in short supply, such competition could produce many losers. However, as the early experience of charter schools has shown, many talented individuals who do not want to teach in schools that have no control over their climate or instructional programs do want to teach in schools that have significant freedom of action. Caroline Hoxby and Julia Koppich, Patricia Holmes, and Margaret Plecki have shown that many public school teachers who chose early retirement have returned to teach in charter schools.[40] Moreover, many highly educated young people who had never considered teaching are joining charter school faculties.

Thus reciprocal teacher-school choice can facilitate accountability in two ways: by strengthening individual schools as organizations able to deliver on promises about instruction and by improving the pool of potential teachers from which schools choose.

RELATIONSHIPS WITH INDEPENDENT DONORS AND SUPPORTERS. Help from independent parties can strengthen schools. Though school districts try to provide everything from advice to new instructional materials to maintenance of physical plants, they often fail to meet schools' needs. Bureaucratic organization begets standardization. Schools suffer if they need something that the district cannot offer or if they require help more urgently than the district can provide it.

A school that is serious about providing an effective instructional program has no choice but to rely on sources other than its school district, at least some of the time. Most schools receive donations of all kinds from many sources, including teachers and parents. Only schools whose parents and faculty have no contacts in the broader community do entirely without donations from independent sources.[41]

Moreover, the more clearly schools are held accountable for performance, the more they need, and seek, independent help. That is true of conventional public schools that come under scrutiny for low performance and of charter schools that face performance challenges. Schools of all kinds seek cash donations to purchase assistance and materials and enter relationships with independent parties that can help them.

Such relationships are necessary, and there is no denying that they affect accountability. Schools that rely on independent providers and donors become accountable to them in some way. On the whole, an accountability relationship with an independent donor or provider reinforces a school's instructional program and thus its performance. Though for-profit providers will seek to maximize efficiencies and profits to benefit stockholders, when subject to effective oversight from authorizers and governing boards, they also have strong incentives to demonstrate the value of their services.[42] As with any independent provider, the question that school leaders and government overseers must ask is whether the contractor's services contribute to school effectiveness.

Redefining Roles in Public Education

Many states have committed themselves to the theory of standards-based reform without knowing exactly how to make it work. How can officials in charge of the public school system tell the difference between low-performing schools that are on the road to improvement and those that are unlikely to improve? What can be done for children stuck in permanently low-performing schools? What freedoms do schools need if they are to be held accountable fairly for performance?

The answers promise to transform public oversight of schools. Until recently, states and school districts operated on the theory that if everyone's rights were protected and the inputs were well regulated, school quality would be the inevitable result. Standards-based reform makes accountability based on the "inputs" theory untenable. Command and control is replaced with a minimalist approach to regulation, one that relies as much as possible on problem solving by people who deliver services. Central determination is replaced by a decentralized balancing of objectives and capabilities. However, many states and districts are clueless about how to oversee schools in this new environment. They will have to create capacities, either in their own bureaucracies and school districts or among independent vendors, to do many things few public agencies have ever done.

We cannot resolve here all questions of how government can play a more constructive role in public education. However—and this is the bottom line—we can conclude that both charter schooling and implementation of the federal No Child Left Behind Act of 2001 are the laboratories in which governments and schools can learn how to operate according to their own comparative advantages. Once considered odd and marginal, chartering can become, through the mechanism of standards-based reform, a template for public school accountability. Rather than being an alternative to standards-based reform, chartering can be the logical conclusion of it. Rather than being a barrier to charters, standards-based reform might be the route by which chartering becomes the normal way of providing public education.[43]

By making the individual school the locus of accountability, standards-based reform and charter schools are reintroducing the principle of subsidiarity to public education. This can lead to a revolution in public oversight of K–12 education, replacing our accidental governance system with one designed deliberately. If schools are to be accountable for whether students meet rigorous expectations, public oversight must focus on performance, not compliance. Schools must have the freedom of action and control of resources that enable them to perform well. A system of balanced accountability, in which schools are largely self-regulating and answer directly to families, teachers, donors, and government, can allow standards-based reform to fulfill its promise.

Notes

1. See James E. Ryan, "The Tenth Amendment and Other Paper Tigers: The Legal Boundaries of Education Governance," in this volume.

2. Compulsory attendance laws are less controlling than they sound. In every state, parents can send their children to private schools, and these are loosely regulated. More-

over, the growth of home schooling shows that states have little ability to compel parents who want to keep their children out of school. In nine states (Arkansas, Idaho, Illinois, Iowa, Michigan, Missouri, New Jersey, Oklahoma, and Texas) parents who keep children home are required to teach certain subjects, but these requirements are not backed up by any application or review processes. See the Home School Legal Defense Association website (www.hslda.org/laws/default.asp).

3. 374 U.S. 483 (1954).

4. Martha M. McCarthy and Nelda H. Cambron-McCabe, *Public School Law: Teacher and Student Rights,* 3d ed. (Newton, Mass.: Allyn and Bacon, 1992), pp. 2–7.

5. For a full account of this review, see the appendixes written by lawyer Kelly Warner-King in Paul T. Hill and others, *Big City School Boards: Problems and Options* (Seattle: Center on Reinventing Public Education, 2003).

6. Robert W. Flinchbaugh, *The 21st Century Board of Education* (Lancaster, Pa.: Technomic Publishing, 1993), p. 32.

7. See Anthony S. Bryk and others, *Improving School-Community Connections: Ideas for Moving toward a System of Community Schools* (Baltimore: Annie E. Casey Foundation, 1999).

8. Howard Fuller and others, *An Impossible Job? The View from the Urban Superintendent's Chair* (Seattle: Center on Reinventing Public Education, 2003).

9. Marguerite Roza and Karen Hawley Miles, *A New Look at Inequities in School Funding: A Presentation on the Resource Variations within Districts* (Seattle: Center on Reinventing Public Education, 2002).

10. See Fuller and others, *An Impossible Job?*

11. Richard F. Elmore and Deanna Burney, *Investing in Teacher Learning: Staff Development and Instructional Improvement in Community School District #2, New York City* (Philadelphia: Consortium for Policy Research in Education, 1997).

12. Fuller and others, *An Impossible Job?*

13. Marshall S. Smith and Jennifer O'Day, "A National Curriculum in the United States?" *Educational Leadership,* vol. 49, no. 1 (September 1991), pp. 74–81. See also, by the same authors, "National Curriculum, American Style: Can It Be Done? What Might It Look Like?" *American Educator,* vol. 14, no. 4 (Winter 1990), pp. 10–17, 40–47.

14. See Paul T. Hill and Robin J. Lake, "Standards and Accountability in Washington State," in Diane Ravitch, ed., *Brookings Papers on Education Policy 2001* (Brookings, 2001).

15. National Task Force on the Future of Urban Districts, *School Communities That Work* (Providence, R.I.: Annenberg Institute, 2002).

16. Noel Epstein notes that many European countries do not apply the principle of subsidiarity to schools, instead regulating them closely. This reflects historic practice and predates formation of the European Community. This paper argues for subsidiarity because it fits the circumstances of American public education, not because the Europeans pioneered it.

17. Pius XI, *Quadrigesimo Anno, 1931.*

18. Charles Taylor Kerchner, Julia E. Koppich, and Joseph G. Weers, *United Mind Workers: Unions and Teaching in the Knowledge Society* (San Francisco: Jossey-Bass, 1997).

19. See Paul T. Hill, "Schools, Government, and the Federal Role in Education," in Diane Ravitch, ed., *Brookings Papers on Education Policy 2000* (Brookings, 2000).

20. See Susan Fuhrman, "Less than Meets the Eye: Standards, Testing and Fear of Federal Control," in this volume.

21. Paul T. Hill and Mary Beth Celio, *Fixing Urban Schools* (Brookings, 1998).

22. On regulated vouchers, see Terry M. Moe, "The Structure of School Choice," in Paul T. Hill, ed., *Choice with Equity* (Hoover Institution Press, 2002).

23. Jacob Adams and I make a similar argument for the convergence of standards and regulated vouchers in Jacob Adams and P. Hill, *A Regulated Market Model of Educational Accountability* (Denver: Education Commission of the States, 2003).

24. Katrina Bulkley, "Education Performance and Charter School Authorizers: The Accountability Bind," *Education Policy Analysis Archives,* vol. 9, no. 37 (October 1, 2001).

25. Analysts differ on who should bear the consequences of government's failure to fulfill its responsibilities under charters and standards-based reform. Both Richard Rothstein and Amy Stuart Wells caution against the expansion of charter schools, not because of the schools' failures but because of the failures of public oversight. The trouble with this argument is that it allows opponents of charter schools on school boards and in central offices to thwart the development of charter schools by unilaterally deciding to ignore their oversight responsibilities. See Richard Rothstein, "Charter Conundrum," *American Prospect,* vol. 9, no. 39 (July–August 1998). See also Amy Stuart Wells and others, "Charter Schools as Postmodern Paradox: Rethinking Social Stratification in an Age of Deregulated School Choice," *Harvard Educational Review,* vol. 69, no. 2 (Summer 1999), pp. 172–204.

26. Richard F. Elmore, *Leadership of Large-Scale Improvement in American Education* (Washington: Albert Shanker Institute, 1999), p. 5.

27. We developed the ideas for this paper in the course of conducting a three-year, federally funded study of charter school accountability. The results of that study are reported in Paul T. Hill, Robin J. Lake, and Mary Beth Celio, *A Study of Charter School Accountability* (U.S. Department of Education, 2001).

28. Note that the best-known proposal for education vouchers, John Chubb and Terry Moe's in their book *Politics, Markets, and America's Schools* (Brookings, 1990), calls for government oversight via licensing, management of admissions lotteries, and provision of unbiased school performance information. See also Moe, "The Structure of School Choice."

29. Standards-based reform expressly identifies local school district boards as the state agency responsible for direct school oversight. Though some charter school laws identify other possible public authorizers, every charter law empowers local districts to charter schools.

30. The 2002 issue of *Brookings Papers on Education Policy* documents the accountability challenges that standards-based reform poses for school districts. It includes analysis of accountability challenges in several states that are considered on the "leading edge" of standards-based reform. In general, districts are struggling to measure school performance reliably, judge the performance of individual schools, and intervene on behalf of children whose schools do not prepare them to meet minimum state standards.

31. See, for example, Hill and Lake, "Standards and Accountability in Washington State."

32. The arguments in this section are drawn from a larger analysis of the requirements of accountability under standards-based reform. See Sarah R. Brooks, *The Strong Schools Model of Accountability: Lessons for States Designing Standards-Based Reform* (Seattle: University of Washington Center on Reinventing Public Education, 2000).

33. Bryk and others, *Improving Community-School Connections.*

34. For a detailed comparison of special-purpose authorizers with school districts that resist the chartering role, see Hill, Lake, and Celio, *A Study of Charter School Accountability,* ch. 3.

35. For resources, see Bryan C. Hassel and Paul Herdman, *Charter School Accountability: A Guide to Issues and Options for Charter Authorizers* (2001) (www.uscharterschools.org/gb/account_auth/index.htm [May 2004]). See also Bryan C. Hassel and Sandra Vergari, "Charter Granting Agencies: The Challenges of Oversight in a Deregulated System," *Education and Urban Society,* vol. 31, no. 4 (August 1999), pp. 406–28, and Bryan C. Hassel, Gina Burkhardt, and Art Hood, *The Charter School Review Process: A Guide for Chartering Entities* (Tallahassee, Fla.: Southeastern Regional Vision for Education, 1998).

36. See, for example, Marc Dean Millot and Robin J. Lake, *So You Want to Start a Charter School?* (Seattle: Center on Reinventing Public Education, 1997).

37. Hill, Lake, and Celio, *A Study of Charter School Accountability.*

38. See, for example, ibid., ch. 2.

39. For a more elaborate development of this point see Paul T. Hill, "The Educational Consequences of Choice," *Phi Delta Kappan,* June 1996, p. 671.

40. Caroline M. Hoxby, "Would School Choice Change the Teaching Profession?" Working Paper 7866 (Cambridge, Mass.: National Bureau of Economic Research, August 2000);.Julia E. Koppich, Patricia Holmes, and Margaret L. Plecki, *New Rules, New Roles? The Professional Work Lives of Charter School Teachers. A Preliminary Study* (Washington: National Education Association, 1998).

41. See for example Mary Beth Celio, *Random Acts of Kindness* (Seattle: Center on Reinventing Public Education, 1997).

42. See, for example, Hill, Lake, and Celio, *A Study of Charter School Accountability,* ch. 4.

43. For an excellent analysis of how an all-charter district—or a district designed around standards-based reform—would operate, see Chester E. Finn, Bruno V. Manno, and Gregg Vanourek, *Charter Schools in Action: Renewing Public Education* (Princeton University Press, 2000).

5

A Solution That Lost Its Problem: Centralized Policymaking and Classroom Gains

LARRY CUBAN

> "No, no!" said the Queen. "Sentence first—verdict afterwards."
> —Lewis Carroll, *Alice's Adventures in Wonderland*

Today's education reforms are curious. They seek to slay demons that no longer exist. They apply uniform approaches to dissimilar problems. They take power away from local school boards and educators, the only people who can improve what happens in classrooms, and give it to distant officials, who have little capacity to achieve results. In short, the Queen of Hearts would have felt at home with them.

Education reforms are fashioned, of course, to address real or perceived problems, which sometimes rise to a "crisis," as, for example, when Americans fear that foreign forces might take over the country. After the 1957 Soviet launch of *Sputnik*, the first man-made satellite, the crisis, as a cold war–era film put it, was "The Russians Are Coming! The Russians Are Coming!" The result for schools was the National Defense Education Act, which chiefly promoted increased learning of mathematics, science, and foreign languages. Not surprisingly, as the sense of crisis faded, so, too, did the attendant education policies, much to the dismay of some academics.

In the early 1980s, Americans had nightmares of a different kind. Amid a sputtering economy and intense global competition, they feared economic dominance by foreigners. The main worry, especially in the business community, was that the Japanese were outstripping America, and U.S. woes were blamed heavily on the schools. Thus in 1983 a federally appointed commission issued the ultimate in crisis reports, *A Nation at Risk*. Drawing powerful conclusions based on students' test scores, it declared that mediocre school performance was endangering "our very future as a nation and a people." If a foe had instigated such academic results said the report, "We might well have viewed it as an act of war." National and state leaders moved aggressively to control millions of classrooms—to require uniform academic standards, aligned curriculum, more tests, and sanctions for lagging schools.[1] This move greatly extended a trend begun in the 1970s by southern governors who had hoped that education reform would help attract more firms and jobs to their states.

Needless to say, neither the Japanese nor anybody else has achieved economic dominance over America, and U.S. jitters have evaporated. Yet while the problem that reforms were created to solve no longer exists, the centralization of school power and imposition of standards-based reforms on all local schools have been thriving, especially since enactment of the No Child Left Behind Act of 2001. The question is why. Are such policies based on valid assumptions? Are they likely to accomplish much? Are they targeted at the schools that need them? Are there better ways to address the challenges facing American education? This analysis examines each question in turn.

The Assumptions

As a teacher and local superintendent as well as a researcher, I have worked in schools and studied these economically driven reforms for more than four decades. Pushed by a broad coalition of business executives, public officials, union leaders, and educators, the policies, as reflected in an array of reports, commentaries, and legislation, are chiefly rooted in the following assumptions:[2]

—As measured by national and international tests, American students have insufficient knowledge and skills. This mediocre performance imperils U.S. economic performance.

—Student deficits have occurred because local school boards and practitioners are hostile to competition, have been unaccountable for student outcomes, have little managerial expertise, and have relaxed academic standards. They lack the political will and grasp of the larger situation needed to solve the problems.

—More authority over schools must therefore be shifted to state and federal agencies to develop uniform academic standards, require more tests, hold local schools accountable, and promote school choice and competition.[3]

These assumptions, advanced by the business-oriented reformers who have dominated education policy since the 1970s, are mostly mistaken.

That students from some Asian and European countries outstrip U.S. students at certain ages on particular tests is well known. The results for the last three international tests in mathematics and science, though, were mixed: U.S. students were ahead of European and Asian counterparts in some areas and grades. For the past three decades, moreover, results on the National Assessment of Educational Progress have been mixed, with alternating gains and losses in reading and mathematics performance.[4] These and other standardized test scores suggest, however, that U.S. students do have a spotty record on school-learned knowledge and skills compared with that of pupils in other industrialized nations.

The problems begin, however, when public school critics link these outcomes to worker productivity and the national economy. In 1991, for example, a U.S. assistant secretary of education asserted that "faltering academic achievement between 1967 and 1980 sliced billions of dollars from the U.S. gross national product." Support for such a linkage is conspicuously underwhelming.[5] Consider the lack of substantial evidence in three areas: the assumed connection between test scores and productivity, the reliance on a theory of mismatched worker skills and employer demands to explain wage differentials among jobs and youth unemployment as well as labor productivity, and the tie between workers' supposed skill deficits and America's global competitiveness.

Test Scores and Wages

Economists connect standardized test scores to hourly wages by taking gains in the scores and computing corresponding increases in dollars earned. They also use broad supervisory ratings of employees (high, medium, and low) to estimate worker productivity. Both measures are, of course, proxies for actual productivity, and they certainly stretch reality. Using standardized achievement tests, for example, assumes that these instruments measure the analytic, creative and practical skills, and positive attitudes valued by employers.

Gauging the results against hourly wages assumes that pay is set by equals, by employer and worker negotiating in fully competitive markets. Furthermore, the measures require complex manipulation of data and substantial interpretation and contain many methodological problems. Little wonder that experts disagree on the worth of such data in estimating worker productivity. Yet debatable conclusions commonly are issued as indisputable facts.[6]

Skills Deficits

In this argument, not only low worker productivity and decreasing global competitiveness but youth unemployment and a widening gap between high-salary and low-wage jobs stem from the inadequate knowledge and skills that high school graduates bring to the workplace. The skills-deficit argument first appeared in the late nineteenth century, when industrial leaders were deeply concerned about global competition, at that time from German and British manufacturers. In 1898, for example, the president of the National Association of Manufacturers told members at the group's annual conference: "There is hardly any work we can do or any expenditures we can make that will yield so large a return to our industries as would come from the establishment of educational institutions which would give us skilled hands and trained minds for the conduct of our industries and our commerce."[7]

As a result, a broad coalition of civic, business, labor, and education leaders pressed district, state, and federal policymakers to introduce vocational curricula so U.S. students would be better prepared for the industrial workplace. By 1917, Washington decided to subsidize high school industrial arts and home economics courses, while states and districts adopted vocational education and guidance in all schools.[8] Through the Great Depression, World War II, the cold war, and Vietnam, moreover, vocational education received enormous political and economic support from business and civic elites. Yet youth unemployment still rose and fell, remaining especially high among minority populations—and even in flush times, employers grumbled that high school graduates were unprepared for the workplace.[9]

Unfortunately, those who complain of skills deficits rarely specify what knowledge and skills are needed to succeed in an information-based economy, and they generally overlook the wealth of evidence showing that employers are far more concerned about applicants' attitudes and behavior than their school-based knowledge in math or science. In fact, the supposed mismatch between worker skills and employer desires has little evidence to support it other than sturdy popular and media-amplified assertions. The suggestion that students who are pressed by centralized, standards-based reforms to take more math and science courses or who do well on standardized achievement tests will succeed in entry-level jobs or in college is simply rash.[10]

Global Competitiveness

Finally, the central claim is that insufficiently educated workers have slowed U.S. productivity and threatened America's position in global markets. This argument is beset with several problems. For one, it does not explain how the United States enjoyed nearly a decade of unbroken prosperity in the 1990s. For another, U.S. productivity rates have increased (not decreased) during the past fifteen years. For a third, even with the weaker U.S. economy of 2000–02, the World Economic Forum found that the United States had the world's second most competitive economy, after Finland's (thankfully, nobody is warning that the Finns are coming). In short, few economists or public officials doubt the predominance of the U.S. economy today.[11]

In light of such prosperity and competitiveness and the pivotal role that student achievement is supposed to play in U.S. economic performance, one might reasonably have expected public schools to be commended for producing the graduates who contributed so much to this remarkable record. Yet corporate leaders, governors, policy analysts, and Oval Office occupants have uttered no such praise. Why? Could it be that economic gains do not depend so heavily on student test scores as public school critics contend? This has, indeed, dawned on various observers. As economist Kevin Hollenbeck of the W. E. Upjohn Institute for Employment Research has put it, "The evidence seems to suggest that mediocre educational results do not threaten economic performance."[12]

It is worth bearing in mind what historian Lawrence Cremin wrote in 1990:

> American economic competitiveness with Japan and other nations is to a considerable degree a function of monetary, trade and industrial policy, and of decisions made by the President and Congress, the Federal Reserve Board, and the federal Departments of the Treasury and Commerce and Labor. Therefore, to contend that problems of international competitiveness can be solved by education reform, especially education reform defined solely as school reform, is not merely utopian and millennialist, it is at best foolish and at worst a crass effort to direct attention away from those truly responsible for doing something about competitiveness and to lay the burden instead on the schools.[13]

To the list of those responsible for economic perforn
add inventors of technologies that contribute significantl'
ductivity and managers (or mismanagers) of U.S. busin
accounting executives who have been issuing so many f
recent years.

The list that most needs expanding, however, is the one on the purposes of our schools, which are more than boot camps for future employees. Schools are expected to instill civic, social, and humanitarian
attitudes and skills that will shape our democracy and influence how
graduates lead their lives in their communities. Schools are expected to
build respect for differences in ideas and cultures. Schools are expected to
be decent and livable places for the young to spend a large portion of
their waking time. These historic aims of public schools often have been
neglected in the mistaken rush to turn schools into engines for the larger
economy.[14]

Are the Reforms Likely to Accomplish Much?

The problem is not only that the nation's economic fate does not depend on
student test scores. It is also that, as a rule, reforms emanating from the
states and the federal government do not improve student achievement. In
other words, neither historic nor contemporary evidence has shown much
of a cause-and-effect relationship between the federal government or the
states mandating goals, establishing uniform standards, administering tests,
requiring accountability, or pushing school choice and students gaining academically. The academic programs that governors began pressing in the
1970s accomplished little, if anything, prompting President George H. W.
Bush and the governors in 1989 to establish six goals that the nation was to
meet by the year 2000. None of the goals—including those linked to student
test performance—was achieved by then or has been achieved since. There
have been improvements here and there. But researchers and policymakers
will need to look carefully at what scattered successful states and districts do
over time to improve teaching and learning—the "black box" of improved
schooling—before they can say with confidence that particular policies
caused particular academic gains.[15]

To underscore what little evidence of achievement gains exists to warrant
major governance changes, we can begin with past state and federal efforts
to alter *local* governance, especially by adopting business management models, as is the fashion.

.istrict-to-School Governance Reform

Consider the hullabaloo that surrounded site-based management (SBM) when it swept across the nation beginning in the mid-1980s.

This devolution of key decisionmaking authority from district officials to professionals in each school can be traced back to the mid-1960s. Under pressure from civil rights advocates and others who charged that control by district officials had lowered teacher morale and stunted parental participation in schools, officials made determined efforts to decentralize decisionmaking. Headline-capturing innovations seized urban schools. Individual schools controlled by parents, alternative schools run by teachers, large districts divided into smaller administrative divisions, and autonomous, model subdistricts blossomed. By the mid-1970s, however, the drive for decentralized decisionmaking was spent.[16]

Then in the early to mid-1980s, spurred by an array of critical education reports, including *A Nation at Risk,* state and local officials showed renewed enthusiasm for shifting district decisions downward to school-site professionals. Borrowing heavily from corporate efforts to restructure companies on the principle that those closest to customers need to participate in key decisions, school reformers launched scores of SBM reforms (initially in cities and counties and later in states).[17] For example, in the mid-1980s Superintendent Joseph Fernandez of Florida's Miami-Dade County School District initiated "shared decisionmaking" for the county's 260 schools. By 1990, half of those schools had adopted SBM. The central office moved from directing to serving local sites. Individual schools selected textbooks, hired teachers, and redesigned report cards. Fernandez even convinced the New York City board of education that SBM would work in the nation's largest district, and he became chancellor there in 1990.[18]

Numerous cities and suburbs adopted SBM throughout the early 1990s, and at least four states mandated some form of shared decisionmaking in district schools. In 1988, the Illinois legislature authorized Chicago to embark on the nation's largest SBM venture. That district's 600 schools held elections for school-site councils, on which nonprofessional majorities had authority to hire and fire principals, staff schools, allocate funds, and determine curriculum and instruction. Such school autonomy in Chicago and elsewhere dominated policy talk. The central office, said two corporate cheerleaders for SBM, "should be a service center, not a command post barking orders."[19]

Unfortunately, researchers who have investigated and practitioners who have participated in a range of SBM programs agree that school autonomy has been, in the words of two researchers, "a fairly weak intervention in the arsenal of school reform measures." Or as the principal of a Miami-Dade County school put it: "Our job is to teach children, not decide how many rolls of toilet paper we need."[20]

Some researchers believed that school-based decisionmaking established the organizational and learning conditions on which a staff could then improve teaching and learning and thereby the academic performance of students. One group identified thirty schools in nine U.S. districts and ten schools in Canada and Australia that had implemented SBM for at least three years in concert with other ambitious instructional, curricular, and organizational reforms such as teaching for higher-order thinking skills, using technology as a learning tool, employing nongraded classrooms, mainstreaming students with special needs, and individualizing instruction. They concluded:

> Although school performance has been the ultimate outcome of most SBM plans, we found this quite difficult to measure for a number of reasons. . . . Most schools did not have meaningful trend data about the educational outcomes that they were pursuing. School personnel had low comfort levels with issues of outcome measurement and accountability. For this reason, some schools did not rigorously evaluate changes, nor did they collect and array outcome data even for problem-solving purposes.[21]

In short, in the best cases of SBM in U.S., Canadian, and Australian districts, school-based governance has yet to show a direct causal link to improved school quality and student academic performance.

Federal and State Interventions

If devolving authority to individual schools has not been proved to enhance school quality, imagine the tenuous connections to student outcomes when state and federal authorities increase their control of schools. Actually, one does not need much imagination. Ample studies demonstrate what state and federal officials have long known: that having central authorities exact local compliance with new academic standards seldom leads to students' scoring higher on standardized tests.

Instead state and federal officials can invest time and money in developing the expertise of district staffs, who do the work and often do not have enough knowledge, skills, and commitment to carry out the policies. But such assistance will drain limited resources even from wealthy states and obviously be even harder for less endowed ones, and it will impose signific costs on the federal government as well. Thus these policymakers must calculate the trade-off between rendering assistance and securing compliance with their rules. This is the conundrum they have faced for decades: while local school control is viewed as the core problem, without local expertise and commitment no sustained improvement can occur. More often than not, state and federal policymakers opt for compliance. It is simply easier to have regulations requiring higher standards, more tests, stricter accountability, or more choice than to improve classroom teaching and learning.

In examining what happens when policymaking authority is shifted upward in our layered system of school governance, then, three crucial questions must be asked. What do state and federal policymakers want to happen in schools? What parts of the desired policies do teachers implement? What do students gain from the policies?

The answers are straightforward: at each link in the policy chain, from federal and state officials' declared intentions to student learning, unintended adaptations occur and affect student outcomes. Rather than sum up that considerable literature, I interpret and condense its four primary lessons as follows.[22]

STATE AND FEDERAL SCHOOL POLICIES ARE STATED INTENTIONS, NOT SCHOOL PRACTICES. Almost every state has mandated standards-based reforms. Yet while they share the same label, different incarnations, not some generic, factory-produced model, exist in states and districts. That is because policy goals are intentions (some say "hypotheses"), often inspirationally (and vaguely) worded, that policymakers seek to put into practice with a small set of blunt-edged tools.

State and federal officials use mandates, incentives, technical assistance, court decisions and sanctions (and mixes thereof) to prod local school boards, principals, and teachers to convert policymakers' aspirations into daily practices. But there are many links in the causal chain between ambiguous policy intentions and classrooms filled with students clamoring for attention. Principals' and teachers' perceptions, knowledge, beliefs, attention, motivation, and capacities come into play when state and federal policies arrive at the schoolhouse door. Other factors also shape practitioners' ～ including their preservice education, the classroom materials ˙ ˙ linkages between policies and tests students take.[23]

kers securing token obedience often trump achiev-
first twenty-five years, for example, Title I of the Ele-
ry Education Act got most districts finally to target
h poor children. As it turned out, however, because

funds have been aimed at low-income schools rather than students who meet the poverty criteria, about one-third of needy students— 4 million in 1999—go unserved. Under the complex Title I formula, funds essentially were sent to schools that met the minimum threshold for poverty but where half the students attending were not poor. Whether those funds produced the intended improvement in test scores has been debated ever since. Far more important to practitioners than compliance with regulations is whether capacity building—that competing value that state and federal officials have wrestled with for decades—occurs.[24]

FEW POLICIES ARE IMPLEMENTED AS INTENDED. What occurs is a process of mutual adaptation at every point in the path from Washington, D.C., or a state capital to the school and classroom. If state and federal policymakers expect flawless local implementation of higher standards and accountability measures, they are engaging in wishful thinking. Everyone's thumbprints are on educational policies as they wend their way into classrooms. State and federal officials interpret the legislation when they draft rules to govern local officials as they comply with the law. Officials seldom budget enough money to cover costs of the policy, so local officials inexorably make adjustments—and the list goes on. Thus determining whether a policy "works" depends on specifying exactly what was put into practice. Even more variations result from different contexts.[25]

CONTEXT SHAPES IMPLEMENTATION. States differ in their histories, political cultures, resources, and populations. A federal education policy that officials expect to be implemented uniformly in Rhode Island and California inevitably will yield disappointment. Within a state, differences in context also matter. Los Angeles Unified School District and Beverly Hills' school district may abut one another, but their differences in size, capacity to finance schools, and children's ethnicity, race, and social class mean that each district's students and practitioners will respond differently to state and federal policies aimed at their classrooms. The same holds true within districts. In Boston, for example, Burke High School and Boston Latin are very different schools in student demography, teachers, administrators, and available resources. Consequently, each will respond differently not only to district directives but also to those from the state commissioner of education and from the federal government.[26]

Thus contexts matter for teachers. As gatekeepers, they determine how they will accept, reject, or modify a mandate from their principal, superintendent or state legislature, or Congress and the president of the United

States. Teachers are, in the crisp phrase used by Andrew Porter and his colleagues, "policy brokers." Sorting out which of the teachers' adaptations of
the policy, the policy itself, or the factors just described have produced the
intended or unintended student outcomes is enormously complex and just
barely within the grasp of most researchers.[27]

ASSESSING STUDENT LEARNING FROM THE IMPLEMENTED POLICY
REMAINS PRIMITIVE. For policies intended to improve student academic achievement, effectiveness (or ineffectiveness) has been severely
narrowed to gains and losses in scores on standardized tests. Most federal
and state policymakers are familiar with the weaknesses of such tests.
Nonetheless, scores on state and national tests are used to evaluate whether
standards-based reforms are successful.

In narrowing achievement to test scores, moreover, policymakers ignore
the critical issue of whether the policy has been partially, moderately, or
fully implemented. After all, without evidence of teachers putting all, most,
or even a tad of the policy into practice, the overall value of the venture
can hardly be judged. For example, if a state called for teachers to teach
math or reading differently, were teachers afforded sufficient opportunities
to learn about the new approaches? Were special lessons and materials made
available and demonstrated to them? Did teachers employ the different ways
of teaching mathematics or reading? Were tests tied to policy aims, professional development opportunities, and classroom materials? Although some
researchers have begun to construct measures that begin to answer such questions, their work, sadly, remains on the periphery of most policy research.
Instead, the easiest and least useful measure—test scores—dominates policymakers' judgments.[28]

Clearly, the four lessons emerging from the literature on state and federal
interventions raise serious doubts about the wisdom of centralizing school
authority to improve teaching and learning.

Glimmers of Hope

For those who yearn for silver linings, glimmers of hope can be found in a
few cases in which state and federal policies have achieved their aims. In
these isolated instances, state and federal policymakers have indeed culti-
vated local educators' capacities to innovate, gain knowledge and skills,
and become committed to improving student achievement.

The federally initiated National Diffusion Network (1974–85), for example, helped local educators implement faithful replicas of research-based

programs that had demonstrated their effectiveness. Subsequent federal efforts along the same line can be seen in the evolution of whole school reform.[29]

Changing one school at a time is part of a tradition dating back to the late 1970s. At that time researchers allied with federal and state reformers identified "effective" urban elementary schools—those that exceeded expectations by scoring higher than predicted, given their numbers of poor and minority students. The "effective schools" movement throughout the 1980s spawned school-by-school reform and in 1998 became the federally funded Comprehensive School Reform Demonstration Program. Districts and states can now choose from many models in federally approved menus of whole school reform programs.[30]

Yet changing one school at a time makes state and federal policymakers impatient. States generally have been raising academic standards, adopting curriculum frameworks, and launching more aligned tests to raise student achievement in all schools at once, not one by one. In only a few states, moreover, have policymakers gone beyond gaining local compliance to render assistance to principals and teachers. Kentucky and California offer instructive examples.

With Kentucky's State Supreme Court ordering an overhaul in the financing and operation of schools and with subsequent passage of the Kentucky Education Reform Act (KERA) in 1990, the past decade has seen compliance and capacity building coupled with standards-based reform, testing, and accountability. School curricula are more sharply focused on state standards. Classrooms are better equipped, and teachers have undergone considerable professional development. Researchers have concluded that increases in elementary school test scores can be attributed to KERA, though they make it clear that much remains to be done, especially in building practitioners' expertise and commitment to classroom changes.[31]

David Cohen and his colleagues capped a decade-long research effort to examine how California, one of the leaders in setting standards, built the capacities of math teachers to engage in deeper, more complex, and more ambitious teaching. They found that when consistency among policy instruments—curricular materials, tests, professional development, and teacher education—were aligned and sustained, about 10 percent of the teachers who attended state-sponsored opportunities to gain knowledge and skills changed "their practices . . . appreciably and students' learning improved."[32]

A small number of urban districts, building on state and 1 dates and incentives, have centralized control of instructic strong school and classroom support, and prodded practitioners to develop school-level instructional coherence. In San Diego and Boston, for example, building a system of instructional coaching helped teachers and principals focus sharply on literacy and math, and allocating resources to support teacher-coaches, smaller classes, earlier interventions, and curricular align-ments has coincided with steady improvements in elementary (but not secondary) school scores on state tests. Using different managerial and instructional strategies, Houston has seen elementary school scores on state tests rise dramatically but with far less success in secondary schools. It is premature to suggest causal links for even limited gains in these districts—careful studies must be done over five to ten years—but these cases nonetheless do provide some flickers of hope.[33]

Despite these encouraging signs, though, the overall evidence provides meager support for reducing the power of local decisionmakers and increasing authority at the state and federal levels. Essentially, the well-documented, failure-studded record of state and federal implementation efforts and the repeated cases in which seeking compliance has over-whelmed the building of local capacity combine to darken the few rays of light.

The reasons for the sorry centralization record, then, are clear. First, state and federal officials seek uniformity and, in doing so, policy compliance overwhelms all else. This is not surprising in light of what state and federal policymakers face. Funds often are short. Constant turnover among local elected officials is inescapable. Popular demands for swift results are shrill. State educators simply find it much easier to submit reports that adhere to the letter of federal requirements than to make often difficult and expensive changes; local educators do pretty much the same with state officials.

A substantial lack of coordination prevails between and among the layers of school governance. That increased state and federal authority has meant new webs of relationships, new forums where local, state, and federal offi-cials can negotiate decisions and blend resources, is evident. Even such new relationships, however, cannot hide the many holes in instructional, cur-ricular, and managerial coordination among government levels.

Finally, local school boards, superintendents, principals, and teachers act as policy brokers who revise state and federal policies. Centralizing state and federal policymaking has not left local officials impotent. On the con-trary, local practitioners still determine what happens in schools.

This is certainly true, for example, in the handful of cities where mayors now appoint school boards and superintendents. To these urban leaders, the shift in governance from an elected board to the mayor means that direct control over schools can, with mayoral appointees in charge and the resources of the city behind them, lead to key changes in school operations. This has happened, for example, in Chicago, Boston, and New York. If some enthusiasts can cite Chicago or Boston as examples of success, however, others can point to stubborn counterexamples in Baltimore or Detroit, where mayoral control has led to rocky results. It is far too soon to say whether moving school authority to city hall generally leads to better teaching and learning.[34]

Nor does the skimpy and often ambiguous evidence on school choice support the argument that competition improves public school management, efficiency, and effectiveness. Policymakers introduced more parental choice through alternative schools, intradistrict and interdistrict transfers, and charter schools in the 1980s and 1990s, with the federal government joining the push for public school options. Advocates have not made much headway, though, on other approaches: only a handful of districts and states have adopted vouchers or tuition tax credits for private school attendance. To date, in any case, there are few signs that choice schools, public or private, are producing more efficient or effective academic results, let alone that public school systems are being transformed or making notable gains out of fear of such competition.[35]

Targeting the Right Schools

Atop of all this is another important problem—that reforms and required resources are not concentrated on the schools that need them. Rather, state and federal policymakers have taken a broad-brush approach aimed at all schools, which has muddled matters. Although few policymakers will say so publicly, they and most Americans know from direct experience that in urban, rural, and suburban districts there are "good" schools, "good enough" schools, and mediocre to awful schools.[36] With nearly 15,000 public school districts containing close to 90,000 schools and serving almost 50 million students, the social, academic, and cultural diversity among and within districts is stunning. Think of New York City, Los Angeles, and Chicago, where some high schools send 90 percent of their graduates to college while others send just 10 percent on for more education.

This diversity is patterned. Generally speaking, we have a three-tiered system of education across the nation. The first tier, about one in ten schools, already exceeds the academic standards and test-score thresholds set by their states. Another four to five of every ten schools—the second tier—already meet or come close to meeting their state standards and cut-off scores. The rest, the third tier, do not. Most third-tier schools are in urban and rural districts with high concentrations of poor and minority families, where the nation's chief education challenges lie.[37]

State and federally driven reforms are really designed for this tier, for the large number of urban and rural schools struggling with students who perform at the lowest academic levels and who often drop out. That's why the No Child Left Behind Act (NCLB), as well as state policies, seeks to close the achievement gap between these students and their more advantaged peers. That is why charter schools, voucher experiments, and other choice mechanisms have emerged as devices to help disadvantaged students. That is why mayoral takeovers of school systems have occurred in big cities like Boston or Chicago and why former corporate executives, ex-generals, and other noneducators now head half a dozen other urban school systems like those in San Diego and Seattle. None of these policies is aimed at more affluent suburbs.

For elected officials to admit this publicly, however, would be politically risky, because most voters who are middle class, white, and live in those more affluent suburbs might be distressed at such targeted use of their tax dollars, at not getting considerable resources for their own school systems. This kind of political calculus has created resistance to equalizing school finance in many states and has required funds for the disadvantaged under Title I of NCLB (which is the latest reauthorization of the Elementary and Secondary Education Act) to be spread among virtually all school districts in the nation. So now academic standards initially aimed at low-performing schools have been transformed to apply to all schools, seeking to hammer our three-tiered system into a single mold. As in the past, reformers have confused setting standards with standardization.[38]

Specifically, forty-nine states have adopted standards for what all students should know and do and tests to assess their performance. The ranks of states administering student tests aligned with published standards in at least one subject grew from thirty-five in 1998 to forty-one in 2000. Twenty-seven states rate schools primarily on the basis of test scores; fourteen states have authorized their education departments to close and take over low-performing schools. In eighteen states, students who fail the statewide graduation test do not receive diplomas; ten more states have ordered that penalty enforced by 2008. In thirteen states (as of 2000), cash payments or awards flowed to schools that met their targets and showed continuous improvement. By 2001, all fifty states had produced or required local school boards to publish district or school report cards that included data on students' test performance, attendance, dropout and graduation rates, school discipline, and student-teacher ratios.[39]

At the federal level, NCLB requires all schools receiving federal funds to test every student annually in grades 3 through 8 in reading and math and, by 2007, to test students in science at least once in grades 3–5, 6–9, and 10–12. All schools are responsible for each ethnic and racial group of students making "adequate yearly progress" (AYP) toward becoming "proficient" in state standards. By 2014, every student must be proficient. NCLB also mandates that those schools showing improvement will be rewarded and those that fail to meet AYP targets two years in a row will face "corrective action" and, ultimately, "restructuring." If a student is in a school identified as failing, the family may choose to send their child to another school at the district's expense (but not across district lines to another school system).

There are problems, however, with such a broad-brush approach. On the one hand, these measures make little positive difference for the thousands of elementary schools that perform far above the new academic standards in such places as La Jolla, California, Arlington, Texas, or Newton, Massachusetts. Nor do they do anything for the hundreds of elite high schools like Bronx High School of Science in New York City, New Trier High School in Evanston, Illinois, or Lowell High School in San Francisco.

On the other hand, uniform, nationwide prescriptions not only drain attention and resources from where they are most needed. They also are ill suited for struggling urban schools, where poor academic performance stems from an entangled blend of in-school and out-of-school factors. In-school problems involve uncredentialed teachers, large class sizes, and insufficient resources for individual student help, early intervention, and sustained assistance. Out-of-school factors include such elements as family poverty, students' medical needs, and neighborhood crime. Yet current policy assumes that if students, teachers, and principals in big city schools just stop whining, roll up their sleeves, work harder, and are held accountable, test scores will increase, more students will earn diplomas, and jobs in an information-based economy will await graduates.

This view certainly contains an element of truth. Much has been written about urban principals' and teachers' low academic expectations for poor and minority students, and studies show that schools that seldom meet academic standards suffer few consequences.[40] What weakens the prescription, however, is evident to anyone who visits an urban elementary or secondary school to sit in classes, listen to teachers and students, and observe lunchrooms, playgrounds, corridors, and offices. They begin to appreciate a simple but inescapable truth: an urban school is deeply influenced by the neighborhood from which it draws its students, by the community's racial, ethnic, and social class strengths and limitations. In middle-class and wealthy neighborhoods, focusing only on what the school can do is reasonable; civic institutions thrive there, and families have the money and networks to provide help if their children have academic, health, or emotional problems. That is not the case in poor communities. Many families lack the personal and institutional resources. They depend on the school and other public agencies. In short, in cities schools cannot do it alone.

This fundamental fact has been ignored in the process of centralizing standards-based school reforms in state and federal policymakers' hands. After all, to strive for school improvements by including the social geography of families and neighborhoods would entail major expenditures by states and particularly by the federal government. Reconceptualizing schools, for example, as youth-serving agencies, rather than places where the single most important job is producing higher test scores, means reorganizing existing cultural, civic, and social services. Policymakers often stammer when faced with the scale of such changes.

Broadening the policy agenda to encompass a community-based strategy to school improvement does not mean that students, teachers, and principals should be held less responsible for higher academic achievement. Nor does recognition of a school being nested in the larger community suggest that there should be different academic standards for the poor and the privileged. The obvious fact that schools are entangled in their communities only makes clear the knotty issues facing urban district leaders. They need to mobilize civic and corporate elites while educating state and federal officials and business and civic opinion setters to the plain fact that raising academic achievement in big city schools involves far more than increasing parental choice, threatening teachers and principals, or withholding high school diplomas for students who fail a graduation test.

In the face of this seemingly out-of-reach complexity and cost in transforming urban schools and their communities, it is far easier for state and federal policymakers to embrace a deeply embedded U.S. reform tradition: change who makes decisions and how they get made. For more than two centuries, reformers have argued again and again for centralizing and decentralizing decisionmaking while searching for mechanisms that better balance competing centers of power and do not paralyze authorities. From this history has come an unbreakable faith in changing the structures of decisionmaking to improve the quality of decisions.[41]

This belief in the quasi-magical powers of new governance structures to solve national and local problems is at work in the thirty-year consolidation of state and federal governance over schools. Policymakers claim that such changes can make a difference in daily classroom practices and in how students connect to their teachers. They believe that governance changes can steer U.S. schools onto a course that will make the economy more productive, improve the quality of urban life, reduce poverty and crime, and solve other social ills. Governance reform, then, becomes the vehicle for transforming classroom practices and relationships as it solves major social and economic problems. If ever a hall of infamy existed for mismatched solutions to problems, in a nanosecond I would nominate state and federally driven governance reforms aimed at raising academic achievement and strengthening the economy.[42]

Are There Better Ways?

The nation's economic fate is not determined by student test scores, federal and state efforts to increase student achievement have not accomplished much, and current education policies are not concentrated in ways that do the most good. In short, the belief in centralizing education authority to impose standards-based reforms and more parental choice does not inspire great confidence. So I end this analysis with reflections on the two arenas in which authority to govern schools has shifted: local school officials and state and federal policymakers.

Local School Officials

Be they business and civic leaders, state and federal policymakers, union leaders, or activist parents, reformers are caught in a conundrum: the people who are viewed as the problem—the local school board and its agents—are also the people who can solve the problem. School board members hire superintendents, principals, and teachers to implement district, state, and federal policy. These are the people—not business executives, governors, U.S. presidents, state or federal legislators, education officials, or policy analysts—who do the daily work. The current governance reform agenda mandates and prescribes what local officials must do. State and federal policymakers use their limited tools of cheerleading and scolding, supplying carrots and wielding sticks, to get locals to do their bidding. Since millions of teachers and students are at the end of a long chain of authority stretching from

1600 Pennsylvania Avenue through state capitals to districts to local schools and finally into classrooms, the chances of securing intended outcomes year after year through rules, demands, threats, and cash bonuses are slim. One alternative to managing the conundrum—too often rejected by the current spate of reformers—is to partner with local boards and invigorate local capacities to meet higher academic standards and the many goals that tax-supported public schools in a democracy are expected to achieve.

According to opinion polls, most communities trust their school boards to do the right thing. More often than not, these polls reveal far more public confidence in local school board members to make sound decisions than in business leaders or elected officials.[43] This support of local schools has long frustrated critics. As one, a former assistant secretary for education in the Reagan administration, remarked in the late 1980s:

> Nearly everyone now acknowledges that the United States has lapsed into a grave state of educational and social decay from which it needs to extricate itself. Yet most Americans are also satisfied with their own immediate situations, the education of their children, and the performance of the schools they know best.[44]

Although this critic called such confidence in local authorities "schizophrenic," and galling as it must have been to him, he recognized that the public wants local control, that it trusted neighbors far more than those in state capitals and federal offices. Even when mayors control public schools and dispense with elected boards of education, they are still politically accountable to a city's voters. Moreover, they can coordinate broader services for children, carry clout with state and federal officials, and be ousted or reelected on their record of improving schools. A mayor is a far more visible figure to constituents than a governor, president, or distant bureaucrats telling practitioners what they must do.[45]

When one considers the discouraging record of state and federal authorities cajoling or coercing local officials to comply with rules, a strategy unfolds that plays to the strength of the local agents and to the limited policy tools of central authorities. That strategy: capacity building.

For school boards, capacity building means learning to solve problems and manage dilemmas. For superintendents it means becoming better political, managerial, and instructional leaders. For principals it means better leadership in their schools, and for teachers it means becoming more expert in knowledge and skills. Yes, it also means far more resources devoted to sustained professional development for those responsible for student learning. And, yes, it will be as expensive an investment as Fortune 500 companies make annually to train their top executives, middle-level managers, shop-floor stewards, and production workers.

Another question arises: capacity building toward what ends? More expertise and better leadership for what purposes? A central point of this analysis is that the flawed drive to improve the economy by improving schools and placing increased authority in state and federal offices has made schools more uniform academically by seeking to prepare all students for college and jobs in a knowledge-based economy. This narrowing of purposes for public schools to basically one aim ignores the rich, broader, and historic purposes that tax-supported public schools have served in a democracy. Civic engagement, learning to deal with different ideas and cultures, participating in the arts, and even appreciating productive labor have been historic goals for public schools that have been largely ignored in the past quarter century, except in retirement speeches, conferences, and national reports where they are mentioned in passing.[46] Building the capacity of local boards of education, administrators, and teachers should have a more generous vision of what public schools are for than the current constricted one.

Even were development of local expertise accepted as the single most important strategy, and even were it agreed that public schools must be far more than employment boot camps, the question is where locals would get the money for capacity building. Here is where state and federal authorities enter the picture.

The Role of State and Federal Authorities

As I see the decentralized system of U.S. public schooling, local, state, and federal authorities have acted more as rivals than as partners. Their roles should tilt far more to partnership. State and federal authorities can build local capacity to govern well, monitor the progress of districts in reaching agreed-upon standards, and intervene on issues of equity of access and fairness in treatment. They can provide resources to local schools for such activities as recruiting, training, developing, and retaining good teachers, and focusing more intently on poor and minority schools, where good principals and teachers are especially needed.

This is not intended to suggest that standards-based reform should be abandoned. Rather, it should be reconfigured. I can imagine, for example, a strategy in which federal and state authorities work closely with local officials to build better schools—especially in urban districts—that achieve state academic standards but that also ensure that students, among other things, become engaged in the community, know how to deal with different ideas and cultures, and participate in the arts.

Summary and Conclusions

The century-old expansion of the public school's role as an agent of social reform has prompted subsequent generations of reformers to turn to schools to solve national social, political, and economic problems. Reformers' fixation in recent decades on reducing local decisionmakers' powers while concentrating more authority in state and federal policymakers as the mechanism to solve these problems has roots in U.S. ambivalence toward consolidated power and strong beliefs in changing decisionmaking structures as the best avenue for producing desired outcomes.

As to the worth of school governance reforms achieving the goal of better teaching and learning, higher academic achievement, and improved quality of schooling, the lack of substantial evidence makes the most determined optimist cry. A few flickers of light may offer hope to chronic romantics who seek links between governance changes and higher-quality schools, but overall the conclusion can only be: if you want better schools, governance changes may be a starting point, but in themselves they are powerless to improve teaching and learning, much less to fortify the economy.

Thus, to the larger and most important question—whether current conditions warrant further concentration of state and federal authority over schools—my answer is no. My answer is based on the lack of evidence during the past century when governance changes directed toward improved schooling were put into practice. If substantial evidence is the primary basis for making rational policy decisions, the stunning absence of compelling research findings should give even the most eager of governance reformers pause. My answer is also based on contemporary policymakers' stealth attempt to target urban schools while offering national prescriptions for all public schools regardless of where they are in the three-tiered U.S. system of schooling.

Finally, my answer is anchored in rejecting the widespread policy assumption that better schools can strengthen the U.S. economy and society through centrally driven standards-based curriculum, testing, and accountability reforms. The assumption born of a problem that no longer exists was flawed from the start. It was worthy of a pronouncement the queen would make in *Alice in Wonderland*. Furthermore, this assumption has neglected historic commitments to building students' civic engagement and problem-solving skills, accepting differences in ideas and cultures, and appreciating the arts and the worth of productive labor. There are important and different roles for state and federal policymakers to play in allocating resources, setting standards, intervening when necessary, and monitoring progress or regress in reaching desired goals. Partnerships among governing authorities in a decentralized democratic system of schooling, not destructive rivalries among parties bent on control, are what students need to do well in school.

Notes

1. National Commission on Excellence in Education, *A Nation at Risk* (Government Printing Office, 1983). Standards-based curriculum, testing, and accountability measures are strategies that evolved from "systemic reform" efforts in the early 1990s. See Marshall Smith and Jennifer O'Day, "Systemic School Reform," *Politics of Education Association Yearbook,* 1990, pp. 233–67.

2. For details on the formation of this business-inspired coalition concentrating on school reform, see Thomas Toch, *In the Name of Excellence* (Oxford University Press, 1991), and Larry Cuban, *Why Are Good Schools So Hard to Get?* (Teachers College Press, 2003). Gordon Lafer maps a sequence of events in the same quarter-century when employers focused on workers' lack of skills and the need for more training and education to equip employees for the future workplace. See *The Job Training Charade* (Cornell University Press, 2002). Economists and widely respected analysts also produced best sellers in these years that judged schools as failures in teaching students to think and solve problems. See Ray Marshall and Marc Tucker, *Thinking for a Living: Education and the Wealth of Nations* (Basic Books, 1992); Robert Reich, *The Work of Nations* (Alfred A. Knopf, 1991); and Lester Thurow, *Head to Head: The Coming Economic Battle among Japan, Europe, and America* (Morrow, 1992).

3. For a brief history of the movement toward standards-based reform with its accountability and testing, see Richard Elmore, *Building a New Structure for School Leadership* (Washington: Albert Shanker Institute, 2000).

4. National Assessment of Educational Progress, *The Nation's Report Card, Reading 2002* (U.S. Department of Education, 2003); Audrey Amrein and David Berliner, "High-Stakes Testing, Uncertainty, and Student Learning" *Education Policy Analysis Archives,* vol. 10, no. 18 (2002).

5. Chester Finn Jr., *We Must Take Charge: Our School and Our Future* (Free Press, 1991), p. 113.

6. An example of connecting tests to wages and productivity is John Bishop, "Is the Test Score Decline Responsible for the Productivity Growth Decline?" *American Economic Review,* vol. 74, no.1 (1989), pp. 178–97. Bishop's answer to his question is yes. For those who doubt these assumptions of test scores and worker productivity, see Henry

Levin, "High-Stakes Testing and Economic Productivity," in Gary Orfield and Mindy Kornhaber, eds., *Raising Standards or Raising Barriers? Inequality and High-Stakes Testing in Public Education* (New York: Century Foundation Press, 2001), pp. 39–49; Robert Balfanz, "Local Knowledge, Academic Skills, and Individual Productivity: An Alternative View," *Educational Policy*, vol. 5, no. 4 (1991), pp. 343–70.

7. Herbert M. Kliebard, *Schooled to Work: Vocationalism and the American Curriculum, 1876–1946* (Teachers College Press, 1999), p. 29.

8. Harvey Kantor, "Vocationalism in American Education: The Economic and Political Context, 1880–1930." In Harvey Kantor and David Tyack, eds., *Work, Youth, and Schooling* (Stanford University Press, 1982), pp. 14–44; Marvin Lazerson and Norton Grubb, eds., *American Education and Vocationalism: Documents in Vocational Education, 1870–1970* (Teachers College Press, 1974).

9. Kliebard, *Schooled to Work*; Harvey Kantor, *Learning to Earn: School, Work, and Vocational Reform in California, 1880–1930* (University of Wisconsin Press, 1988).

10. Levin, "High-Stakes Testing and Economic Productivity"; John P. Smith III, "Tracking the Mathematics of Automobile Production: Are Schools Failing to Prepare Students for Work?" *American Educational Research Journal*, vol. 36, no. 4 (1999), pp. 835–78. Also see Lafer, *The Job Training Charade* (2002), chs. 2 and 3, for a comprehensive summary of evidence revealing how workplace demands are inconsistent with the theory and beliefs of those who argue for more well-trained graduates from high school and college. Critics of using standardized test scores as the only or best indicator of improved teaching and learning have often referred to other important measures that are either ignored or missing because of measurement difficulties. These include the quality of intellectual work in school, the links between classroom teaching and assessment, and other measures of student performance. See Lorrie A. Shepard, "The Role of Assessment in a Learning Culture," *Educational Researcher*, vol. 29, no. 7 (2000), pp. 4–14.

11. For growth in productivity in the 1990s, see Louis Uchitelle, "Big Increases in Productivity by Workers," *New York Times*, November 13, 1999, p. B1; Hal Varian, "The Economic Scene," *New York Times*, June 6, 2002, p. C2; Michael Porter, Jeffrey Sachs, and John McArthur, *Global Competitiveness Report 2001–2002* (New York: World Economic Forum, 2002).

12. Kevin Hollenbeck, *Education and the Economy* (W. E. Upjohn Institute for Employment Research, January 2001).

13. Lawrence A. Cremin, *Popular Education and Its Discontents* (Harper and Row, 1990), p. 103.

14. David Labaree, "Public Goods, Private Goods: The American Struggle over Educational Goals," *American Educational Research Journal*, vol. 34, no.1 (1997), pp. 39–81; John Goodlad, *A Place Called School* (Macmillan, 1984).

15. For national goals, see Jack Jennings, "From the White House to the Schoolhouse: Greater Demands and New Roles," in William L. Boyd and Debra Miretzky, eds., *American Educational Governance on Trial: Change and Challenges*, part 1 (Chicago: National Society for the Study of Education, 2003), pp. 291–310; David Grissmer and Ann Flanagan, *Exploring Rapid Achievement Gains in North Carolina and Texas* (Washington: National Education Goals Panel, 1998).

16. Mario D. Fantini, *Free Schools of Choice* (Simon and Schuster, 1973); Marilyn Gittell, *Participants and Participation: A Study of School Policy in New York City* (Praeger, 1967); Diane Ravitch, *The Great School Wars* (Basic Books, 1974).

17. Jane David, "Site-Based Management: Making It Work," *Educational Leadership*, vol. 53, no. 4 (December 1995/January 1996), pp. 4–9; Carnegie Forum on Education and the Economy, *A Nation Prepared: Teachers for the 21st Century* (Hyattsville, Md.: Carnegie Forum on Education and the Economy, 1986).

18. Joseph Berger, "Miami Brings Democracy to School Management," *New York Times*, January 1, 1990, p. A10.

19. For the spread of SBM in the late 1980s and early 1990s, see Rodney Ogawa, "The Institutional Sources of Educational Reform: The Case of School-Based Management," *American Education Research Journal*, vol. 31, no. 3 (1994), pp. 519–48. See also Lynn Olson, "In San Diego, Managers Forging 'Service' Role," *Education Week*, March 8, 1989, pp. 1, 8–9; Ann Bradley and Lynn Olson, "The Balance of Power: Shifting the Lines of Authority in an Effort to Improve Schools," *Education Week*, February 24, 1993, pp. 9–13. The quote is cited in Olson's 1989 article in *Education Week*, p. 8. The New York City Board of Education fired Fernandez in 1993. In 1995 the Illinois legislature gave the mayor of Chicago expanded authority to appoint the school board and the superintendent and to run the district schools, sharply reducing the previous powers that elected school-site councils had gained from the 1988 legislation. In effect, Chicago recentralized governing authority into the hands of the mayor and his appointees. See Dorothy Shipps, "Invisible Hand: Big Business and Chicago School Reform," *Teachers College Record*, vol. 99, no. 1 (1997), pp. 73–116.

20. Lynn Beck and Joseph Murphy, *The Four Imperatives of a Successful School* (Thousand Oaks, Calif.: Corwin Press, 1995), p. viii; Berger, "Miami Brings Democracy to School Management."

21. Priscilla Wohlstetter and others, *Organizing for Successful School-Based Management* (Alexandria, Va.: Association for Supervision and Curriculum Development, 1997), p. 54.

22. Milbrey McLaughlin, "Lessons from Past Implementation Research," *Educational Evaluation and Policy Analysis*, vol. 9, no. 2 (1987), pp. 171–78; Hugh Davis Graham, *The Uncertain Triumph: Federal Education Policy in the Kennedy and Johnson Years* (University of North Carolina Press, 1984); Paul T. Hill, "The Federal Role in Education," in Diane Ravitch, ed., *Brookings Papers on Education Policy 2000* (Brookings, 2000), pp. 11–57; Andrew Porter and John Smithson, "Are Content Standards Being Implemented in the Classroom? A Methodology and Some Tentative Answers," in Susan H. Fuhrman, ed., *From the Capitol to the Classroom: Standards-Based Reform in the States* (University of Chicago Press, National Society for the Study of Education, 2001), pp. 60–80; James Spillane, "Challenging Instruction for 'All Students': Policy, Practitioners, and Practice," in Fuhrman, *From the Capitol to the Classroom*, pp. 217–41; Suzanne Wilson and Robert Floden, "Hedging Bets: Standards-Based Reform in Classrooms," in Fuhrman, *From the Capitol to the Classroom*, pp. 193–216; Richard F. Elmore and Milbrey Wallin McLaughlin, *Steady Work: Policy, Practice, and Reform of American Education* (Santa Monica, Calif.: RAND, 1988); Michael Fullan, *The New Meaning of*

Educational Change (Teachers College Press, 1991); for teachers adapting instructional policies, see Cynthia Coburn, "Collective Sensemaking about Reading: How Teachers Mediate Reading Policy in Their Professional Communities," *Educational Evaluation and Policy Analysis,* vol. 23, no. 2 (2001), pp. 145–70.

23. For policy as intentions and the relationship to instructional implementation, see Milbrey McLaughlin, "Learning from Experience: Lessons from Policy Implementation," in Alan Odden, ed., *Education Policy Implementation* (SUNY Press, 1991), pp. 143–55; David Cohen and James Spillane, "Policy and Practice: The Relations between Governance and Instruction," in Susan H. Fuhrman, ed., *Designing Coherent Education Policy: Improving the System* (San Francisco: Jossey-Bass, 1993), pp. 35–88; David Cohen and Heather Hill, *Learning Policy: When State Education Reform Works* (Yale University Press, 2001); James Spillane, Brian Reiser, and Todd Reimer, "Policy Implementation and Cognition: Reframing and Refocusing Implementation Research," *Review of Educational Research,* vol. 72, no. 3 (2002), pp. 387–431.

24. Figures for unserved poor children come from *Biennial Evaluation Report, FY 1993–1994,* "Education of Disadvantaged Children (Chapter 1, ESEA) Formula Grants to Local Education Agencies" (U.S. Department of Education); and Nina Rees, "How the Senate Can Reform Title I to Empower Parents and Help Children Achieve," *Executive Memorandum no.* 659 (Washington: Heritage Foundation).

25. Elmore and McLaughlin, *Steady Work;* Lorraine McDonnell and Milbrey McLaughlin, *Education Policy and the Role of the States* (Santa Monica, Calif.: RAND, 1982); Jerome Murphy, "Progress and Problems: The Paradox of State Reform," in Ann Lieberman and Milbrey McLaughlin, eds., *Policy Making in Education* (Chicago: National Survey of Student Engagement, 1982), pp. 195–214; David Cohen, "Standards-Based School Reform: Policy, Practice, and Performance," in Helen Ladd, ed., *Holding Schools Accountable* (Brookings, 1996), pp. 99–127.

26. Janet Fairman and William Firestone, "The District Role in State Assessment Policy," in Susan H. Furhman, ed., *From the Capitol to the Classroom: Standards-Based Reform in the States,* part 2 (University of Chicago Press, National Society for the Study of Education, 2001), pp. 124–47; Elizabeth DeBray, Gail Parson, and Katrina Woodworth, "Patterns of Response in Four High Schools under State Accountability Policies in Vermont and New York," in Fuhrman, *From the Capitol to the Classroom,* pp. 170–92; Suzanne Wilson and Robert Floden, "Hedging Bets: Standards-Based Reform in Classrooms," in Fuhrman, *From the Capitol to the Classroom,* pp. 193–216.

27. Wilson and Floden, "Hedging Bets"; Larry Cuban, *How Teachers Taught* (Teachers College Press, 1993); Spillane, Reiser, and Reimer, "Policy Implementation and Cognition."

28. Cohen and Hill, *Learning Policy;* Porter and Smithson, "Are Content Standards Being Implemented in the Classroom?"

29. David Crandall and others, *People, Policies, and Practices: Examining the Chain of School Improvement* (Andover, Mass.: The Network, 1983); Michael Huberman, "School Improvement Strategies That Work: Some Scenarios," *Educational Leadership,* vol. 41, no. 3 (1983), pp. 23–27; for the Comprehensive School Reform Demonstration Project, see www.nwrel.org/csrdp/about.html [May 2004].

30. Stewart Purkey and Marshall Smith, "Effective Schools: A Review," *Elementary School Journal*, vol. 83, no. 4 (1983), pp. 427–52; for an examination of the spread of effective schools in the 1980s and 1990s, see Pamela Bullard and Barbara Taylor, *Making School Reform Happen* (Boston: Allyn and Bacon, 1993); for comprehensive school reform, see the National Clearinghouse of Comprehensive School Reform (www. goodschools.gwu.edu/ [May 2004]).

31. Connie Bridge, *The Implementation of Kentucky's Primary Program 1995: A Progress Report* (Lexington: Institute on Education Reform, University of Kentucky, 1995); Betty Lou Whitford and Ken Jones, eds., *Accountability, Assessment, and Teacher Commitment: Lessons from Kentucky's Reform Efforts* (State University of New York, 2000); Patricia Kannapel and others, "The Impact of Standards and Accountability on Teaching and Learning in Kentucky," in Susan H. Furhman, ed., *From the Capitol to the Classroom: Standards-Based Reform in the States* (University of Chicago Press, National Society for the Study of Education, 2001), pp. 242–62.

32. Cohen and Hill, *Learning Policy*, p. 6; see also Michael Knapp, "Between Systemic Reforms and the Mathematics and Science Classroom," *Review of Educational Research*, vol. 67, no. 2 (1997), pp. 227–66. For an insightful synthesis of the issues researchers have to resolve in determining whether state standards do indeed lead to improved teaching and learning in classrooms, see Porter and Smithson, "Are Content Standards Being Implemented in the Classroom?"

33. Larry Cuban and Michael Usdan, *Powerful Reforms with Shallow Roots* (Teachers College Press, 2003); see chapters on Boston and San Diego. For Houston, see Paul T. Hill, "Digging Deeper," *Education Next* (Fall 2001), pp. 18–23; Jane Hannaway and Shannon McKay, "Taking Measure," *Education Next* (September 2001), pp. 9–17.

34. Cuban and Usdan, *Powerful Reforms with Shallow Roots;* James Cibulka and William Boyd, *A Race against Time: The Crisis in Urban Schooling* (Norwood, N.J.: Ablex Publishing, 2003).

35. Jeffrey Henig, *Rethinking School Choice* (Princeton University Press, 1994); Frederick Hess, *Revolution at the Margins* (Brookings, 2002).

36. I place the word "good" in quotation marks to signify that goodness in a school means different things to different people. President George W. Bush, reformer Deborah Meier, and a fundamentalist Christian would define a "good" school differently. I inquire into these meanings of "good" schools in *Why Is It So Hard to Get Good Schools?* (Teachers College Press, 2003).

37. I have drawn this portrait of a three-tiered system from the literature on urban and suburban schools over the past half-century, with their mix of academically successful schools and those enrolling high percentages of poor minority children who have slipped considerably in academic achievement. In suburban schools, high academic aspirations and achievement go hand in hand with family education and income levels. There are, of course, academically mediocre schools in suburbs, but by and large the three-tier system tracks family education and income. See, for example, Patricia Sexton, *Education and Income: Inequalities in Public Schools* (Viking, 1961); Christopher Jencks and others, *Inequality* (Basic Books, 1972). For large urban and suburban districts, see

National Center for Education Statistics, "Characteristics of the 100 Largest Public Elementary and Secondary School Districts" (U.S. Department of Education, 2002).

38. I elaborate on this argument in *Why Is It So Hard to Get Good Schools?*

39. "Quality Counts '99: Rewarding Results, Punishing Failure," *Education Week,* January 11, 1999; Jodi Wilgoren, "For 2000, the GOP Sees Education in a New Light," *New York Times,* August 2, 2000, p. A15. David Sanger, "Bush Pushes Ambitious Education Plan," *New York Times,* January 24, 2001, pp. A1, A14.

40. The literature on urban schools with high percentages of poor minority students failing is enormous. The "effective schools" literature of the late 1970s and early 1980s picked up from the rich literature that emerged in the early 1960s documenting vividly how teachers, administrators, and other adults had low academic expectations and how those low expectations became a factor in the academic failure of low-income minority students. See Robert Rosenthal and Lenore Jacobson, *Pygmalion in the Classroom* (Holt, Rinehart, and Winston, 1968); Ron Edmonds, "Effective Schools for the Urban Poor," *Educational Leadership,* vol. 37, no. 10 (1979), pp. 18–24.

41. For the unique romance that Americans have had with changing governance structures as a mode of reform, see Deborah A. Stone, *Policy Paradox: The Art of Political Decision Making* (W. W. Norton, 1997), pp. 351–72; Aaron Wildavsky, *Speaking Truth to Power* (New Brunswick, N.J.: Transaction Books, 1996), pp. 142–54.

42. For the awesome complexity of trying to change authority structures to reach into the classroom and make improvements, see Cohen and Spillane, "Policy and Practice," and Penelope Peterson, Sarah McCarthy, and Richard Elmore, "Learning from School Restructuring," *American Educational Research Journal,* vol. 33, no. 1 (1996), pp. 119–53.

43. Stanley Elam, *The Gallup/Phi Delta Kappa Polls of Attitudes toward the Public Schools, 1969–1988* (Bloomington, Ind.: Phi Delta Kappa, 1989).

44. Finn, *We Must Take Charge,* p. 94.

45. Anthony Carnevale and Donna Desrochers, *School Satisfaction: A Statistical Profile of Cities and Suburbs* (Princeton, N.J.: Educational Testing Service, 1999).

46. The best summary of the historic goals of U.S. public schools is David Labaree, "Public Goods, Private Goods."

6

Less than Meets the Eye: Standards, Testing, and Fear of Federal Control

SUSAN H. FUHRMAN

W hen Washington starts issuing mandates about standards for student learning and how to assess that learning, controversies begin. Such policies, after all, have strong implications for school curriculums, and federal control of curriculum has long been taboo. Since before the Elementary and Secondary Education Act (ESEA) of 1965, fear of federal dominance over education and worries about preserving local control have kept federal influence over the content of schooling rather circumscribed.

Now, however, the No Child Left Behind Act of 2001 (NCLB) is asserting a strong new role for Washington: directing states to set academic standards, determining how often states assess students, and shaping patterns of accountability among states, districts, and schools. Furthermore, it is reinforcing the standards and assessment policies by holding states accountable for conforming to them. Does NCLB abandon the tradition that reserves control over education to the states, originally embodied in the Tenth Amendment to the U.S. Constitution? Is the United States heading toward federal dominance over education?

In this chapter, following a brief review of the history of federal involvement with standards policies, I discuss the provisions in the No Child Left Behind Act that suggest that the act is a major breach with the past, a new level of federal involvement in policy areas close to curriculum, and a major new assertion of federal power. I then consider some reasons why NCLB may not be the epitome of federal dominance that some imagine. These include the facts that, historically, Washington has lacked the capacity and political will to enforce its policies fully and that NCLB accountability depends entirely on enforcement by the states, which is limited at best. I examine alternative approaches to assigning responsibility for standards, assessments, and accountability among different levels of government, rejecting the notion of definitively sorting out responsibilities as unrealistic and concluding that a strategic partnership is inevitable and in some senses desirable. Finally, I lay out some principles for shaping intergovernmental relations on these issues. Without attention to these principles, NCLB is unlikely to lead to improvements in classroom practice or student learning.

Education Standards and the Federal Government

Federal interest in standards for student learning began in the late 1980s. It is commonly believed that before this time curriculum was largely left up to local schools. For decades, however, groups with national purview, such as the College Board and textbook and test publishers, exerted considerable influence over what was taught.[1]

The federal government also grew in influence in the twentieth century, through programs such as the National Defense Education Act, which chiefly supported foreign-language and science instruction.[2] In part because of controversial curriculums that the National Science Foundation supported under that act,[3] federal statutes, starting in 1970, incorporated the following prohibition: "No provision of any applicable program shall be construed to authorize any department, agency, officer or employee of the United States to exercise any direction, supervision or control over the curriculum, program of instruction [or] administration . . . of any educational institution . . . or over the selection of library resources, textbooks, or other printed or published instructional materials. . . ."[4]

Although states historically had delegated decisions about the substance of school curriculums to localities, they increasingly began to mandate specific courses, such as state or U.S. history. That trend escalated after the

1983 publication of *A Nation at Risk,* with its bleak picture of American education. State policymakers reacted by rushing to develop large, comprehensive reform packages, with new, higher graduation requirements, standards for teachers, and more testing.[5]

By the mid- to late 1980s, states such as California had begun to design approaches that brought together these previously discrete policy instruments. Using substantive standards for student learning as the anchor, new reform approaches attempted to tie curriculum, textbook adoption, teacher professional development, and testing policies together in a more coherent fashion. Other states, discouraged that reforms adopted in response to *A Nation at Risk* had failed to translate into much school improvement, followed suit.[6]

In 1989 the nation's governors and President George H. W. Bush held the first Education Summit, which produced the National Education Goals. Goals 3 and 4, in particular—calling for students to leave the fourth, eighth, and twelfth grades with "competency in challenging subject matter" and for the nation to be "first in the world in science and mathematics achievement"—had obvious implications for standards policies. As Diane Ravitch put it, "It quickly became apparent that the [Goals] panel had no way to monitor progress toward goals 3 and 4 without some clear definition of the 'challenging' subject matter to be learned and the 'competency' to be demonstrated."[7] Congress established the National Council on Education Standards and Testing (NCEST) to "advise on the desirability and feasibility of national standards and tests," as well as to "recommend long-term policies, structures and mechanisms of setting voluntary education standards and planning an appropriate system of tests."[8]

At the same time, professional associations, led by the National Council of Teachers of Mathematics (NCTM), began developing explicit standards for student learning. NCTM became a model, showing that it was possible to create a powerful, nationwide vision of what students should know and be able to do.

As NCEST deliberated, the U.S. Department of Education began supporting development of such standards in other subject areas. In this context, NCEST not surprisingly recommended the development of standards and assessments that, importantly, were to be not mandatory or "federal," but rather, voluntary and "national"—developed by states, districts, and professional associations. President Bush and President Bill Clinton both acted on the NCEST recommendations and proposed legislation to support state standards reform and the development of a national standards and assessment system. And in March 1994 Goals 2000, which included grants to states and federal support for development of voluntary standards, became law.

Two vigorous debates characterized this period. One concerned the propriety of emphasizing expectations for student learning and measuring the results without a concomitant focus on whether students have equal access to the content to be assessed. Many reformers and advocates, especially Democrats in the House of Representatives, called for standards (first termed "school delivery" standards and then "opportunity-to-learn" standards) for the resources and supports students should receive before they or schools were held accountable on new standards-based assessments.

Others, including many Republicans and state policymakers, feared that such standards would dictate school operations, getting into issues such as class size or teacher assignments that traditionally have been reserved to local policymaking. Thus the final version of Goals 2000 did not require states to develop such process-related standards; it merely encouraged them.

A second issue involved the creation of a national body to certify state standards and assessments and the new voluntary national versions. To some, this body, eventually embedded in Goals 2000 as the National Education Standards and Improvement Council (NESIC), personified the specter of federal control over education.[9] In the words of South Carolina governor Carol Campbell, chair of the National Governors Association, a national role in approving state standards would lead to "a federalization of what has been, until now, a pact that recognized and respected the preeminent role of states in education reform."[10]

Within six months after the Republicans regained the House in 1994, NESIC was effectively dead. The 1994 reauthorization of the Elementary and Secondary Education Act, called the Improving America's Schools Act (IASA), included no mention of opportunity-to-learn standards. It tied aid for Title I, bilingual education, and a number of other federal programs to state standards developed under Goals 2000. Children in Title I schools were expected to make progress toward challenging content and performance standards expected of all children in each state and to participate in performance-based state assessments, intended to replace standardized tests that had focused on low-level skills. The bill lowered the threshold that high-poverty schools had to meet to use Title I funds for all children in the school.

IASA came at a time when most states already had started down the path to standards-based reform. By 1994 more than thirty states were engaged in developing standards; fifteen more reported that they were already implementing standards-based reform.[11] Both Goals 2000 and IASA were cast by the Clinton administration as ways of supporting and furthering state standards reform efforts.[12]

The No Child Left Behind Act continues the standards-based reform approach of the IASA, but it is less open to a variety of approaches to standards, assessment, and accountability policies and more constraining on policies that states must have in place to receive Title I funds. It seems paradoxical that a Republican administration put forth a bill that appears to extend federal control over education, especially given the mid-1990s debates over whether NESIC went too far. Richard Elmore of Harvard University noted, "What's particularly strange and ironic is that conservative Republicans control the White House and the House of Representatives, and they sponsored the single-largest—and single-most-damaging— expansion of federal power over the nation's education system in history."[13]

It should be remembered, however, that a Republican president, the senior President Bush, first proposed support for national standards and assessments and for a federal role in encouraging state standards policies. In addition, the vigorously partisan arguments over Goals 2000 focused more on the federal role in providing sufficient resources and curricular support (opportunity-to-learn standards) than on the idea of outcomes or standards-based reform; both parties strongly supported the latter theme. Finally, NCLB, though proposed by a Republican president, had strong bipartisan support in Congress. It was negotiated by two Democrats and two Republicans, representing each chamber's education committees, and passed the full Congress overwhelmingly.

No Child Left Behind: New Federal Powers

NCLB has been characterized as asserting a new level of federal control over education, chiefly because of its standards, assessment, and accountability provisions. These go further than previous law in detailing what states are supposed to do and require significant changes in state policies. In addition, sanctions for noncompliance are clearer and more specific.

Standards

NCLB requires all states to adopt challenging academic content standards, not only in reading and mathematics, as was mandated under the IASA, but also in science. Student achievement standards, the descendants of the performance standards called for in the 1994 legislation, must describe at least three levels of achievement: advanced, proficient, and basic. All states but one currently have content standards in reading and mathematics—Iowa, the exception, requires districts to develop them—and nearly all have science standards. The status of state achievement or performance standards is more variable. A number of states were in compliance agreements with the U.S. Department of Education at the time of NCLB's passage because they missed the original deadline for developing these standards.

The U.S. Department of Education reviews the development of standards by the states. This review may be kept in check by a provision in NCLB that is a holdover from the 1994 IASA.[14] Section 1905 of NCLB reads: "Nothing in this title shall be construed to authorize an officer or employee of the federal government to mandate, direct or control a state, local educational agency or schools' specific instructional content, academic achievement standards and assessments, curriculum or program of instruction."

Assessments

NCLB requires states to test all students in grades 3 through 8 each year in reading/language arts and mathematics. Science testing is required later. As in the past, states also must test students at least once in math and language arts in grades 10 through 12, but the annual testing in the lower grades and the inclusion of science represent significant innovations. Not only must tests be given to all students in each elementary class above grade 2 (IASA permitted sampling and testing at benchmark grades), but states also must produce individual score reports, no later than the beginning of the following school year.

Other notable provisions concern English language learners. All who have attended U.S. schools for at least three years must take reading assessments in English, although states are encouraged to develop assessments in other languages as well. Moreover, states must ensure that districts administer annual English proficiency tests for English language learners.

Many other assessment provisions in NCLB are similar to those in the IASA. Score reports must be disaggregated by major subgroups, for example, and tests must be aligned to standards and meet appropriate technical criteria. NCLB's testing provisions, however, are not only more numerous than the IASA's, but also are more specific, defining the shape of state testing programs. The IASA's requirement for annual reading or language arts and math exams in benchmark grades gave states great flexibility. They could test in grades 4, 8, and 10 or 5, 7, and 11. They could test reading or language arts in grade 3 and math in grade 4. They could sample students.

For example, they could use exams that covered many domains of content and cognitive demand, such as the National Assessment of Educational Progress, but minimize actual testing burdens and test-taking time by administering different questions to different students. Now states must test every student every year.

Given the added costs of such universal administration, one important concern is that states will be driven to choose relatively inexpensive, off-the-shelf assessments and more sophisticated exams specifically designed to meet state standards will fall by the wayside. While the testing requirements are in fact contingent on Washington providing yearly funding to cover development costs, the administration and scoring of new, secure assessments for so many grades is expensive. Moreover, the requirement that all students take the same exams makes sampling to cover more domains and varieties of items a luxury on top of everything else.

NCLB's additional and more specific testing requirements stand out in bold relief because states must make so many changes to meet them. In spring 2002, only seven states met the assessment requirements in math, language arts, and science. Only fifteen states plus the District of Columbia had annual reading and math tests in grades 3 through 8, and it is not clear how many of those exams would be judged appropriately aligned with standards.[15] Since the NCLB provisions for reading and mathematics take effect in 2005–06 and those for science in 2007–08, states have several years to adjust their systems. Nonetheless, the changes they must make are significant. More than two-thirds of the states need new annual assessments in additional grades in three subjects; even more may require new tests if current exams are not deemed to be aligned to standards or are not compatible with testing planned for the additional grades.

Accountability

NCLB has a number of provisions regarding state systems of accountability for school performance. These are among the most controversial because they (1) govern how states are supposed to assist and sanction schools and districts, their own delegates; (2) are exceedingly specific, seeming to leave little room for flexibility; and (3) expect progress in achievement that many argue is not feasible. Although a number of provisions are noteworthy—such as those describing state report cards and reports to Congress or others providing recognition for high performance—two issues are particularly important: the definition of adequate yearly progress (AYP) and the consequences for failing schools.

ADEQUATE YEARLY PROGRESS. States must have a single accountability system for all schools, for Title I and for all other purposes. They must
define adequate yearly progress in both reading and math in a way that
brings all students to proficiency (as defined by the state) within twelve
years. Progress is to be judged primarily on achievement indicators, but at
the high school level graduation rates are also included, and at least one
other academic indicator, of the state's choice, must be used at the elementary level. Not only must schools and districts make progress on average by
the AYP measures, they also must set AYP goals and track progress by student subgroups according to economic disadvantage, major racial or ethnic categories, and disability and English language learner status. At least
95 percent of students in each subgroup must participate in the assessment (or a legal accommodation) used for AYP.

The AYP provisions are particularly controversial because they are such a
departure from previous law, which let states decide how annual yearly
progress was to be measured. Although they contain some options, such as
the ability to average scores over two or three years or to use cross-grade
data in schools (to smooth out measurement errors), the twelve-year timeline and the subgroup requirements permit few alternative designs. Moreover, the choice of twelve years seems entirely arbitrary, not based on any
empirical evidence about how much progress can realistically be expected
from year to year. According to Robert Linn, codirector of the National Center for Research on Evaluation, Standards, and Student Testing, score
increases typically average 1 percent to 1.5 percent, not the 12 percent or
so annually that would be required in many states to bring all students up to
the proficient level by 2014.[16]

Most states are far from total student proficiency. In Massachusetts, for
example, in 2000 only 1 percent of schools had more than 80 percent of
students scoring at the proficient or advanced level, while a quarter had
fewer than 20 percent of students scoring at proficient.[17] In Virginia, only
22 percent of schools met the state's 70 percent proficient target in 2000.[18]
The numbers reaching proficiency undoubtedly would be even lower if the
subgroup requirement were factored in.[19] One possibility is that states
will use whatever flexibility they can find—for example, in defining "proficient" or in specifying the minimum size of a subgroup for valid school-
specific measurement—to make the twelve-year deadline feasible. This
would subvert the intent of the law, but it is hard to imagine how states that
have set very challenging standards and currently define most of their students as nonproficient could meet the deadline without resorting to such
measures.

Because AYP was left to states in the past, state definitions varied considerably and few approximated the NCLB model. Only twenty-two states had a "unitary" accountability system in 2000–01; more than half have had systems that measured AYP differently for Title I and non-Title I schools.[20] States, moreover, have used three approaches to AYP: (1) setting an absolute target (or threshold) for schools and districts to meet yearly; (2) setting relative growth targets for schools, depending on where they are in the distribution curve; and (3) requiring that the number or percentage of those in the lowest-performing group be reduced. By contrast, NCLB makes absolute the demand that schools and districts meet annual growth targets toward the goal of proficiency for all in twelve years.[21]

Only a few states, including Vermont and Oregon, had timelines similar to NCLB; most had longer timelines, such as the twenty-year period set by Kentucky and California. Some did not expect all students to reach the proficient level; in Maryland and Virginia, for example, the goal was to bring 70 percent of students to proficiency. Finally, few states collected and reported disaggregated achievement data in the manner required by NCLB. According to the Education Commission of the States, only four states were capable initially of reporting achievement by all subgroups required, and other states did not have mechanisms to tie income data to individual student records. Worries about data security and confidentiality also are likely to surface.[22] In short, states have had a considerable way to go to redesign performance targets to conform to the new AYP requirements, which are so specific and often differ so much from preexisting practice that they are drawing considerable fire from state policymakers.

CONSEQUENCES FOR LOW-PERFORMING SCHOOLS. Schools and districts that fail to meet their AYP requirements face a series of consequences, from technical assistance and the provision of other public school options for students to restructuring. The severity of the consequences relates to the number of years that AYP has not been met. Schools that have failed for three years, for example, must offer low-income pupils the chance to receive instruction from a supplemental service provider, whereas those that have failed for four years must take such corrective actions as replacing school staff or changing the school structure. The clock on AYP started the minute the legislation was enacted, making schools already identified as in "school improvement" or "corrective action" status eligible for the new remedies on the new timeline.

About half the states already sanctioned both schools and districts for poor performance, so these provisions are not such a departure from preexisting practice as some others in NCLB. States, however, are required to take on a number of new responsibilities, such as reviewing supplemental service providers to assure quality and developing assistance and intervention programs based on scientific research, as defined by the legislation.

The number of Title I schools identified as needing improvement in the past also varies considerably from state to state. In some there were very few; Texas had sixty-one. Furthermore, not all schools needing improvement have received help, even though it was required in the past as well. In the 1998–99 National Longitudinal Survey of Schools, only 47 percent of principals in Title I schools identified for improvement said that they had received additional technical assistance or professional development.[23]

Stricter new AYP provisions might mean that many more schools will need and must receive intervention than in the past. Because states are likely to find these new requirements challenging, they might take advantage of the fact that the consequences specified are required only for schools and districts receiving Title I funds. Even though all schools must be measured by the same AYP provisions, only Title I schools must get the NCLB-specified interventions. So it is possible that states will maintain some form of "dual accountability," following different procedures for Title I and non-Title I schools that fail to meet AYP.

What makes NCLB seem especially far-reaching is that states face specific consequences for failing to enforce standards, assessment, and accountability provisions. Congress evidently was frustrated that states had not sufficiently complied with the 1994 IASA, in particular, not producing performance standards and assessments on schedule.[24] All states that were still not in compliance with the 1994 requirements risked 25 percent of state administrative funds.

State administrative funds also may be withheld in the future if new NCLB requirements are not met. NCLB has extensive requirements for state reporting—of results of schools identified for improvement and of measures taken. The U.S. Department of Education will conduct an annual peer review of state AYP results to assure they are met for each subgroup, that all students reach targets, that English proficiency targets are met, and the like. If a state fails to make AYP, the U.S. secretary of education must provide reliable and rigorous technical assistance and constructive feedback.

As an additional way to hold their feet to the fire, NCLB requires that states participate every other year in the National Assessment of Educational Progress (NAEP) reading and math tests for grades 4 and 8, beginning in the current school year. Assessing state NAEP performance is intended as a way of verifying the rigor of state assessments and proficiency standards, and providing independent measurement of state progress. Most states, but not all, have participated in NAEP in the past, when it was voluntary; now the stakes are much higher.

Clearly, NCLB's standards, assessment, and accountability provisions pose challenges for states. They offer considerably less flexibility than previous law and require most states to make important policy changes. The seriousness with which Congress views these provisions is evidenced by the law's compliance aspects, including the potential to shame states by holding their performance up against the independent national NAEP. Neither the language itself nor Congress's resolve, however, guarantees enforcement.

The Realities of the Federal System

Like other laws, NCLB will be one creature on paper and quite another in practice. If the past is any guide, the measure will not be implemented as written, and the specter of unprecedented new federal domination may remain more illusory than real.

All laws change as they are translated into practice. Modifications are particularly likely in this case, as the tasks are daunting, federal enforcement capacity is limited, and the politics are fierce. Moreover, enforcement relies entirely on states' capacity to hold local schools accountable, even though experience shows that states are not holding schools accountable even to the extent that their own laws require. The messy realities of implementation do not necessarily mean that states will be free to pursue their own previously designed accountability approaches. Nor do they mean that classrooms will be protected from potential consequences. They do mean, however, that federal domination of standards, assessments, and accountability is far from certain.

Implementation

Ever since the first ESEA, it has been apparent that implementers—states, districts, and schools—alter policies as they translate them into practice. Sometimes they resist new policies, but more often they shape them to meet their own needs, a practice that has been called "mutual adaptation."[25] Schools or districts sometimes are ahead of states in creating new policies, attempting to forge potential policy models and to shape legislation to fit their own pioneering efforts.[26]

Recently, policy analysts have been applying the principal-agent framework—a concept borrowed from economics—to explain why implementers typically do not see eye to eye with policymakers.[27] In this view, the policymaker (the "principal") "hires" educators ("agents") to further a goal, since the principal is at some distance from the classroom and cannot achieve the educational goal himself. The principal and the agent operate in different contexts, have different information, and face different constraints; the agent will not necessarily do the principal's bidding upon request. So the principal's challenge is to design incentives strong enough to induce agents to further the principal's goal. The agent, however, may not entirely control the factors affecting the results or have the necessary knowledge and skill to achieve the goal. So to some extent, the principal must compromise, accepting the best outcome possible, given that he must hire an agent rather than accomplish the goal himself.

If implementation is always problematical and dependent on complicated relationships, the execution of policies related directly to student learning is especially demanding. Instruction is a highly complex and dynamic process that is very difficult to influence through policy.[28] What happens in the classroom is the product of continual, ever-changing interactions between teachers and students over curricular content. It is highly dependent on teachers' knowledge, skills, and dispositions; on students' attitudes and prior learning; and on the properties of curricular materials, such as their specificity and elaboration.[29]

Recent standards and accountability reforms pose even greater implementation challenges than most policies. They envision that all students will be taught rigorous content, a goal our society has not set in the past. They require the development of standards expressing these ambitions, as well as of aligned assessments that are sophisticated enough to yield valid measures of instructional improvement. They require new knowledge and skills on the part of teachers, in addition to imposing new expectations about the ability of all students to learn more complex material. They require new curriculums and materials that are aligned to standards and that develop content further. They require sufficient expertise to assist schools and districts where performance does not improve. In other words, they require not just compliance but also substantial new effort and learning on the part of the "agents"—the state and local educators. Studies of how standards reform policies are being translated into practice certainly confirm these challenges.[30]

In this context, it is hard to see how the federal government—a principal who is so far removed from the classroom—can provide sufficient inducements or sanctions to get states, districts, and schools to do the unprecedented and complex work required. In fact, the history of federal standards-based reform programs suggests that Washington will face great difficulty getting states to comply. Consider the implementation of the 1994 IASA. As of mid-April 2002, only nineteen states had won full approval of their standards and assessments, even though the 2000–01 deadline had long passed. Most states had waivers of one to three years. Four states and the District of Columbia, which were judged to be especially behind, entered into compliance agreements with the U.S. Department of Education. These agreements were spurred by a provision in NCLB giving the department a deadline ninety days from the signing of the act beyond which no state could get extra time to meet the 1994 requirements. Clearly, most states did not implement the standards and assessment provisions in a timely way, and several needed extreme pressure.

Some of this enforcement difficulty is to be expected; with the implementation of any new federal law, some states lag, just as others are out ahead. Much of the difficulty in compliance with the IASA has been due to the specific challenges of the standards reforms. The GAO (now the Government Accountability Office) found that states were struggling with requirements to test all students, including those with limited English proficiency, and that "some also have more intractable problems, such as assessments that are not aligned with state standards."[31]

Michael Cohen, former assistant secretary for elementary and secondary education, thinks an important reason for compliance lags is the distance states had to go in meeting the 1994 requirements, particularly those dealing with assessments. "Full compliance required significant changes in test design, administration and reporting practices. Meeting these requirements required states to shift from norm-referenced to standards-based assessments, to end long-standing practices of excluding students with disabilities and limited-English-proficient students from the state testing, reporting and accountability programs."[32]

Some of the difficulty also reflects the limits of federal enforcement capacity. Federal compliance monitoring is generally pro forma, more concerned with checking off activities than investigating quality, and relies mostly on state self-reports. The GAO reported that the U.S. Department of Education's own inspector general found federal compliance visits—one-week reviews every four years—to be too cursory. The inspector general "cited insufficient time to conduct the reviews, lack of knowledge among Education staff about areas they were reviewing, and a lack of consistency in how the reviews were conducted."[33] The U.S. Department of Education did not engage in substantive reviews of state standards and assessments. In the case of standards, it satisfied itself that an appropriate process is in place. With accountability systems, a peer-review process was begun but ultimately dropped.[34] A new process was just getting under way in fall 2001.

Political Realities

To the extent that Washington can detect noncompliance, politics limits its ability to inflict punishment. The ultimate threat is to withhold federal program funds, which in the case of NCLB amount to large portions of school spending, particularly in cities and high-poverty rural areas that depend heavily on Title I. But because refusing this money punishes the very children who need the aid, the political pressures to keep the funds flowing are intense.

Cohen recounts a famous story about Washington backing down on enforcement in response to local political pressure. In the mid-1960s U.S. Commissioner of Education Francis Keppel attempted to withhold federal funds from Chicago because it failed to comply with certain desegregation requirements. Mayor Daley called Lyndon B. Johnson directly to complain. Keppel was fired, the funds were not withheld, and as Cohen put it, "No one has been foolish enough to try anything like that since."[35]

NCLB, however, does not threaten to withhold any program funds. Rather, it says that states will lose a portion of their administrative funds for continued noncompliance with IASA provisions and that they also may lose such funds for noncompliance with NCLB in the future. There is reason to question whether states will be impressed by this less-serious threat. For one thing, there was considerable opposition from state policymakers to the law as it was being developed. In September 2001, for example, the National Conference of State Legislatures told Congress that the testing requirements in the emerging legislation were "an egregious example of a top-down, one-size-fits-all federal reform."[36] Republican governors also expressed objections to AYP provisions in early versions of the measure and pushed the president to make them more realistic and somewhat easier on states.[37] Such opposition could be seen as laying the groundwork for noncompliance.

State Capacity and State-Local Relations

For NCLB to result in a new level of federal control, then, it would have to alter state policy toward standards and assessments, and many states would be required to make substantial changes, especially in testing policies. Some have done so readily.

Other states, in any case, may resist. Still others may take advantage of whatever flexibility federal rules and guidance permit and comply minimally. Many will be limited by their own capacity, in terms of resources, manpower, and expertise. As the GAO noted, states are finding it difficult to develop appropriate accommodations for special learners and to disaggregate data as required. The same report said that most states do not sufficiently monitor scoring by assessment contractors (contractors hired by states to score assessments), so there is no way to verify the contractors' results.[38] In addition, states still have separate departments or offices responsible for federal programs and for state standards and assessments, hindering development of a coherent standards, assessment, and accountability system.[39]

NCLB, however, aims not only to change states' own policies but also to affect relationships between states and localities. The accountability provisions for districts and schools are left entirely to states to design (within the confines of AYP and other NCLB provisions) and execute. It is not Washington that identifies schools needing improvement or fashions the remedies. For accountability, NCLB relies totally on states' capacity to influence districts and schools. And in this realm in particular, the law's straightforward explication of the improvement process and the sanctions that states may impose assumes far more powerful and competent state education governance than exists.

As noted previously, states only recently have expressed a policy interest in areas such as curriculum, instruction, and testing. Until the 1970s, the attention of most states was confined chiefly to education finance. Then, as a result of legislative redistricting and associated professionalization of state legislatures and governors' offices, modernized state governments began taking a more serious look at many policy areas. In particular, as states reformed school finance systems and increased education spending, they wanted more say over substantive education issues, such as assessments and curriculum, that formerly had been left to districts and schools. The urgency surrounding education reform in the years following *A Nation at Risk* accelerated these developments.

Despite states' newfound attention to what is taught, though, the tradition of deferring to locals on such matters has been hard to change. States find themselves unable simply to dictate to districts. In a loosely coupled education system, states are most often in the position of persuading districts, creating incentives, and mobilizing opinion, just as any "principal" must do with respect to "agents."[40] States frequently face serious political backlash when they are seen as interfering with local school control.

State education agencies and boards, after all, have no direct constituents, while all school districts have legislators who are attentive to their needs, especially needs expressed by politically savvy superintendents who know that legislative activity is central to their jobs. When districts object to assertions of state power, legislatures are their first recourse. Often states find themselves defending agency and board policies against an onslaught of bills. In 2001, for example, Massachusetts legislators introduced forty-six bills designed to alter or remove the state's policy on high school exit exams.[41]

Like Washington, states also suffer from a lack of enforcement capacity. State agencies' budgets have consistently decreased over the past twenty or so years, even as their responsibilities have grown. The political imperative is to send money to districts and schools; legislatures generally keep state agencies' budgets down, and when money is tight, these are often among the first casualties. Moreover, within agencies subject-matter experts and other substantive personnel are among the first to go; they may have the most expertise on standards reform, but they are seen as more dispensable than the managers needed to keep the programs running.

Agencies simply lack expertise for many of the challenges created by new policies. As Cohen points out, the 1994 legislation, just like NCLB, required states to identify and assist low-performing schools, but it included no substantive guidance about how to provide such help. State agency officials, and the education community in general, know relatively little about improving instruction at scale. NCLB's specification of remedies—restructuring, changing governance, and so forth—does not help this problem, focusing as it does on structural changes at some remove from the classroom. It is extremely difficult to turn around a failing school; it requires a better knowledge base than is readily available to most state policymakers and more expert technical assistance than most state agencies have or have access to.[42]

Evidence that states lack the capacity to enforce accountability policies is plentiful. Most schools identified as needing improvement under the 1994 Title I provisions did not receive help, and a number of states have been unable to apply sanctions to schools that fail to meet their performance criteria. In Massachusetts, of eighty-one schools designated by test scores as eligible for intervention in 2001, only four were declared underperforming, largely because the state lacked the capacity to undertake the in-depth reviews required by law.

In Maryland, 108 schools had been declared eligible for reconstitution as of January 2001. Only four were reconstituted by the state; three were being managed by a private vendor. California designated 3,244 schools as underperforming in 1999–2000, but it had funds to assist only 1,270.[43] In early 2002 the California Board of Education quietly lowered standards so that many fewer schools than originally predicted would face state takeover. According to the *Sacramento Bee,* state officials said the number of schools facing sanctions would fall from 122 to about thirty-six, and "even three dozen potential takeovers are too much for the state to handle."[44]

These trends do not bode well for NCLB enforcement. In sum, implementation of federal policy is always variable, and even more so in the case of complex instructional policies. The track record of the 1994 reforms is not encouraging, and the politics surrounding compliance with NCLB is already fierce. Washington depends entirely on the states for the success of these policies, but these are areas where states have not shown great competence. NCLB is not likely, as a consequence, to be the epitome of federal dominance that some have feared.

The educational consequences of this muddy outlook for enforcement are troubling. NCLB, essentially a test-driven improvement strategy, is already raising questions about whether the curriculum will be narrowed around tested areas and whether schools will have sufficient capacity to make meaningful, long-term improvements as well as immediate test score gains.[45] The possible consequences of states' efforts to water down NCLB or of dependence on states for capacities they lack may make matters worse. Will there be fifty definitions of "proficiency," with many set quite low to make a twelve-year timeline feasible? Will states rely on relatively poorly aligned off-the-shelf tests that measure only part of what students need to know? Will there be combinations of state and local testing, of customized and commercial testing, that send mixed and muddled messages about what is important for students to know? Will there be "overadoption" or superficial adoption of policies, so that, for example, states and districts pick programs with some "scientifically rigorous" stamp of approval, without thoughtful examination of how such programs will work in the specific context? Will more schools be identified for improvement, since all schools must make progress for each subgroup, but even fewer given meaningful assistance?

The educational consequences of NCLB must be carefully monitored and the effects on the federal system studied. Even if the act is not going to lead to unprecedented federal domination of the education system, it will have important consequences for federal-state-local relationships. It is appropriate, then, to ask whether a federal role in this area is necessary. Could there be a regression to dual federalism, as originally implied by the Tenth Amendment? Could education policy be handed back to the states?

Education and Views of Federalism

If the Tenth Amendment were strictly applied today, functions would be sorted by layers of government according to which powers were delegated to Congress and which were reserved to the states. This theory of federalism, characterized as "dual" federalism, or "layer-cake" federalism, prevailed from George Washington's time until the Great Depression and the New Deal. Since then, federal-state-local sharing in virtually all functions has developed and matured. Under "cooperative" federalism (sometimes called "marble-cake" or "chocolate-chip cookie" federalism), the various levels of government are seen not as adversaries but as colleagues trying to achieve common purposes.[46]

Despite the extent to which cooperative federalism has become entrenched—sanctioned by the judiciary and embedded in countless grant-in-aid and regulatory relationships—it has many detractors. State and local advocates argue that Washington is heavy handed, incapable of providing true assistance, and short when it comes to funding the programs it develops. Furthermore, if states are supposed to be "laboratories of democracy," federal interference into how they perform functions can reduce the variation necessary to uncover the most effective and efficient solutions.

David Walker of the University of Connecticut characterizes the current federal system as ambivalent.[47] It is both "overloaded" (in terms of programs to administer) and "undernourished" (in terms of money to fund those programs fully). It is both "top heavy" (in terms of a federal presence in so many areas) and "bottom heavy" (because Washington must rely on states and localities to implement its programs). It is both "overregulated" (meaning not just program regulation, but also across-the-board rules in areas such as civil rights, the environment, and others) and "underregulated" (in the sense that oversight is often lax). It is both "activist" (in terms of continual program expansions and identification of new problems needing federal solutions) and "passive" (particularly when it comes to the implications of a growing national debt). It is both "co-optive" (in the sense that arbitrary federal actions continue) and "cooperative" (in that many newer policies stress consultative processes). It is both "competitive" (characterized by federal-state confrontations over issues like unfunded mandates) and "collaborative" (in that everyone sees value in working together over shared problems like crime). Walker calls these characteristics of "conflicted federalism" and argues for a sorting of functions that would leave primary and secondary education entirely to the states.[48]

Certainly in the field of education, particularly with respect to standards, assessments, and accountability, there is reason to question whether federal policy initiatives are necessary. In these areas, the states were pioneers, working on the precursors to standards reforms in the early and mid-1980s and developing standards-based reforms in the late 1980s and early 1990s.[49] Federal support for standards reforms did not come until 1994, through Goals 2000 and the IASA. Virtually every state has standards and an assessment or accountability system, even though they might vary from the design put forward in NCLB. The states have demonstrated they are proactive and can produce results. Research is beginning to show that states with strongly developed accountability systems are seeing increases in student achievement.[50]

Moreover, it is not clear that Washington will provide sufficient resources to support the extensive new workload that states must assume to comply with NCLB. While praising NCLB, Massachusetts senator Edward Kennedy complained that the president's 2003 education budget fell seriously short: "Under [these] reforms, states and communities are asked to do more than ever before," whereas "President Bush's budget provides only a 2.8 percent increase—not even enough to keep up with inflation."[51] Virginia state delegate Jim Dillard put it this way: "The bill preempts state laws on accountability, standards, testing, and data collection. And it threatens to be a huge unfunded mandate."[52]

In light of weak federal capacity to enforce its policies and concern about underfunded mandates—mandates that many states view as unnecessary anyway—why not endorse a dual federalism approach here and leave standards, assessment, and accountability policy to the states? In this view, the federal role in these areas would be minimized, if not eliminated. The way to assess this possibility is to ask whether the states are sufficient "principals" in the standards reforms. Do they need to be joined by Washington in this arena, even though the federal presence may complicate the relationship with the "agents"—the local educators?

Historically, the primary justification for Washington's policies on elementary and secondary education has been the provision of equal opportunity for all students. According to this argument, without a federal role through programs such as Title I, poor and other needy students would not receive the resources or services they do. There is substantial empirical support for this position. Even recently, after decades of school finance reform and efforts to shift state monies to needier districts, the GAO found that far more federal funds than state and local funds continue to be targeted on poor districts. Federal funding provided an extra $4.73 per student on average nationally for every dollar that students in these districts received from state and local sources.[53]

Washington has both political and fiscal comparative advantages in supporting redistributive programs. Interest groups seeking redistribution, those that represent poor and minority voters, focus on the federal level, where they can aggregate their power across states and capitalize on the fact that their members are strongest in high-turnout elections, particularly those for president. In addition, states compete with one another on their economic and tax bases and are reluctant to raise taxes by the amount necessary to provide sufficient compensatory, redistributive aid.[54]

With respect to standards, assessments, and accountability, even though the states developed their own systems without federal prodding, certain aspects of federal policy in this arena are focused on redistributive goals that the states do not champion as clearly. At the most basic level, federal accountability provisions assure that federal money, targeted on poor students, is spent to further these students' performance, not simply to provide services.

Many states, as noted, have run two accountability systems, holding children served by Title I to lower standards than students in higher-wealth schools. In addition, Washington's interest in disaggregated data about performance by race, sex, and ethnic group, as well as by economic disadvantage, shows equity concerns that do not appear as prominent at the state level. Few states collected and publicly reported achievement data in this fashion. Only ten reported achievement data by one subgroup or more.[55]

Equity concerns have always been a prime motivator of standards-based reforms.[56] Holding all students to high standards requires a common, rigorous curricular vision. Furthermore, aligned assessment and accountability systems can highlight where such instruction is not occurring, where opportunities to learn are not being provided, and direct both attention and resources to those settings. These issues have motivated advocates of equity like the Education Trust to take strong positions in support of NCLB's major provisions.[57]

Arguably, federal support for standards-based reforms over the years has promoted these policies and made progress toward equity goals that much more tangible. As Cohen pointed out, "Though the standards movement began among the states, there can be little doubt that the combination of Goals 2000 and the 1994 reauthorization of ESEA helped move every state, as well as the broader education, business and policy communities, in that direction."[58] In turn, those reforms appear to be furthering equity goals. Martin Carnoy and Susanna Loeb of Stanford University have found that students in states with stronger accountability systems made greater gains on the NAEP mathematics test at the basic-skill level than those in other states and that "the impact of stronger accountability on disadvantaged minority students' scores is relatively greater than on white students' scores."[59]

A second reason for the federal and state governments to continue sharing the role of "principal" for standards, assessment, and accountability policy concerns the states' weaknesses in designing and implementing standards reforms. Those weaknesses mean not only that Washington cannot rely on states to the extent that legislation such as NCLB requires but that additional assistance, if correctly crafted, could be welcome. Washington's ability to fund and draw on research that crosses state boundaries, to invest additional support in capacity-building functions such as professional development, and to hold up a mirror to state efforts through evaluation studies, NAEP, and cross-national assessments can provide important support for state reforms. The federal government's role would have to be deliberately designed to meet such ends, but excluding it from standards-based reforms would eliminate the possibilities that such a constructive partnership would offer.

Finally, Washington's education expenditure is so large, relative to other nonentitlement domestic spending, that accountability for these sums is inevitable. It is the way of most grants-in-aid to acquire more and more regulation to make sure funds are spent as intended; this is especially true of redistributive funds, which without such regulation would just be folded into the distributive spending patterns of states and localities.[60] The regulations accompanying Title I are not going to go away, and the focus on standards, assessments, and accountability is arguably, and politically, as important to redistributive goals as is the funding.

Principles of a Federal-State-Local Partnership

If one assumes that standards, assessment, and accountability policies are likely to emanate from all government levels, to be "shared" within a "cooperative" federalism framework, it is appropriate to ask how such a partnership can generate improvements and avoid some of the problems noted above. How can intergovernmental partnerships promote good education practice, capitalize on the comparative advantages of each government level, and recognize the limits of enforcement capacity throughout the system? How can they avoid overloading, unduly restricting, and underfunding both schools and other levels of governance?

Here I lay out a set of principles that can guide future intergovernmental partnerships in the education arena. The assumption is that it is more useful to establish general principles relevant to future policies than to specify how NCLB guidance might be written or enforced, though the principles have evident implications for NCLB implementation.

1. Flexibility, or Maximum Discretion for States and Localities without Compromising Program Goals

Federal policymakers talk about promoting flexibility, but more often than not in recent years flexibility has been the exception for states and localities, rather than something assumed to be their right. Laws often read restrictively, as if the worst implementers, the "bad apples," were the modal case.[61] Those who can handle more flexibility are encouraged to request it, and decisions are then made on a case-by-case basis.

The Ed-Flex program of 1999, which made states eligible for waivers from the IASA if they developed standards and accountability policies, is one example. The state and local flexibility provisions of NCLB, which permit seven states and up to eighty school districts in other states to consolidate funds under a number of programs for any NCLB purpose, are another. Such exemptions would be unnecessary, however, if considerably more flexibility were written into policy to begin with. As Martha Derthick of the University of Virginia, has noted, "In education, as in welfare, the subject of waivers would never have arisen had not a vast body of law and regulation developed from which relief had to be sought."[62]

Applying the flexibility principle in the case of standards, assessments, and accountability would mean presuming that the states need options in how they design these policies and acknowledging that one size does not fit all. It would mean maintaining the goal of encouraging state standards-based reform and equity for all children, while permitting variety in how states reached this goal. This was the presumption in the IASA; the failure of all states to reach "compliance" apparently was judged by Congress as evidence that permitting a variety of approaches was not productive. One could ask, however, whether slow progress, including the fact that many still have dual accountability systems, is more reflective of the difficulty of the task and of their own capacity issues than of the discretion permitted by the IASA. Restricting states' freedom of choice will not help those states hindered by their own lack of expertise or staff capacity.

If some states are truly recalcitrant, federal guidance, assistance, and special attention may be required. Given the limits on federal capacity in these areas, there is little to gain by writing laws that are so restrictive that many states will require such intense attention. Rather, it makes sense to let states find their own best path, within guidelines that are more general than restrictive, and attend to building the relevant capacity at both the state and federal levels.

2. Design Federal Policies in Partnership with States and Localities

This second principle closely follows the first. State and local policymakers and educators should be consulted as part of the development process, as individuals and as members of relevant organizations. Only by consulting these "agents" can the federal "principals" understand the constraints and opportunities of various contexts. In this way they can design policies that permit options and can be tailored to individual circumstances. Of course, consultation also promotes buy-in, but its main value lies in making federal policymakers aware of state and local differences.

One current example of differences among states concerns the definition of adequate yearly progress. As noted above, states have taken one of three approaches. Some set relative growth targets for individual schools, depending on where they are at baseline. Under this approach, even higher-achieving schools that score above any statewide goal of percentage proficient would be given a target. Other states focused on narrowing the gap between high- and low-achieving students. Only one-third previously used the approach specified in NCLB, requiring all schools to meet an absolute target of proficiency over a set period.[63] These differences and the reasons behind them—such as the desire to set continuous improvement goals for all schools, not just the lowest-achieving schools—should inform federal policy as NCLB is implemented and future reauthorizations considered.

Consultation also permits Washington to learn from the states about the advantages and disadvantages of various policy approaches. At the turn of the twentieth century, Supreme Court Justice Louis Brandeis coined the term "laboratories of democracy" to describe the states in his epigrammatic characterization of the federal system's genius. He saw the states as places where Progressive activists could experiment with approaches to improving social and economic welfare. New ideas could be tested on a limited basis to see if they succeeded; the federal government could learn from the state laboratories before imposing ideas on the whole nation.

3. Avoid Unfunded or Underfunded Mandates

The charge most consistently lodged against Washington by aggrieved states is that it mandates services without providing sufficient support or reimbursement. This is true in all policy areas, but examples that particularly irk the states are in the field of education. In special education, for instance, federal cost reimbursement has always been a fraction of the expectations raised with the passage of Public Law 94-142 (now known as the Individuals with Disabilities Education Act). Title I itself has never been "fully funded," or supported at the level originally projected.

Many years of protest and action by state and local policymakers and opponents of increasing federal regulation led to the "Unfunded Mandates Reform Act of 1995," which requires the Congressional Budget Office to estimate the costs of mandate compliance. It also states that it is out of order for the House or Senate to consider legislation that would increase direct costs of federal mandates above a statutory threshold without providing new budget, entitlement, or direct spending authority. The law, however, construes the concept of compliance costs narrowly. Cost estimates focus only on the "direct" costs of compliance, though some indirect costs may be just as severe. For example, NCLB provides funds for the states to develop new annual assessments, but the states will have to absorb additional administration and scoring costs.

The costs to states and localities in standards-based reforms are much broader than those involved in simply producing standards, assessments, and scores. Given the challenges of these reforms, as discussed previously, cost assessments should include significant expenditures for elaboration of standards into curricular models, professional development for teachers, assistance in data analysis and information use, and technical assistance for schools that are not doing well. New money in Title I and support in other NCLB titles, such as new funding for reading instruction, should help.

In general, however, states are underfunding these important functions, and the new increment of federal dollars is unlikely to compensate sufficiently. All levels of government have underestimated the resources needed to make standards-based reforms work effectively; any future intergovernmental partnerships in this area should be based on more extensive and realistic assessments of the challenges.

4. Extensive Investment in the Capacity of Educators and the Systems That Support Them

The fourth principle, borrowed from Richard Elmore, who has used it with reference to state and local accountability reforms, is "the reciprocity of accountability and capacity—for each increment in performance I require of you, I have an equal and reciprocal responsibility to provide you with the capacity to produce that performance."[64]

Under NCLB, the federal government—"the principal"—is holding the states—"the agents"—accountable for improvements in student performance, depending on them to ensure that each school and subgroup makes such improvements. In turn, states, as "principals," both hold accountable and depend on locals and schools as "agents." NCLB, as well as current state and local standards and accountability policies, place emphasis on the accountability side of the equation, not on whether the "agents" have the wherewithal to do the job.

Policy has stressed developing standards, assessing students to measure performance on the standards, reporting that information, and attaching rewards and sanctions to provide additional motivation. The fact that accountability policies depend on "agents"—at other levels of governance and in the schools—to improve student achievement without assuring that they have the ability to do so has received much less attention. Motivating them by focusing on performance goals, providing information about performance, and applying consequences to various levels of progress may make "agents" more willing, but it does not make them more capable.

Additional capacity is needed at each level. Start with classrooms. Instructional improvement depends on complex interactions among teachers, students, and materials. If students are to perform better, schools need well-prepared teachers who believe that students can learn, students who are prepared to learn, and excellent curricular materials. Capacity investments in regard to teachers include attention to preparation and licensure, assignment, professional development and continued learning, evaluation, and compensation. Capacity investments in regard to students include attention to readiness, special needs, and diverse learning styles. Capacity investments also include the development of good curriculums that are aligned to standards and supported by rich arrays of materials.

At the school level, capacity includes organizational cohesion, some shared norms, and collective acceptance of responsibility for student learning.[65] Leadership that knows and supports good instruction is essential. So, too, is the ability of a school to develop and use good information about performance. This includes data from state accountability tests, as well as many other indicators of student performance, attainment, school processes, and instruction. Schools need to understand what performance data tell them about where students are or what gains they have made. But they also need an array of other measures and information to help them understand the reasons for gains or losses and to craft remedies as needed.[66]

Districts, states, and the federal government all must play roles in assuring that classrooms and schools have the necessary capacities. But if governments are to help schools, they must have sufficient capacity themselves. And if higher levels of government are to hold accountable and depend on lower levels to play their role in building classroom and school capacity, they must, according to Elmore's principle, ensure that these levels have the capacity to do so.

Districts must be able to provide or help schools fund and choose programs leading to good professional development and curriculums, implement human resource policies promoting good leadership and teacher expertise, and assist schools coping with special needs of students. Because of student mobility, they must pay attention to coherence not just within but across schools. They must assist schools that are not doing well, helping them develop and use information to determine remedies and to fund and implement appropriate solutions. The states and Washington have a role in helping districts perform these tasks, by providing funding, technical assistance, models, and materials.

In turn, states need sufficient capacity to develop the elements of standards-based reforms and to assist both districts and schools. These are not simple matters. Take assessment. By a number of estimates, current assessments in use in many states are not well aligned to student standards.[67] The evidence of their validity and reliability is often sparse; measurement errors are large, and as a result both students and schools are often misclassified.[68] Assessments typically are incapable of measuring growth in learning, and even longitudinal, value-added accountability models suffer from shortcomings that limit their ability to inform states about year-to-year student progress.[69]

These technical problems in part reflect the state of the art, but they also stem from lack of sufficient staff expertise in both the state agencies that contract for assessments and the testing companies, where burgeoning demand is outstripping capacity. More money must be invested, but it will take time to grow the necessary expertise. As for assisting districts and schools, states lack both the people and the know-how and consequently are backing away from applying remedies for school failure. More investment by states in these tasks certainly is warranted; it is also clear that if the federal government is to depend on states, it too must develop state capacity through technical assistance, funding of research and development, the provision of models, and the like.

As to the federal government, attending to the capacity of its "agents" requires investment in its own capacity. The U.S. Department of Education needs more technical expertise to provide wise guidance to states and districts, and it must strengthen its own ability to learn about the implementation and enforcement of its own regulations. A major challenge for Washington is to learn how standards, assessment, and accountability policies are working in practice and to use that knowledge to inform its own policies.

5. Additional Investment in Research and Commitment to Use New Knowledge to Refine and Improve Policy

Research is needed to build the knowledge base about what works in school improvement and to inform policymakers about how standards-based reforms are being implemented. For example, more knowledge is needed about how to develop assessments that actually measure the growth of students' knowledge in specific subjects, how to best prevent or deal with the "behindness" that afflicts so many urban students by the time they reach middle school and high school, and how to turn around large numbers of failing schools.[70]

Even though a consensus may be forming on the characteristics of "good" professional development, little is known about the mechanisms through which professional development works to improve instruction.[71] Research also is needed on implementation, on how states are defining proficiency, developing and administering new assessments, and aiding and sanctioning low-performing schools. For example, do problems seen in implementation reflect capacity issues that can be directly affected by additional investments, or is the policy design flawed and in need of adjustment? Washington undoubtedly has a comparative advantage in funding more basic and multistate implementation studies, but all levels of government should commit to better evaluation and information gathering.

New knowledge will be of limited value, though, without a greater commitment to using such evidence in policymaking at all levels of government. That commitment has been lacking. For example, accountability policies typically have not incorporated what is known about good assessment practices. While testing experts have developed research-based standards for assessment systems, especially those used in accountability policies, these standards are honored more often in the breach than in practice. They call, for example, for consequential decisions to employ more than a single test (since no test is perfectly reliable and since a single measure is unlikely to cover the entire domain of interest), for documentation of validity for every use of an assessment (since validity is dependent on use), and for documentation that tests are sensitive to differences in instructional quality and student effort (tests that focus instead on student ability are not useful for system improvement).[72] Intergovernmental efforts on standards, assessment, and accountability should employ and depend upon the best available knowledge; instead they too often suffer from underinvestment and the drive to do things on the cheap.

Summary

Using these principles to guide intergovernmental policies will be a challenge. Federal commitments to grant the states maximum flexibility, while consulting with them about different policy approaches; to provide sufficient funding, particularly for capacity building; and to enhance and facilitate research would make good rhetoric but difficult politics. These principles require more patience, longer time frames, and larger budgets than most policymakers bring to the process. Investments in capacity, for example, mean years of outlays without near-term results.[73] Even rhetorical commitment, however, would clarify and improve the debates around intergovernmental policies, and perhaps over time the rhetoric would begin to influence practice. Without attention to such principles, policies on standards, assessment, and accountability are likely to be both constraining, in terms of narrowing the options for lower levels of government, and empty, in terms of enforcement and the promotion of better education.

Notes

1. For example, see Arthur G. Powell, "Motivating Students to Learn: An American Dilemma," in Susan H. Fuhrman and Jennifer A. O'Day, eds., *Rewards and Reform: Creating Educational Incentives That Work* (San Francisco: Jossey-Bass Publishers, 1996), pp. 19–59; Brian Rowan, "The Ecology of School Improvement: Notes on the School Improvement Industry in the United States," unpublished ms., University of Michigan, School of Education, 2001.

2. Carl F. Kaestle and Marshall S. Smith, "The Federal Role in Elementary and Secondary Education, 1940–1980," *Harvard Educational Review,* vol. 52, no. 4 (1982), pp. 384–408.

3. Peter B. Dow, *Schoolhouse Politics: Lessons from the Sputnik Era* (Harvard University Press, 1999).

4. General Education Provisions Act, Public Law 103-33, Sec. 432, as quoted in Diane Ravitch, *National Standards in American Education: A Citizen's Guide* (Brookings, 1995), p. 158.

5. Lorraine McDonnell and Susan H. Fuhrman, "The Political Context of Education Reform," in Van D. Mueller and Mary P. McKeown, eds., *The Fiscal, Legal and Political Aspects of State Reform of Elementary and Secondary Education* (Cambridge, Mass.: Ballinger, 1985), pp. 43–64.

6. Susan H. Fuhrman, "Introduction," in Susan H. Fuhrman, ed., *From the Capitol to the Classroom: Standards-Based Reform in the States* (University of Chicago Press, National Society for the Study of Education, 2001), pp. 1–12.

7. Ravitch, *National Standards in American Education,* p. 58.

8. Ibid., p. 139.

9. Ibid.

10. As quoted in ibid., p. 152.

11. Ellen Pechman and Kate Laguarda, *Status of New Curriculum Frameworks, Standards, Assessments and Monitoring Systems* (Washington: Policy Studies Associates, 1993).

12. Susan H. Fuhrman, "Clinton's Education Policy and Intergovernmental Relations in the 1990s," *Publius: 1994 Annual Review of Federalism,* vol. 24, no. 3 (1994), pp. 83–97.

13. Richard F. Elmore, "Unwarranted Intrusion," *Education Next,* vol. 2, no. 1 (2002), p. 31.

14. Dan Goldhaber, "What Might Go Wrong with the Accountability Measures of the 'No Child Left Behind Act'?" paper prepared for "Will No Child Truly Be Left Behind? The Challenges of Making This Law Work," a conference sponsored by the Thomas B. Fordham Foundation, Washington, February 2002.

15. Margaret E. Goertz and Mark C. Duffy with Kerstin Carlson Le Floch, *Assessment and Accountability Systems in the 50 States: 1999–2000* (Philadelphia: Consortium for Policy Research in Education, University of Pennsylvania, 2001); Education Commission of the States (ECS), *No State Left Behind: The Challenges and Opportunities of ESEA 2001* (Denver, 2002).

16. Remarks at the annual meeting of the American Educational Research Association, New Orleans, April 3, 2002.

17. Massachusetts Department of Education, 2001, as cited in Margaret E. Goertz, "The Federal Role in Defining 'Adequate Yearly Progress': The Flexibility/Accountability Trade-Off." Paper prepared for the Center on Education Policy, Washington, 2001.

18. Frederick M. Hess, "Reform, Resistance, . . . Retreat? The Predictable Politics of Accountability in Virginia," paper presented at the Brookings Conference on Accountability and Its Consequences for Students, Washington, May 15–16, 2001.

19. Goertz, "The Federal Role in Defining 'Adequate Yearly Progress.' "

20. Goertz and Duffy, *Assessment and Accountability Systems in the 50 States.*

21. Ibid.; ECS, *No State Left Behind.*

22. ECS, *No State Left Behind.*

23. Mary Jean LeTendre, "Defining Adequate Yearly Progress: Strengthening Responsibility for Results without Toppling State Accountability Systems," paper prepared for the Center on Education Policy, Washington, 2001.

24. Susan Rigney, "How Federal Requirements Are Affecting Inclusion of Special Needs Students on State Assessments," paper presented at the annual meeting of the American Educational Research Association, New Orleans, April 2002.

25. Paul Berman and Milbrey Wallin McLaughlin, *Federal Programs Supporting Educational Change: Implementing and Sustaining Innovations* (Santa Monica, Calif.: RAND, 1978); Milbrey Wallin McLaughlin, "Learning from Experience: Lessons from Policy Implementation," *Educational Evaluation and Policy Analysis,* vol. 9, no. 2 (1987), pp. 171–78.

26. Susan H. Fuhrman, William H. Clune, and Richard F. Elmore, "Research on Education Reform: Lessons on the Implementation of Policy," *Teachers College Record,* vol. 90, no. 2 (1988), pp. 237–58.

27. For example, Paul Milgrom and John Roberts, *Economics, Organization and Management* (Upper Saddle River, N.J.: Prentice-Hall, 1992); Robert Gibbons, "Incentives in Organizations," *Journal of Economic Perspectives,* vol. 12, no. 4 (1998), pp. 115–32.

28. Richard F. Elmore and Milbrey Wallin McLaughlin, *Steady Work: Policy, Practice, and the Reform of American Education* (Santa Monica, Calif.: RAND, 1988).

29. David K. Cohen and Deborah Loewenberg Ball, "Making Change: Instruction and Its Improvement," *Phi Delta Kappan,* vol. 83, no. 1 (2001), pp. 73–77.

30. For example, David K. Cohen, "Revolution in One Classroom: The Case of Mrs. Oublier," *Educational Evaluation and Policy Analysis,* vol. 12, no. 3 (1990), pp. 327–45; Suzanne M. Wilson and Robert E. Floden, "Hedging Bets: Standards-Based Reform in Classrooms," in Susan Furhman, ed., *From the Capitol to the Classroom: Standards-Based Reform in the States* (University of Chicago Press, National Society for the Study of Education, 2001), pp. 193–241; Janet C. Fairman and William A. Firestone, "The District Role in State Assessment Policy: An Exploratory Study," in Fuhrman, *From the Capitol to the Classroom,* pp. 124–47; Patricia J. Kannapel and others, "The Impact of Standards and Accountability on Teaching and Learning in Kentucky," in Fuhrman, *From the Capitol to the Classroom,* pp. 242–62.

31. Government Accounting Office (GAO), *Title I: Education Needs to Monitor States' Scoring of Assessments* (2002), p. 3.

32. Michael Cohen, "Implementing Title I Standards, Assessments and Accountability: Lessons from the Past, Challenges for the Future," paper prepared for "Will No Child Truly Be Left Behind? The Challenges of Making This Law Work," a conference sponsored by the Thomas B. Fordham Foundation, Washington, 2002, p. 4.

33. GAO, *Title I,* p. 16.

34. Erik Robelen, "States, Ed Department Reach Accords on 1994 ESEA," *Education Week,* April 17, 2002, pp. 1, 28, 29.

35. Cohen, "Implementing Title I Standards, Assessments and Accountability," p. 10.

36. As quoted in ibid., p. 8.

37. Gail Russell Chaddock, "Bush Education Plan Meets New Foe: GOP Governors," *Christian Science Monitor,* May 10, 2001, p. 2.

38. GAO, *Title I,* p. 21.

39. Cohen, "Implementing Title I Standards, Assessments and Accountability," p. 10.

40. Susan H. Fuhrman and Richard F. Elmore, "Understanding Local Control in the Wake of State Education Reform," *Educational Evaluation and Policy Analysis,* vol. 12, no. 1 (1990), pp. 82–96.

41. Susan H. Fuhrman, Margaret E. Goertz, and Mark C. Duffy, "Slow Down, You Move Too Fast: The Politics of Making Changes in High-Stakes Accountability Policies for Students," in Susan H. Fuhrman and Richard F. Elmore, eds., *Redesigning Account-ability Systems for Education* (Teachers College Press, 2004), pp. 245–73.

42. Cohen, "Revolution in One Classroom"; Consortium for Policy Research in Education, "U.S. Department of Education Regional Forum on Turning around Low-Performing Schools: Implications for Policy" (University of Pennsylvania, 2001).

43. Fuhrman, Goertz, and Duffy, "Slow Down, You Move Too Fast."

44. Jim Sanders, "School Takeover Threat Relaxed: Most Campuses Now Are Facing Softer Sanctions by the State," *Sacramento Bee,* May 1, 2002, p. A1.

45. Elmore, "Unwarranted Intrusion"; Joan L. Herman, "The Effects of Testing on Instruction," in Susan H. Fuhrman and Richard F. Elmore, eds., *Redesigning Account-ability Systems for Education* (Teachers College Press, 2004).

46. Morton Grodzins and Daniel J. Elazar, *American System: A New View of Govern-ment in the United States* (New Brunswick, N.J.: Transaction Books, 1984); Daniel J. Elazar, *Exploring Federalism* (University of Alabama Press, 1987); David Bradstreet Walker, *The Rebirth of Federalism: Slouching toward Washington* (Chatham, N.J.: Chatham House Publishers 1995).

47. Walker, *The Rebirth of Federalism.*

48. Walker, *The Rebirth of Federalism,* quote pp. 12–13, also p. 328; see also Alice M. Rivlin, *Reviving the American Dream: The Economy, the States and the Federal Govern-ment* (Brookings, 1992).

49. Fuhrman, *From the Capitol to the Classroom;* Diane Massell and Michael W. Kirst, "Determining National Content Standards: An Introduction," *Education and Urban Soci-ety,* vol. 26, no. 2 (1994), pp. 107–17; William A. Firestone, Susan H. Fuhrman, and Michael W. Kirst, *The Progress of Reform: An Appraisal of State Education Initiatives* (New Brunswick, N.J.: Center for Policy Research in Education, Rutgers University, 1989); William A. Firestone, Susan H. Fuhrman, and Michael W. Kirst, "State Educational Reform since 1983: Appraisal and the Future," *Educational Policy,* vol. 5, no. 3 (1991), pp. 233–50.

50. David Grissmer and Ann Flanagan, *Exploring Rapid Achievement Gains in North Carolina and Texas* (National Education Goals Panel, 1998); Martin Carnoy and Susanna Loeb, "Does External Accountability Affect Student Outcomes? A Cross-State Analysis," in Susan H. Fuhrman and Richard F. Elmore, eds., *Redesigning Accountability Systems for Education* (Teachers College Press, 2004), pp. 189–219.

51. Edward M. Kennedy, untitled speech to National Education Writers Association, Washington, April 2002.

52. As quoted in Carl Tubbesing, "Federalism's Ups and Downs," *State Legislatures,* vol. 28, no. 2 (2002), pp. 12–17.

53. GAO, *School Finance: State and Federal Efforts to Target Poor Students* (1998).

54. Paul E. Peterson, Barry G. Rabe, and Kenneth K. Wong, *When Federalism Works* (Brookings, 1986); Paul E. Peterson, *The Price of Federalism* (Brookings, 1995).

55. ECS, *No State Left Behind.*

56. For example, Marshall S. Smith and Jennifer A. O'Day, "Systemic School Reform," in Susan H. Fuhrman and Betty Malen, eds., *The Politics of Curriculum and Testing, 1990 Yearbook of the Politics of Education Association* (London and Washington: Falmer Press, 1991), pp. 233–67; Jennifer A. O'Day and Marshall S. Smith, "Systemic Reform and Educational Opportunity," in Susan H. Fuhrman, *Designing Coherent Education Policy: Improving the System* (San Francisco: Jossey-Bass, 1993), pp. 250–312.

57. Joetta L. Sack, "Group Seeks Help for Minority Achievement," *Education Week,* December 15, 1999, pp. 23, 26.

58. Cohen, "Implementing Title I Standards, Assessments and Accountability," p. 6.

59. Carnoy and Loeb, "Does External Accountability Affect Student Outcomes?"

60. Peterson, *The Price of Federalism.*

61. Eugene Bardach and Robert A. Kagan, *Going by the Book: The Problem of Regulatory Unreasonableness* (Temple University Press, 1982).

62. Martha Derthick, "American Federalism: Half Full or Half Empty?" *Brookings Review,* vol. 18, no. 1 (2000), pp. 24–27.

63. Goertz and Duffy, *Assessment and Accountability Systems in the 50 States: 1999–2000.*

64. Richard F. Elmore, "Conclusion: The Problem of Stakes in Performance-Based Accountability Systems," in Susan H. Fuhrman and Richard F. Elmore, eds., *Redesigning Accountability Systems for Education* (Teachers College Press, 2004), pp. 274–96.

65. Charles Abelmann and Richard F. Elmore with others, *When Accountability Knocks, Will Anyone Answer?* (Philadelphia: CPRE, University of Pennsylvania, 1999).

66. Jennifer A. O'Day, "Complexity, Accountability and School Improvement," in Susan H. Fuhrman and Richard F. Elmore, eds., *Redesigning Accountability Systems for Education* (Teachers College Press, 2004), pp. 15–43.

67. Andrew C. Porter and John L. Smithson, "Are Content Standards Being Implemented in the Classroom? A Methodology and Some Tentative Answers," in Susan H. Fuhrman, ed., *From the Capitol to the Classroom: Standards-Based Reform in the States* (University of Chicago Press, National Society for the Study of Education, 2001), pp. 60–80; R. Rothman, "Benchmarking and Alignment of State Standards and Assessments," in Susan H. Fuhrman and Richard F. Elmore, eds., *Redesigning Accountability Systems for Education* (Teachers College Press, 2004), pp. 96–114.

68. Eva L. Baker and Robert L. Linn, "Validity Issues for Accountability Systems," in Susan H. Fuhrman and Richard F. Elmore, eds., *Redesigning Accountability Systems for Education* (Teachers College Press, 2004), pp. 47–72.

69. Dale Ballou, "Sizing up Test Scores," *Education Next,* vol. 3, no. 2 (2002), pp. 10–15.

70. On behindness, see Leslie S. Siskin and Richard Lemons, "Internal and External Accountability: The Challenge of the High School," paper presented at the annual meeting of the American Educational Research Association, New Orleans, April 2002.

71. On the characteristics of good professional development, see, for example, Richard F. Elmore, *Bridging the Gap between Standards and Achievement: The Imperative for Professional Development in Education* (Washington: Albert Shanker Institute, 2002).

72. American Educational Research Association (AERA), American Psychological Association, and National Council on Measurement in Education, *Standards for Educational and Psychological Testing* (Washington: AERA, 1999); National Center for Research on Evaluation, Standards, and Student Testing and the Consortium for Policy Research in Education, *Standards for Educational Accountability Systems,* Policy Brief no. 5 (Los Angeles: CRESST, 2002).

73. Lorraine M. McDonnell and Richard F. Elmore, "Getting the Job Done: Alternative Policy Instruments," *Educational Evaluation and Policy Analysis,* vol. 9, no. 2 (1987), pp. 133–52.

7

A Teacher Supply Policy for Education: How to Meet the "Highly Qualified Teacher" Challenge

LINDA DARLING-HAMMOND AND GARY SYKES

R ecent policy developments have drawn unprecedented attention to teacher quality. To achieve its goals for improved school outcomes, the No Child Left Behind Act of 2001 (NCLB) requires a "highly qualified teacher" in all classrooms, as well as better-prepared paraprofessionals and public reporting of staff qualifications. This concern has been driven by a growing acknowledgment, fueled by accumulating research evidence, of how critical teachers are to student learning. In this recognition policymakers are catching up with parents, who have long believed that teachers matter most.[1]

To turn the NCLB mandate into a reality, however, the nation will have to overcome serious labor market obstacles. For one, inequalities in school funding—along with widely differing student needs and education costs—produce large differentials in staff salaries and working conditions that affect the supply of teachers in different schools. For another, teacher labor markets, although starting to change, have been resolutely local. In many states, most

We are grateful for the research assistance of Lisa Marie Carlson at Stanford University and Debbi Harris and Lisa Ray at Michigan State University.

teachers still teach in schools near where they grew up or went to college.[2] These factors, with other labor market conditions, have meant that some schools traditionally have been "hard to staff." The hardest-hit schools chiefly serve poor, minority, and low-achieving children—the same children whose learning must increase significantly if the central NCLB goal of closing the achievement gap between advantaged and disadvantaged pupils is to be accomplished. To get and keep high-quality teachers in these children's class-rooms will require substantial policy change at all levels.

While more extensive federal roles in curriculum, testing, and school choice are hotly contested, there is long-standing precedent and strong jus-tification for Washington to create a major education manpower program. As in other key professions such as medicine, where the national government has long provided vital support for training and distributing doctors in shortage areas, the ability of schools to attract and retain well-trained teach-ers is often a function of forces beyond their boundaries. But without well-qualified teachers for schools with the neediest students, it will be impossible for them to make the progress on achievement that NCLB demands.

In that case, we will continue the historic pattern of failed federal educa-tion programs, in which low-income, disabled, language minority, and other vulnerable students are taught by the least qualified teachers and untrained aides, rather than the skilled practitioners envisioned by the Elementary and Secondary Education Act and other national laws. The purpose of these multibillion-dollar programs—to ensure equal education opportunity for the disadvantaged—has long been undermined by local inability or unwill-ingness to provide teachers capable of meeting the pupils' needs.

As the importance of well-qualified teachers for student achievement has become increasingly clear, this source of inequality has become more and more difficult to justify or ignore. On equity and adequacy grounds, qualified teach-ers constitute a critical national resource that requires federal investment and cross-state coordination as well as other state and local action. No Child Left Behind provides a standard for equitable access to teacher quality that is rea-sonable and feasible. Meeting this goal, however, calls for a new vision of the teacher labor market and development of a national manpower policy.

Understanding the Problems

To make headway on this agenda, it is essential to correct at least three pop-ular misunderstandings.

—*The hiring of unqualified teachers is generally a result of distributional inequities, rather than overall shortages of qualified individuals.* Contrary to what some believe, the United States does not face an overall shortage of qualified teachers. While some schools have dozens of qualified applicants for each position, others—mostly those with poor and minority pupils—suffer from shortfalls, a mismatch that stems from an array of factors. These include disparities in pay and working conditions, interstate barriers to teachers' mobility, inadequate recruitment incentives, bureaucratic hiring systems that discourage qualified applicants, transfer policies that can slow hiring and allocate staff inequitably, and financial incentives to hire cheaper, less qualified teachers.

—*Retaining teachers is a far larger problem than training new ones—and a key to solving teacher "shortages."* In the years ahead, the chief problem will not be producing more new teachers, as many seem to believe, but an exodus of new teachers from the profession, with more than 30 percent leaving within five years. This, too, chiefly hurts low-income schools, which suffer from turnover rates as much as 50 percent higher than affluent schools.[3] Such churning, which results in a constant influx of inexperienced teachers, is caused largely by insufficient preparation and support of new teachers, poor working conditions, and uncompetitive salaries.

—*While the nation produces far more new teachers than it needs, federal action is needed to address teaching fields that experience shortages.* These include teachers for children with disabilities and those with limited English proficiency as well as teachers of mathematics and physical science, two of the three subjects in which NCLB mandates student exams. Increasing supply in the fields with shortfalls requires both targeted recruitment and supports for preparatory institutions to expand programs to meet select national needs.

To address these problems, we need to recognize that while the supply of and demand for teachers historically have been local affairs, states and districts alone are unable to solve these problems. Teacher issues increasingly are national in origin and consequences, and the vital roles and prerogatives of states and localities must be supported by appropriate national programs. These programs, we argue, should be modeled in good measure on U.S. medical manpower efforts, which have long supplied doctors to high-need communities and eased shortages in specific health fields. Similarly, teacher labor market policy should help induce well-prepared teachers to go into districts that sorely need them—and enable them to succeed and stay there—while relieving shortages in fields like special education, math, and physical science. Policy should help stem the departures of new teachers, which cost the nation billions of dollars a year. Indeed, the cost of the new programs could be entirely sustained by savings incurred by reducing teacher turnover.

The Alternative: Lowering Standards

The alternative to such policies is to lower standards for teacher knowledge and skills, through continued emergency hiring or "quick-fix" programs that send people into difficult classrooms with little training in how to teach or deal with children. This has been the usual answer to teacher shortages, with unhappy results during the better part of a century. There are, fortunately, a growing number of new and rigorous alternate-certification programs based on careful selection, purposeful preparation, and intensive mentoring that are successful in preparing midcareer recruits from other fields. Evidence shows that graduates of such programs feel confident about their teaching, are viewed as successful with children, and intend to stay in teaching.[4] We endorse these approaches.

However, there is also strong evidence that shortcut versions—those providing little training and meager support for new teachers—fail to prepare teachers to succeed or to stay, thus adding to the revolving door of ill-prepared individuals who cycle through the classrooms of disadvantaged schools, wasting district resources and valuable learning time for their students. Unfortunately, as some states develop plans to implement NCLB, they are including entrants into these programs (even before they have completed their modest training) in their definitions of "highly qualified" teachers.

The evidence to date provides cause for concern about this approach. For example, alternate-route teachers whose training lasts just weeks before they take over classes quit the field at high rates. Recent studies have documented such outcomes for recruits from the Massachusetts Institute for New Teachers program, nearly half of whom had left teaching within three years, and the Teach for America program, an average of 80 percent of whom had left their teaching jobs in Houston, Texas, after two years.[5] Analyses of national data show that individuals who enter teaching without student teaching (which some alternative programs omit) leave teaching at rates twice as high as those who have had such practice teaching.[6] Those who enter teaching without preparation in key areas such as instructional methods, child development, and learning theory also leave at rates at least double those who have had such training.[7]

It is not hard to fathom why such teachers swiftly disappear. A former investment banking analyst, for example, tells of the "grim" circumstances she faced in a New York City elementary school, scarcely trained, unsupported, and realizing that "a strong academic background and years in an office are not preparation for teaching." Enthusiasm does not compensate for inexperience, she found, and teacher turnover is "so high that a school's 'veteran' teachers have frequently been around only three years, which makes it hard for new teachers to find experienced mentors." She quit after a year, part of the problem, not the solution.[8]

Despite these outcomes, the push to lower teacher standards, especially through quick-fix programs or back-door entry paths that skirt preparation, has strong adherents. These include some with influence in the U.S. Department of Education, as evidenced by the secretary of education's report to Congress on teacher quality. Called *Meeting the Highly Qualified Teachers Challenge,* the report is highly critical of teacher education.[9] It views certification requirements as a "broken system."[10] The report also urges that attendance at schools of education, coursework in education, and student teaching become "optional."[11] By contrast, it regards alternate-route programs—especially ones that eliminate most education coursework, student teaching, and "other bureaucratic hurdles"—as the model option, getting teachers into classrooms on what it calls a "fast-track" basis. The report's prescription is for states to redefine teacher certification to stress content knowledge and verbal ability and to deemphasize knowledge of how to instruct, assess, motivate, or manage pupils.

The problem is not only that the report ignores and misrepresents research evidence, as has been documented in detail elsewhere.[12] It is also that, together with other signals from Washington, D.C., it raises questions about how the Department of Education will enforce the requirement for all teachers to be highly qualified by the end of the 2005–06 school year. "Highly qualified," according to NCLB, means that all teachers "must be fully licensed or certified by the state and must not have had any certification or licensure requirements waived on an emergency, temporary, or provisional basis." Teachers also must demonstrate competence in subject matter.[13]

Now, however, the department appears to be signaling that states can comply in ways that dilute or undercut the law's standard. The statute permits "highly qualified" teachers to obtain full certification through traditional or alternative routes. However, the final regulations indicate that the department will accept state plans that designate as "highly qualified" those who have simply *enrolled* in alternative-certification programs, even if they have not completed them, demonstrated an ability to teach, or met the state's standards for a professional license. Such teachers may "assume the functions of a teacher" for up to three years without having received full certification and be considered "highly qualified."[14] The department's comments on the final regulations note that teachers in alternative routes to certification are to be considered an exception to the requirement that "highly qualified" teachers may not have had certification requirements "waived on an emergency, provisional, or temporary basis."[15] The comments further suggest that "these alternative routes can also serve as models for the certification system as a whole."[16]

Some states are proposing to meet NCLB requirements by lowering certification standards even further. For example, bills introduced in the 2002–03 legislative sessions in Texas, Florida, and California would allow candidates who have no preparation to teach to be certified as long as they have a bachelor's degree and pass a state test. In pressing for the Texas bill, the state comptroller argued that Texas should eliminate teacher education entirely from certification requirements.[17] As her primary supporting evidence she cited the secretary of education's report to Congress and speeches at a conference sponsored by the department.[18] The department, moreover, has signaled that it would welcome this further lowering of the bar on teacher standards.

Such interpretations of NCLB involve sleight of hand on teacher qualifications. If certification requirements are redesigned to require less stringent standards than at present, meeting such standards will be an even poorer guarantee of teacher quality than what already exists. If some teacher education programs have their flaws, essentially unregulated pathways lie almost completely beyond careful scrutiny. At this juncture in our history, encouraging the proliferation of pathways without preparation raises the specter of a legally sanctioned, two-tiered staffing system. Schools that cannot afford competitive salaries, cannot provide attractive working conditions, and educate the most needy students will be staffed with emergency hires and recruits from untested alternatives, while more advantaged schools will continue to recruit teachers with more complete professional education. This certainly is not the intent of NCLB, but it may well be the result.

As we describe in the following paragraphs, there is no research support for this approach. There *is* evidence, however, that it could reduce teacher effectiveness and contribute to attrition. The chief victims will be the most vulnerable children in the hardest-to-staff schools, where underprepared teachers commonly work during their initial teaching years, before they meet licensing standards or leave the profession. This will extend the historic pattern of shortchanging disadvantaged students, even as evidence mounts that teacher quality is critical to student achievement. To cite just one of many studies, a 1991 analysis of 900 Texas school districts found that combined measures of teacher expertise—scores on a licensing examination, master's degrees, and experience—accounted for more of the interdistrict difference in students' reading and mathematics achievement in grades one through 11 than any other factor, including students' family income.[19] The effects were so strong and the variations in teacher quality so great that after controlling for socioeconomic status, the large disparities in achievement between black and white students were almost entirely accounted for by differences in teacher qualifications.

On the central importance of teachers there is, in fact, little disagreement, even among advocates for eased entry requirements. For example, the Thomas B. Fordham Foundation states, "The research shows that great teachers are the most important ingredients in any school. Smart, caring teachers can help their students overcome background problems like poverty and limited English proficiency."[20] However, putting teachers with less preparation in classrooms for the neediest children will not provide equal opportunity or an adequate education. The far better strategy, we believe, is to craft a national teacher supply policy to ensure that well-prepared teachers are available to high-need districts, produce more teachers in fields with shortages, and stem high attrition rates. Even with such a system, of course, most decisions on teachers will remain the domain of state and local school officials, some of whom have made important strides toward filling their classrooms with high-quality teachers—in part by doing exactly the opposite of what advocates for shortcuts recommend.

A Compelling State Interest

Those urging few certification requirements want to shift more decisions away from the states and to the local level. But states have a compelling interest in setting meaningful teacher standards. Harvard University professor Richard Murnane and colleagues note, for example, that traditional economic assumptions about consumer competence, priorities, knowledge, and information do not always hold for teacher hiring, that "some local districts (the purchasers of teachers' services) are underfunded, incompetent, or have priorities that the state finds unacceptable."[21] If poor information were the only problem, then states could concentrate on requiring tests and other measures of the "right stuff," however defined. Local districts could then select teachers based on scores and other information. However, if some local districts are likely to hire teachers whom the state finds unacceptable, then information alone will not solve this problem. The consequences of poor choices are not only local:

> States are concerned because equal opportunity is threatened when incompetent teachers are hired, and the costs of inadequate education are borne not only by the children themselves, but also by the larger society. Dimensions of these costs include a lower rate of economic growth, higher incidence of welfare, greater crime rates, and higher unemployment rates.[22]

Columbia University Professor Henry Levin makes a similar point:

> [T]he fact that we expect the schools to provide benefits to society that go beyond the sum of those conferred upon individual students, that it is difficult for many students and their parents to judge certain aspects of teacher proficiency, and that teachers cannot be instantaneously dismissed, means that somehow the state must be concerned about the quality of teaching. It cannot be left only to the individual judgments of students and their parents or the educational administrators who are vested with managing the schools in behalf of society. The purpose of certification of teachers and accreditation of the programs in which they received their training is to provide information on whether teachers possess the minimum proficiencies that are required from the teaching function.[23]

Without strong, meaningful, and well-enforced certification requirements, not only will districts lack important information about candidates, but parents also will lack important safeguards regarding those people entrusted with their children. In addition, states will lack the policy tools needed to encourage improvements in training and to equalize access to the key educational resource of well-prepared teachers.

To demonstrate why combining a national teacher supply program with state and local reform is the wiser way to meet the "highly qualified" teacher challenge, we need to examine the evidence on five issues:

—The kinds of teacher preparation that make a difference for student achievement;
—The evidence on alternative routes to certification;
—The current workings of the teacher labor market;
—The factors influencing teacher distribution; and
—The steps some states and districts have been taking to ensure teacher quality.

We then turn to the elements of a national manpower policy for education.

What Preparation Makes a Difference in Student Learning?

There is wide agreement on some teacher attributes that seem related to teacher effectiveness and student learning. For example, almost everyone acknowledges the importance of teachers' verbal ability and knowledge in the subjects taught. Those qualities, along with a liberal arts grounding, are at the heart of most state certification processes, which began requiring tests and coursework to ensure competence in these areas in the early 1980s. These qualities are also central to the National Board for Professional Teaching Standards' voluntary certification process and other efforts to strengthen teacher education and professional development. The fact that some alternative-certification advocates focus intently on such skills can only be welcomed. The problem is that many advocates very nearly stop there, as if little else mattered. Common sense and research evidence, however, tell us otherwise.

The Importance of Knowing How to Teach

Research shows that beyond verbal skills, knowledge of subject matter, and academic ability, teachers' professional knowledge and experience also make an important difference in student learning. Many other characteristics also matter for good teaching—enthusiasm, flexibility, perseverance, concern for children—and many specific teaching practices make a difference for learning.[24] The evidence suggests, in fact, that the strongest guarantee of teacher effectiveness is a combination of *all* these elements.[25] It is this combination that most licensure processes seek to encourage, through requirements for courses, tests, student teaching, and the demonstration of specific proficiencies.

It is difficult to settle a research debate about which factors matter most because few large-scale databases allow a comprehensive set of high-quality measures to be examined at once. Estimates of the relationships between particular teacher characteristics and student learning vary from study to study, depending on the factors examined and when and where the study was conducted. Moreover, many variables that reflect teacher quality are highly correlated with one another. For example, teachers' education levels typically are correlated with age, experience, and general academic ability. Similarly, licensure status is often correlated with academic skills, content background, education training, and experience.

Studies linking teacher scores on tests of academic ability to student achievement have led some analysts to suggest that general academic or

verbal abilities are the primary measurable predictors of teacher quality.[26] However, these studies typically have lacked other measures of teachers' preparation.[27] When studies have looked directly at teachers'
knowledge of both subject matter and how to teach, they have found that
knowing how to teach also has strong effects on student achievement.
Indeed, such studies show that knowledge of teaching is as important as
knowledge of content.[28]

For example, based on national survey data for 2,829 students, David
Monk found, not surprisingly, that teachers' content preparation, as measured by coursework in the subject field, was often positively related to
student achievement in math and science.[29] But courses in such subjects as
methods of teaching math or science also had a positive effect on student
learning at each grade level in both fields. For math these teaching methods courses had "more powerful effects than additional preparation in the
content area."[30] Monk concluded that "a good grasp of one's subject area
is a necessary but not a sufficient condition for effective teaching."[31]

Harold Wenglinsky looked at how math and science achievement levels
of more than 7,000 eighth graders on the 1996 National Assessment of Educational Progress (NAEP) were related to measures of teaching quality,
teacher characteristics, and social class background of students.[32] He found
that student achievement was influenced by both teacher content background (such as a major or minor in math or math education) *and* teacher
education or professional development coursework, particularly in how to
work with diverse student populations (including limited-English-proficient
students and students with special needs). Measures of teaching practices,
which had the strongest effects on achievement, were related to teachers'
training: students performed better when teachers provided hands-on
learning opportunities and focused on higher-order thinking skills. These
practices were, in turn, related to training they had received in developing
thinking skills, developing laboratory skills, and having students work with
real-world problems. The cumulative effect of the combined measures of
teacher quality outweighed the effect of socioeconomic background on student achievement.

Teacher Certification and Student Learning

Since teacher certification or licensure has come in for criticism, we
should look more closely at this factor. Although some analysts view licensure—and the teaching preparation that has typically been one of its major
components—as unnecessary, the preponderance of evidence indicates that

it, too, is associated with the effectiveness of teachers. Indeed, studies using national and state data sets have shown significant links between teacher education and licensure measures (including education coursework, credential status, and scores on licensure tests) and student achievement. These relationships have been found at the level of the individual teacher,[33] the school,[34] the school district,[35] and the state.[36] The multilevel findings reinforce the inferences that might be drawn from any single study.

Daniel Goldhaber and Dominic Brewer concluded, for example, that the effects of teachers' certification on student achievement exceed those of a content major in the field, suggesting that what licensed teachers learn in the pedagogical portion of their training adds to what they gain from a strong subject matter background:

> [We] find that the type (standard, emergency, etc.) of certification a teacher holds is an important determinant of student outcomes. In mathematics, we find the students of teachers who are either not certified in their subject . . . or hold a private school certification do less well than students whose teachers hold a standard, probationary, or emergency certification in math. *Roughly speaking, having a teacher with a standard certification in mathematics rather than a private school certification or a certification out of subject results in at least a 1.3 point increase in the mathematics test. This is equivalent to about 10% of the standard deviation on the 12th grade test, a little more than the impact of having a teacher with a BA and MA in mathematics.* Though the effects are not as strong in magnitude or statistical significance, the pattern of results in science mimics that in mathematics.[37]

In this study, beginning teachers on probationary certificates (those who were fully prepared and completing their initial two- to three-year probationary period) from states with more rigorous certification exam requirements had positive effects on student achievement, suggesting the value of recent reforms to strengthen certification.[38]

Similarly, a number of studies from states with large numbers of underprepared teachers have found strong effects of certification on student achievement. California is a case in point. There, three recent school-level studies found significant negative relationships between the percentage of teachers on emergency permits and student scores on state exams.[39] Similarly, studies have found that students in Texas schools with smaller proportions of certified teachers were significantly less likely to score well on Texas state tests, after controlling for students' socioeconomic status and teacher experience.[40]

This and other evidence suggests that it is a mistake to believe that one or two characteristics of teachers can explain their effects on student achievement. The message from the research is that many factors are involved and that teachers with a combination of attributes—knowing how to instruct, motivate, manage and assess diverse students, strong verbal ability, sound subject matter, and knowledge of effective methods for teaching that subject matter—hold the greatest promise for producing student learning. Those aspects of preparation that enable teachers to teach students with the greatest educational needs are, of course, most needed for teachers who will work with such children, a point often missed by advocates of reduced standards for teachers in hard-to-staff schools, which serve these children. States and local districts should be pursuing fully prepared teachers, whose training includes all of the attributes intended by the NCLB definition of "highly qualified," especially for the neediest students.

Alternate Routes to Certification

The evidence on alternate-route programs is consistent with the research described: in general, efforts that include a comprehensive program of education coursework and intensive mentoring have been found to produce more positive evaluations of candidate performance than models that forgo most of this coursework and supervised support.

Just as a quality distribution exists for conventional programs of teacher education, so there appears to be an even wider quality distribution for alternate programs.[41] At one end of the spectrum is a state alternative-certification program in New Hampshire that provides little structure or support. Candidates take "full responsibility for students prior to any preparation, and [have] three years to acquire 14 state-identified competencies through workshops or college courses."[42] A study found that these alternate-route teachers were rated significantly lower than traditional teachers on instructional skills and instructional planning by their principals, and they rated their own preparation significantly lower than did traditionally certified teachers.

Some programs impart more systematic training and support. In a 1992 study of Connecticut's alternative-certification program—whose two-year training model provided "a significantly longer period of training than in any other alternate-route program" at the time—supervisors gave mixed reviews of recruits' performance.[43] In relation to other teachers, the recruits were rated lower in classroom management, but some strengths were noted in their teaching skills. A study of the Los Angeles Teacher Trainee Program, another two-year training model, also produced mixed results: university-trained English teachers were rated as more skillful than alternate-route (intern) teachers, while the levels of skill appeared more comparable but lower overall for math teachers from both groups.[44]

In California, the Commission on Teacher Credentialing has worked to overcome shortcomings found in many local internship programs.[45] A recent study of California State University teacher education graduates, however, found that those who prepared to teach after having entered teaching through emergency routes or internships felt less well prepared than those who had experienced a coherent program of preservice preparation, and they also were perceived as less competent by their supervisors.[46] A recent study by Stanford Research International echoed these concerns:

> Principals reported that interns were less well prepared than fully cre-dentialed recent hires in terms of their subject matter knowledge, their knowledge of instructional and assessment techniques, and their ability to teach basic skills to a diverse student population.[47]

The Dallas Schools' alternative-certification program provides summer training and then places recruits in mentored internships during the school year while they complete other coursework. In a study of this program, supervisors' perceptions of recruits were positive for the 54 percent who completed the intern year without dropping out or being held back because of "deficiencies" in one or more areas of performance.[48] The study also reported data from an evaluation of the program by the Texas Education Agency,[49] which surveyed principals, finding that:

> The principals rated the [traditionally trained] beginning teachers as more knowledgeable than the AC interns on the eight program variables: reading, discipline management, classroom organization, planning, essential elements, ESL methodology, instructional techniques, and instructional models. The ratings of the AC interns on nine other areas of knowledge typically included in teacher preparation programs were slightly below average in seven areas compared with those of beginning teachers.[50]

Only two controlled studies of student achievement outcomes of alternate-route and traditionally trained teachers have been reported, again with mixed results. One, examining data from the Dallas program, found that students of traditionally prepared teachers experienced significantly larger gains in language arts than those of alternate-route teachers.[51] The other,

using data from a well-designed program with strong pedagogical preparation and mentoring, found student outcomes comparable across the two
groups.[52] This study focused on a university-sponsored program that provided fifteen to twenty-five credit hours of coursework before interns
entered classrooms. There they were intensively supervised and assisted by
university personnel and school-based mentors while they completed additional coursework needed to meet full state licensure requirements. Because
this design is so different from the many quick-entry, alternate-route programs, the researchers concluded that these results:

> provide no solace for those who believe that anyone with a bachelor's
> degree can be placed in a classroom and expect to be equally successful
> as those having completed traditional education programs. . . . The three
> studies reported here support carefully constructed AC programs with
> extensive mentoring components, post-graduation training, regular in-
> service classes, and ongoing university supervision.[53]

One other program often cited in reference to alternative certification is
Teach for America (TFA), although TFA is a recruiting program rather than
an alternative-certification program. Recruits in some cities are placed in
alternative certification programs operated by universities or districts after
they have been hired. After controlling for teacher experience and school
and classroom demographics, one study found that TFA recruits in Houston
were about as effective as other inexperienced teachers in schools and classrooms serving high percentages of minority and low-income students,
which is where most underqualified teachers in the district are placed.[54] In
1999–2000, the last year covered by the study sample, about 50 percent of
Houston's new teachers were uncertified, and these teachers were even more
heavily concentrated in high-minority, low-income schools, so TFA teachers were compared with an extraordinarily ill-prepared group. This study
did not report how TFA teachers' outcomes compare with those of trained
and certified teachers. However, a separate study in Arizona that examined
this question found that students of TFA teachers did significantly less well
than those of certified beginning teachers on math, reading, and language
arts tests.[55] A third study found that TFA teachers did about as well as other
novice teachers in their schools in teaching reading and slightly better in
teaching math but that TFA teachers in these sites had more preparation
than these other novice teachers, who were less likely to be certified and to
have had student teaching than the TFA teachers.[56]

Ideally, we would like to know more about the effectiveness of different
kinds of alternate-route programs with different configurations of training

and support. Although the research is not definitive, most studies to date tend to support more extensive preparation over dropping recruits into classrooms with little preparation or support.[57]

Given the evidence suggesting the importance of the preparation intended by NCLB, the question is whether it is possible for states to comply in the face of what seem to be substantial teacher shortages in some places. The evidence suggests that states can indeed comply—with targeted policies that better organize and more equitably distribute their own teaching force, supplemented with a national system that, among other things, works to correct the maldistribution of well-qualified teachers.

The Teacher Labor Market

To understand how teachers become so inequitably distributed, we need to examine how teacher supply and demand operate, what causes attrition, and why shortages exist in certain fields. We then look at the chief causes of the inequitable distributions that are the target of No Child Left Behind.

More Supply Than Demand

The nation currently is in the midst of a teacher hiring surge that began in the early 1990s. Annual demand recently has averaged about 230,000 teachers— demand that can easily be met with existing well-prepared teachers from our three main supply sources. Only one of these sources is newly prepared teachers, who generally constitute no more than half the teachers hired in a given year.[58] In 1999, for example, when U.S. schools hired 232,000 teachers who had not taught the previous year, fewer than 40 percent (about 85,000) had graduated from college the year before. About 80,000 were from the second source—re-entrants from the reserve pool of former teachers.[59] Of the remaining 67,000, most were from the third source—delayed entrants who had prepared to teach in college but who had taken time off to travel, study, work in another field, or start a family.[60] (See figure 7-1.)

In the aggregate, worries about preparing many more new teachers to meet demand are misplaced. As a nation, we produce many more new teachers than the 100,000 or fewer that are needed annually. In 2000, for example, the 603 institutions counted in the American Association of Colleges for Teacher Education/National Council for Accreditation of Teacher Education joint data system—representing about half of all teacher training institutions and about three-quarters of teachers in training—reported

Figure 7-1. *Sources of Teachers*

Thousands

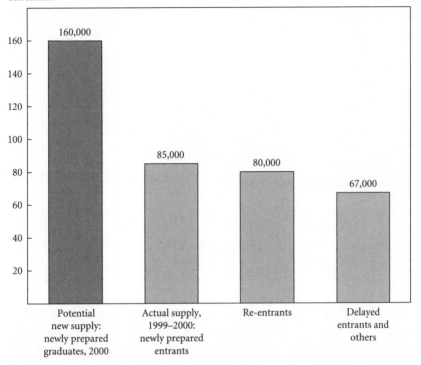

Source: L. Darling-Hammond, based on data from National Center for Education Statistics, Schools and Staffing Surveys, 1999–2000 (Washington).

123,000 individuals who completed programs that led to initial teaching certification. So the newly prepared pool that year was well above 160,000.[61] That was before counting those who entered teaching through alternative pathways that were not university based.[62] Overall, according to the Census Bureau, more than 6 million people in the nation held a bachelor's degree in education in 1993. This represented only a fraction of the credentialed teacher pool, since most teachers now enter teaching with a major in a disciplinary field plus a credential or master's degree in education. Thus, excluding the 2.5 million active teachers at that time, more than 4 million people were prepared to teach but were not doing so.

If we have no overall "shortage" of individuals prepared to teach, why are there so many unqualified teachers in some states and cities? What we do have is a maldistribution of teachers, with surpluses in some areas and shortfalls

Figure 7-2. *Trends in Teacher Entry and Attrition, 1987–2000*

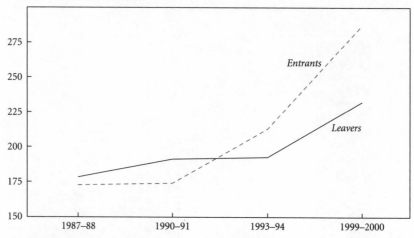

Source: Adapted from Richard M. Ingersoll, "Teacher Turnover and Teacher Shortages: An Organizational Analysis," *American Educational Research Journal*, vol. 38, no. 3 (2001), pp. 499—534.

in others. In 2000, for example, there were surpluses of teachers in most fields in the Northwest, the Mid-Atlantic, and much of the South but shortages in the far West, the Rocky Mountain states, and Alaska.[63] With slowed employment in other sectors of the economy during 2002 and teacher salary hikes in some places that had previously had hiring problems, newspapers across the country carried stories of shortages being resolved.[64] In some growing areas, enrollment increases will likely continue to create hiring pressures, while enrollment declines promise to expand teacher surpluses elsewhere. By 2007, for example, enrollments are projected to climb by more than 20 percent in California and Nevada while shrinking in most parts of the Northeast and Midwest. But enrollment levels are not the central problem.

The Exodus of Beginning Teachers

A much larger challenge than preparing new teachers is retaining existing teachers. Since the early 1990s, the annual outflow from teaching has surpassed the annual influx by increasingly large margins, straining the nation's hiring systems. While schools hired 232,000 teachers in 1999, for example, 287,000 teachers left the profession that year (figure 7-2). Retirements make up a small part of this attrition. Only 14 percent of teachers who left in

1994–95 listed retirement as their primary reason.[65] More than half left to take other jobs or because they were dissatisfied with teaching. Especially for hard-to-staff schools, the largest exodus is by newer teachers who are dissatisfied with working conditions or have had insufficient preparation for what they face in classrooms.[66]

The early exodus of teachers from the profession has been a long-standing problem. Studies indicate that as many as 20 percent of new teachers may leave teaching after three years and that closer to 30 percent quit after five years.[67] Departure rates for individual schools and districts run higher, as they include both "movers," who leave one school or district for another, and "leavers," who exit the profession temporarily or permanently. Together, movers and leavers particularly affect schools serving poor and minority students. Teacher turnover is 50 percent higher in high-poverty schools than in more affluent ones, and new teachers in urban districts exit or transfer at higher rates than suburban counterparts. In addition, teachers quit schools serving low-performing students at much higher rates than schools in which students are high achieving.[68] As a result, these schools are often staffed disproportionately with inexperienced as well as ill-prepared teachers.

The costs of early departures from teaching are large, as evidenced by a recent study in Texas that employed different models to estimate the costs of teacher turnover. Based on the state's current turnover rate of 15.5 percent, which includes more than 40 percent of beginning teachers quitting the field in their first three years, the study found that, "Texas is losing between $329 million and $2.1 billion per year, depending on the industry cost model that is used."[69] This represents between $8,000 and $48,000 for each beginning teacher who leaves. The larger figure, truly a staggering number, stems from a model that includes separation costs, replacement or hiring costs, training costs, and learning-curve loss. If one uses even the lowest estimate for this one state, however, it is clear that early attrition from teaching costs the nation billions of dollars each year.

Such churn among novices reduces overall education productivity, since teacher effectiveness rises sharply after the first few years in the classroom.[70] It drains affected schools' financial and human resources. High-turnover schools, which typically can least afford it, must constantly pour money into recruitment and professional support for new teachers, many of them untrained, without reaping benefits from the investments. Other teachers, including the few who could serve as mentors, are stretched thin by the needs of their colleagues and their students.[71] Scarce resources are wasted trying to reteach the basics each year to teachers who arrive with few tools and leave before they become skilled.[72] Most important, the constant staff churn consigns a large share of children in high-turnover schools to a parade of relatively ineffective teachers.

Shortage Fields

While U.S. teacher supply is sufficient on the whole to meet demand, there are nonetheless long-standing shortages in particular fields. These result largely from more attractive earnings opportunities outside teaching. Increased demand for special education and bilingual education teachers, and the skill sets that trained teachers in these fields possess, have produced shortfalls in many states and localities.[73] Mathematics and science teaching suffer larger wage disparities than such fields as English and social studies. Thus college graduates trained in mathematics and the sciences typically must forgo greater salaries in order to teach.

These shortages, again, particularly hurt disadvantaged students who disproportionately end up with unqualified teachers of science and math. In 1993–94 only 8 percent of public school teachers in wealthier schools taught without a major or minor in their main academic assignment—compared with fully a third of teachers in high-poverty schools.[74] In 1998 the proportions of out-of-field math and science teachers continued to be much higher in schools with more minority students, as well as those with more low-income students (figure 7-3).[75]

The Children Who Suffer Most

With all of these problems—whether the general maldistribution of teachers, the exodus of younger teachers from the profession, or shortages in special fields—the chief victims are disadvantaged students in big cities or poor rural areas. This state of affairs heavily reflects the nation's inequitable funding of education. In most states, the wealthiest districts have revenues and expenditures per pupil that are two or three times those of the poorest districts.[76] Poor rural districts typically spend the least, and urban districts serving students with multiple needs spend much less than surrounding suburbs, where students and families have far fewer challenges. These inequities translate into differentials in salaries and working conditions—resources that greatly affect labor markets for teachers.

A recent report from the Education Trust found that, in many states, the quartile of districts with the highest child poverty rates receives less state and local funding per pupil than the most affluent quartile.[77] The study indicated

Figure 7-3. *Disparities in Access to Qualified Math and Science Teachers, 1998*

Percent of teachers with a major or minor in their main teaching field

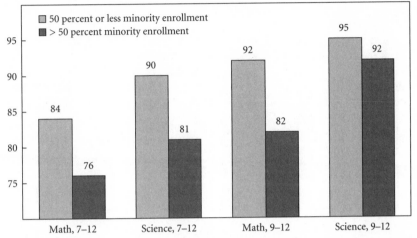

Source: National Center for Education Statistics, *Digest of Education Statistics, 1999* (Washington, 2000).

that, nationwide, this disparity decreased slightly between 1997 and 2000; nevertheless, the disparities persist, and their effects are amplified by the needs that students bring to school.[78] A recent large-scale study of young children found that children's socioeconomic status (SES) is strongly related to cognitive skills at school entry. For example, the average cognitive scores of entering children in the highest SES group are 60 percent above the average scores of the lowest SES group.[79] As the study documents, low-SES children then begin kindergarten in systematically lower-quality schools than their more advantaged peers, no matter what measure of quality is used—qualified teachers, school resources, teacher attitudes, achievement, or school conditions. From the outset of schooling, then, inequalities associated with family circumstances are multiplied by inequalities of education.

Those unequal opportunities continue throughout the students' education. In almost every field, central city schools with the largest numbers of disadvantaged children are much more likely than other schools to report unfilled teacher vacancies.[80] These schools are far more likely than others to fill vacancies with unqualified teachers. The funding inequalities also lead to enlarged class sizes, lack of access to higher-level courses, and poorer teaching.[81]

Figure 7-4. *The Relationship among Elementary School API Scores, Student Socioeconomic Status, and Teacher Qualifications in California, 2000*

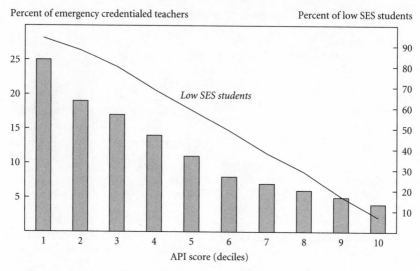

Percent of emergency credentialed teachers   Percent of low SES students

Source: Linda Darling-Hammond, "Access to Quality Teaching: An Analysis of Inequality in California's Public Schools," *Santa Clara Review,* vol. 43 (2003), pp. 101–239.

California data provide a dramatic example of the maldistribution of qualified teachers and its effects. On the one hand, many California districts have little difficulty hiring qualified teachers. In 2000–01, for example, about 47 percent of districts (and 41 percent of schools) had fewer than 5 percent uncredentialed teachers, and about 25 percent hired no unqualified teachers at all.[82] However, in another quarter of California schools, more than 20 percent of teachers were underqualified (that is, lacking a preliminary or professional clear credential), and in some schools most teachers lacked full certification. As figure 7-4 shows, the presence of underqualified teachers is strongly related to student socioeconomic status and to student achievement, with students who most need highly qualified teachers least likely to get them.

Across the nation, disparities in access to qualified teachers occur not only among districts but also among schools within districts. Among other things, recent studies show:

—Nonwhite, low-income, and low-performing students, particularly in urban areas, are disproportionately taught by less qualified teachers.[83]

—Teachers most often transfer out of schools with poor, minority, and low-achieving students.[84]

—School and district disparities in teacher qualifications persist over time and have worsened over fifteen years as teacher demand and funding inequities have increased.[85]

What Factors Influence Teacher Distribution?

Researchers have examined what factors influence who teaches where and how long teachers stay. These factors include wages and benefits and "nonpecuniary" items such as working conditions and student characteristics, teacher preparation, and district personnel policies.[86] Disentangling these factors is essential to the evaluation of policy alternatives. If teachers generally prefer teaching white, middle-class, high-performing students, for example, that preference may be hard to influence. But if teachers object to poor working conditions that often exist in schools serving low-income and minority children, those are potentially alterable. Many analysts contend that districts and schools often fail to hire the best candidates at any given salary level, introducing inefficiencies into the labor market for teachers.[87] So the joint preferences of individuals and organizations interact to determine who teaches and where they teach. A brief tour of this terrain suggests the kinds of policies needed.

The Draw of Home

The first feature of note is the long-standing tendency for many teachers to seek positions close to where they grew up or went to college. As some researchers note, "The importance of distance in teachers' preferences particularly challenges urban districts, which are net importers of teachers."[88] While teachers who grew up in cities often are inclined to teach in their hometowns, the number of urban recruits falls short of the number needed, requiring urban districts to seek teachers from elsewhere. If urban districts cannot offer compensating incentives, their recruits are likely to be less qualified overall than those who teach in suburbs. The differential qualifications of teachers in disadvantaged urban schools seem to be at least in part a function of first-job placements as well as differential exits or transfers. Geography, then, clearly plays a powerful role in determining who teaches in various districts.

Salaries

Even if teachers may be more altruistically motivated than many other workers, teaching must compete for talented college graduates in ways that

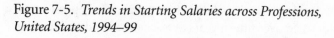

Figure 7-5. *Trends in Starting Salaries across Professions,*
United States, 1994–99

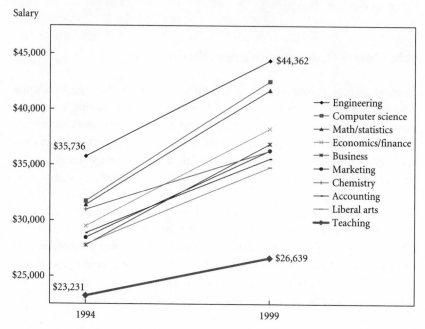

Source: Based on data from the Department of Labor.

include pay. On this score, although overall teacher demand can be met, there is reason for concern. Pay not only is relatively low, but during the 1990s it declined compared with salaries for other professionals (figure 7-5). Even after adjusting for the shorter work year in teaching, teachers earn 15 percent to 30 percent less than college graduates who enter other fields.

Today's troubled economy is temporarily offsetting these trends because of the relative stability of teaching compared with such hard-hit sectors as high technology. Thus in the Silicon Valley area, the flow of technology workers into math and science teaching recently has swelled, and reports indicate that applications are up elsewhere too.[89] The profession needs to maximize this temporary opportunity, ensuring that enough new entrants, especially from high-need fields, receive sufficient training and support to succeed, adding to the long-term supply of high-quality teachers. Otherwise, demand from career-switchers may increase pressure for fast-track training, creating teachers who may soon become part of the exodus from the profession. Moreover, the economy's cycles are temporary, so before

too long many career-switchers may return to mor
they do not find satisfying work in teaching. What h
enues, teacher salaries, and subsidies for decent trai
entrants will determine whether schools can benefit from

There is evidence that wages are at least as important to te
decision to enter and quit the profession as they are to work
occupations.[90] Teachers are more likely to leave the field when the
districts with lower pay and when their salaries are low compared with
wage opportunities.[91] These factors are strongest at the start of the te
ing career and for teachers in high-demand fields like math and science.[9

But do pay increases result in better educational results? To find out,
some analysts have examined the relationship between changes in teacher
salaries and student achievement. Based on a meta-analysis of about sixty
production function studies, Greenwald, Hedges, and Laine found larger
effects for student achievement associated with increased salaries (as well
as experience and education, which are rewarded in salary schedules) than
for other resources such as reduced pupil-teacher ratios.[93] Ronald Ferguson's
analysis of student achievement in Texas also concluded that student gains
were associated with the use of resources to purchase higher-quality teachers.[94] An analysis of hiring practices and salaries in California counties
found that higher salaries appeared to attract better-prepared teachers.[95]
Finally, in a study looking across states from 1960 through 1990 and across
districts in California from 1975 through 1995, Loeb and Page found that
student educational attainment increased most in states and districts that
increased wages for teachers.[96]

Studies confirm that salaries are widely disparate within and across
states—and that school systems serving large numbers of low-income and
minority students often have lower salary levels than surrounding districts.[97] Nationally, teachers in schools serving the largest concentrations of
low-income students earn, at the top of the scale, salaries one-third less than
those in higher-income schools, while they also face lower levels of
resources, poorer working conditions, and the stresses of working with
students and families who have an array of needs.[98] One study found that
large differences in teachers' wages across school districts within the same
county are a significant factor in explaining the use of emergency permits
and waivers.[99]

Once teachers begin work, however, transfers to other schools often
appear to be influenced only modestly by salaries and more by other factors.[100] One study found that teacher transfers tended to improve salary
slightly.[101] Another found that salary variation seemed to contribute little to

:lude, then, that teacher salaries are
aching from the college-educated
vior. They also have an effect on
eachers' decisions about whether

e lucrative occupations if
appens to school rev-
ing for these new
hese trends.
chers in their
rs in other
work in
other
ch-

ions greatly influence teachers'
ssion. Reasons for remaining
ed with how teachers view
sources, input into decision-
... Moreover, there are large differences in the
... teachers receive in affluent and poor schools. Teachers in more advantaged communities experience easier working conditions, including smaller class sizes and pupil loads, more materials, and greater influence over school decisions.[104] In 1994–95, more than a quarter of all school leavers listed dissatisfaction with teaching as a reason for quitting, with those in high-poverty schools more than twice as likely to leave as those in wealthier schools.[105]

A number of studies have found that attrition appears related to student demographics, with teachers transferring out of high-minority and low-income schools or out of low-performing schools into better-performing ones.[106] Given the confluence of negative conditions in schools serving low-income and minority students, the question is whether these demographic variables can be disentangled from other nonpecuniary factors that are amenable to policy influences.

There is evidence that working conditions are an important independent cause of attrition, beyond the student characteristics frequently associated with them. For example, a survey of California teachers found that teachers in high-minority, low-income schools reported significantly worse working conditions, including poorer facilities, fewer textbooks and supplies, less administrative support, and larger class sizes.[107] Furthermore, the teachers were significantly more likely to say that they planned to leave a school soon if working conditions were poor. The relationship between teachers' plans to leave and schools' demographic characteristics was much smaller.

A multivariate analysis of these California data found that turnover problems at the school level are influenced by student characteristics, but that demographic variables become much less significant when working conditions and salaries are considered. Working conditions—ranging from large class sizes and facilities problems to multitrack, year-round schedules and faculty ratings of teaching conditions—proved to be the strongest predictors of turnover problems, along with salaries.[108] We believe that such conditions constitute a primary target for policies aimed at retaining qualified teachers in high-need schools.

Finally, a new aspect of working conditions that affects teacher retention may be traced to unexpected consequences of the new accountability. In many states today, schools that fail to meet performance standards on state assessments are being targeted for special attention, often associated with new labels. Low-performing schools frequently are identified in the local press and may be subject to sanctions and interventions. Such targeting can be valuable in identifying schools that need more help, but it can also stigmatize such schools, affecting staff morale and leading to a teacher exodus. Evidence of such effects is beginning to emerge. A Florida report described teachers leaving schools rated "D" or "F" in "droves."[109] A North Carolina study found "failing" schools lagging behind others in their ability to attract more highly qualified teachers, a trend researchers attribute to the accountability system.[110] In the California study noted earlier, teachers rated more negatively than any other working condition the state tests they are required to administer. This was a component of the measure that significantly predicted turnover.[111]

Teacher Preparation and Support

Often overlooked in economic analyses is the effect of preparation on teacher retention. A growing body of evidence indicates that attrition is unusually high for those with little initial preparation. A recent National Center for Education Statistics (NCES) study found, for example, that 49 percent of uncertified entrants left the profession within five years, more than triple the 14 percent of certified entrants who did so.[112] This report and an analysis of another NCES database showed that attrition rates for new teachers who lacked student teaching were double those who had had student teaching.[113]

In California, the state standards board has found that 35 percent to 40 percent of emergency permit teachers leave the profession within a year.[114] National data from the Recent College Graduates Survey indicate that about two-thirds of novices who enter without teacher education (that is, neither certified nor eligible for certification) leave teaching within their first year.[115] As noted previously, moreover, studies of entry paths to teaching that offer only a few weeks of training before assumption of full teaching responsibilities have also found high attrition rates.

Figure 7-6. *Average Retention for Different Pathways into Teaching*[a]

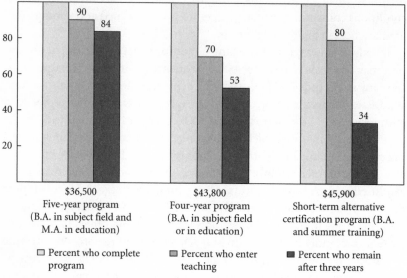

Percent of individuals

□ Percent who complete   ▨ Percent who enter   ■ Percent who remain
  program   teaching   after three years

Source: Linda Darling-Hammond, *Solving the Dilemmas of Teacher Supply and Quality* (New York: National Commission on Teaching and America's Future, 2000).

a. Dollar amounts are the estimated cost per third-year teacher.

Conversely, accumulating evidence indicates that better-prepared teachers stay longer. For example, a longitudinal study of eleven institutions found that teachers who completed redesigned five-year teacher education programs entered and stayed in teaching at much higher rates than four-year teacher education graduates from the same campuses.[116] The five-year programs allow a major in a disciplinary field, intensive training for teaching, and longer-term student teaching. Both four- and five-year graduates enter and stay at higher rates than teachers hired through alternatives that offer only a few weeks of training before recruits are left on their own in classrooms.[117] These differences are so large that, considering the costs to states, universities, and school districts of preparing, recruiting, inducting, and replacing teachers because of attrition, the cost of preparing a third-year career teacher through a five-year program is far less than that of preparing the larger numbers through short-term routes that would yield a third-year veteran (figure 7-6). Graduates of five-year programs also report higher levels of satisfaction with their preparation and receive higher ratings from principals and colleagues.[118]

Figure 7-7. *Teacher Preparation Reduces Attrition of First-Year Teachers*

Percent of teachers leaving after one year

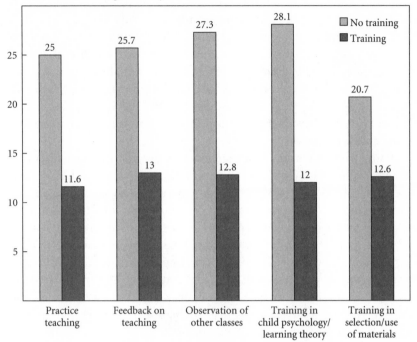

Source: National Commission on Teaching and America's Future, *No Dream Denied* (Washington, 2003).

Similarly, Schools and Staffing Survey (SASS) data for 1999–2000 show big differences in plans to stay in teaching between first-year teachers who felt well prepared and those who felt poorly prepared. On items such as preparation in planning lessons, using a range of instructional methods, and assessing students, two-thirds of those reporting strong preparation intended to stay, compared with only one-third of those reporting weak preparation. The differentials hold true for actual attrition. Analyses of SASS Teacher Follow-up data show that new recruits who had training in aspects of teaching such as selecting instructional materials, child psychology, and learning theory, who had practice teaching experience, and received feedback on their teaching left the profession at rates half as great as those who did not have such preparation (figure 7-7).[119] Similarly, a survey of 3,000 beginning teachers in New York City found that recruits who felt better prepared were more inclined to stay in teaching, feel effective, and say they would enter through the same program or pathway again. Graduates of teacher education programs felt significantly better prepared and more effective than those entering through alternative routes or with no training.[120]

The effects of strong initial preparation are likely to be enhanced by strong induction and mentoring in the early teaching years. School districts such as Cincinnati, Columbus, and Toledo, Ohio, and Rochester, New York, have reduced beginning-teacher attrition rates by more than two-thirds by providing expert mentors with release time to coach beginners in their first year.[121] These young teachers not only stay in the profession at higher rates, but they also become competent more quickly than those who learn by trial and error.

States increasingly are requiring induction programs, some with strong results. Unfortunately, quality can decline as programs expand. For example, assessments of one of the oldest programs, California's Beginning Teacher Support and Assessment (BTSA) Program, found rates of new-teacher retention exceeding 90 percent in the first two to three years on the job for early pilots with carefully designed mentoring systems. However, as the program scaled up with more uneven implementation across the state, a later study reported that only 47 percent of BTSA participants had received classroom visits from their support provider at least monthly, and only 16 percent of novice teachers participating in other induction programs had received such visits.[122] Often, districts provided orientation sessions and workshops rather than on-site mentoring, the most powerful component of induction programs. While the number of states requiring induction programs for beginning teachers rose from seven in 1996–97 to thirty-three in 2002, only twenty-two states fund the programs, and many do not require regular, on-site coaching.[123] To reap the gains that well-designed programs have realized, state-mandated induction programs must include real support and follow-through.

Particularly in hard-to-staff schools, then, policies encouraging strong initial teacher education are warranted, along with strong induction and continuing support. Initial preparation cannot entirely overcome poor working conditions and inadequate support, but it can launch teachers successfully, reducing the odds that they will leave teaching altogether.

Personnel Management

Finally, how districts and schools recruit, hire, assign, support, and manage transfers of teachers—within the constraints of state policies and collective bargaining agreements—plays a large role in determining shortages. Studies in locales ranging from large cities to small rural districts make clear how local management preferences and practices shape who teaches in which schools—and how such preferences can systematically enhance or undermine efficiency and effectiveness.

Some states, for example, enforce redundant requirements for fully qualified and credentialed candidates from other states, making it difficult for them to enter the local teaching force.[124] Additional barriers include late budget decisions by state and local governments, teacher transfer provisions that push new hiring decisions into August or September, lack of pension portability across states, and loss of salary credit for teachers who move. Nor does the list stop there. For example, most districts have salary caps for experienced candidates. As a result, some highly desirable teachers must take pay cuts if they want to teach in new schools where they have moved. Changing professions can look like a better option in those circumstances. Few districts reimburse travel and moving expenses, yet another barrier to mobility in the labor market for teachers.

On top of all of this, many districts do not hire the best applicants because of inadequate information systems or antiquated and cumbersome procedures that discourage or lose candidates in seas of paperwork.[125] For example, before its recent overhaul, the sixty-two-step hiring process in Fairfax County, Virginia, mirrored those of many other large districts that attract a surplus of qualified applicants but cannot find an efficient way to hire them.[126] A process that takes months and features long lines and delays can discourage all but the most persistent.

In districts with high demand relative to supply, late hiring and disorganized hiring processes can undermine the recruitment of qualified teachers. In one recent study, conducted in four states, researchers found that one-third of a sample of new, young teachers were hired after the school year had already started; only 23 percent had any sort of reduced load; 56 percent received no extra assistance; and 43 percent went through the entire first year with no observations from a mentor or more experienced teacher.[127] Another study found that nearly 50 percent of newly hired California teachers were hired after August 1, and 25 percent were hired after the start of the school year.[128] Teachers in schools with large numbers of underprepared teachers were significantly less likely to report that they had been actively recruited or assisted in the hiring process and more likely to report that the hiring process had been slow and filled with obstacles.[129] The California State Fiscal and Crisis Management Team reports hiring and screening procedures that are erratic and fraught with glitches, application processes that are not automated or well coordinated, applicants and vacancies that are not tracked, and recruitment that is disorganized in districts that hire large numbers of underqualified teachers.[130]

Various studies have uncovered still more reasons for district hiring of unqualified teachers. These include patronage, a desire to save money on salaries by hiring low-cost recruits over better-qualified ones, and beliefs that more qualified teachers are more likely to leave and less likely to take orders.[131] Testimony before the California Assembly Select Committee on Low Performing Schools pointed to the prevalence of such concerns:

> In some situations districts hire emergency permit holders because [they] can be paid less; need not initially be provided with benefits; cannot be placed on a tenure track; can be dismissed easily; and need not be provided with systematic support and assistance.[132]

Yet other influences on the assignment of teachers may operate at the school level. In schools serving advantaged families, parents will tolerate less mediocrity in teaching and are more likely to exert pressure to hire and retain well-qualified teachers. At the classroom level, some parents pressure administrators to obtain or avoid certain teachers for their children. Responding to such informal pressures may systematically alter the availability of effective teachers for students who lack vocal and knowledgeable parent advocates. Such informal, "microlevel" processes are likely to operate unless countervailing tendencies are present.[133]

Finally, in many states, collective bargaining agreements influence the effective deployment of teachers. In particular, contract provisions that regulate transfers among schools by seniority often mean that hard-to-staff schools systematically lose experienced teachers. Turnover in such schools is high, with a steady influx of young, inexperienced teachers who often are ill supported by mentor or induction programs. In some locales, progressive labor-management relations have resulted in bargaining agreements that create more equitable staffing patterns, but these are the exceptions.

Several critical points emerge from this thicket of issues. First, incentives that influence teacher entry and mobility often fail to support an equitable distribution of teachers across districts, schools, and classrooms. Salaries and working conditions are unequal, and they fail to provide compensating inducements in support of hard-to-staff schools. Second, teachers' preferences and school system behaviors influence teacher distribution. Many states and districts manage hiring inefficiently for reasons ranging from fiscal conditions to management procedures, contract provisions, and political pressures. Taken together, these factors create a maldistribution of teachers that is systemic in nature and will require coordinated responses across the levels of government and education to solve. Some locales have begun to develop policies and practices that make genuine headway on these problems. These and other exemplars suggest how policies can be developed that directly address the sources of long-standing disparities.

Lessons from State and District Experiences

In the following pages, we describe examples of both states and local school districts that have fashioned successful strategies for strengthening their teaching forces. These approaches inform our recommendations at the end of this chapter.

State Approaches

Beginning in the 1980s, Connecticut and North Carolina enacted some of the nation's most ambitious efforts to improve teaching. On the heels of these efforts, these states, which serve sizable numbers of low-income and minority students, registered striking gains in overall student learning and narrowed achievement gaps between advantaged and disadvantaged pupils.[134] During the 1990s, for example, North Carolina posted the largest student achievement gains of any state in math and sizable advances in reading, putting it well above the national average in fourth grade reading and math, although it had entered the decade near the bottom of state rankings. Of all states during the 1990s, it was also the only state to narrow the achievement gap in fourth grade reading.[135] In Connecticut, also following steep gains throughout the decade, fourth graders ranked first in the nation by 1998 in reading and math on the National Assessment of Educational Progress (NAEP) despite increased poverty and language diversity among its public school students. Its minority-white achievement gap, too, narrowed notably. The proportion of Connecticut eighth graders scoring at or above proficient in reading was first in the nation. In the world, moreover, only top-ranked Singapore could outscore Connecticut students in science.[136]

Among the reforms that contributed to such gains were the significant improvements in both states' teaching forces, including in inner cities and rural areas. How did they accomplish this? With ambitious teacher initiatives that introduced standards, incentives, and professional learning for teachers, along with curriculum and assessment reforms for schools.[137]

Notably, neither state succeeded by relaxing teacher education or licensure. On the contrary, they strengthened both. For a teaching license, for example, Connecticut insisted on additional preparation at entry, including a major in the content area taught, more pedagogical training, and passing basic skills and content tests before entry to teaching. All teachers were also required to take coursework in the teaching of reading and special education. The state eliminated emergency licensing and toughened requirements for temporary licenses. In the initial years of teaching, teachers must complete a master's degree and a rigorous performance assessment modeled on that of the National Board for Professional Teaching Standards to gain a professional license.

North Carolina, too, increased licensing requirements for teachers and principals (in the form of increased coursework in content and pedagogy as well as licensing tests), required schools of education to achieve professional accreditation through the National Council for Accreditation of Teacher Education (NCATE), invested in improvements in teacher education curriculum, and supported creation of professional development schools connected to schools of education. Both states also developed mentor programs for beginning teachers that extended assistance and assessment into the first year of teaching, and both introduced intensive professional development for veteran teachers. A recent study of North Carolina's reforms noted the strong quality of teachers in the state as a whole and in schools serving diverse student populations. The authors write:

> Like the dog that did not bark in the night . . . what is most significant is what is absent. One does not see teachers without pedagogical training, teachers with inadequate content knowledge, or teachers whose own literacy and mathematical skills are poor. . . .[138]

These efforts were successful because both states created strong labor market incentives linked to their teacher standards. Among the measures they adopted were:

—*Increased and equalized salaries, tied to standards.* Both states coupled major statewide increases in teacher salaries with improved pay equity across districts. In Connecticut, for example, the average salary climbed from $29,437 in 1986 to $47,823 in 1991, with the equalizing nature of the state aid making it possible for urban districts to compete for qualified teachers. Because Connecticut's state teacher salary assistance can be spent only for fully certified teachers, districts had greater incentives to recruit those who had met the high new standards, and individuals had greater incentives to meet these standards. North Carolina created standards-based incentives by adopting notable salary increases for teachers to pursue National Board Certification, so that North Carolina now has more teachers certified by the National Board than any other state.

—*Recruitment drives and incentives.* To attract bright young candidates, both states initiated programs to subsidize teacher education in return for teaching commitments. The highly selective North Carolina Teaching Fellows program, for example, paid all college costs, including an enhanced and fully funded teacher education program, for thousands of high-ability students in return for several years of teaching. After seven years, 75 percent of these teachers remained in teaching, and many of the ones remaining held public school leadership posts.[139] Connecticut's service scholarships and forgivable loans similarly attracted high-quality candidates and provided incentives to teach in high-need schools and shortage fields, while the state also took steps to attract well-trained teachers from elsewhere. By 1990, nearly a third of its newly hired teachers had graduated from colleges rated "very selective" or better in the Barron's Index of College Majors, and 75 percent had undergraduate grade point averages of 3.0 or better.[140]

—*Support systems.* Both states bolstered support systems that make a difference in stemming teacher turnover. North Carolina launched a mentoring program for new teachers that greatly increased their access to early career support.[141] Connecticut provided trained mentors for all beginning teachers and student teachers as part of its staged licensing process. For existing teachers, North Carolina created professional development academies, a North Carolina Center for the Advancement of Teaching, and teacher development networks such as the National Writing Project and analogous institutes in mathematics. This was in addition to incentives for National Board Certification. Connecticut, among other things, required continuing professional development, including a master's degree for a professional license.

Such teacher reforms began paying off early on. After Connecticut's $300 million initiative was launched in 1986, for instance, the higher salaries and improved pay equity, combined with the tougher preparation and licensing standards and an end to emergency hiring, swiftly raised teacher quality. An analysis found that within three years, the state not only had eliminated teacher shortages, even in cities, but had created surpluses.[142] Even as demand increased, the pool of qualified applicants remained solid. A National Education Goals Panel report found that in urban districts with sharply improved achievement, educators cited the high quality of teachers and administrators as a critical reason for their gains and noted that "when there is a teaching opening in a Connecticut elementary school, there are often several hundred applicants."[143]

These initiatives occurred alongside other education changes—increased investment in early childhood education and public schools generally, and wide-ranging, standards-based reform—which also contributed to the states' student achievement gains. There is little doubt, however, that higher-quality teachers supplied to all schools were substantial contributors to these other reforms as well as to the overall achievement increases. Both states sought to increase not only salaries and the quality of preparation for teachers, but also the incentive structure for distributing teachers to fields and locations. Both sharply reduced hiring of unlicensed and underprepared staff. Most notably, both held to the course of teacher improvement over a sustained period—more than fifteen years in each case. They demonstrate what state policy in support of good teaching can accomplish.

District Approaches

District success stories reflect the importance of recruiting, inducting, and supporting qualified teachers through policy tools available at the local level and by leveraging state assistance. Following are just four examples of what urban districts in high-demand states have done.

NEW YORK CITY. New York City illustrates how a focus on recruiting qualified teachers, coupled with necessary salary increases, can have a large effect in a brief period. The city long had hired thousands of underprepared teachers, typically filling as many as half of its vacancies with uncertified applicants, many well after September. The state, however, pressured the city to hire qualified teachers and mandated that uncertified teachers could no longer teach in low-performing schools. This move, and awareness of pending NCLB requirements, led to the improvements. The district focused on more aggressive recruitment and hiring of qualified teachers and implemented a steep increase in salaries—averaging 16 percent overall and more than 20 percent for beginning teachers—to make them more competitive with surrounding suburban districts. With these policies, within less than a year, vacancies for 2002–03 were filled by July, and 90 percent of new hires were certified, up from 60 percent the year before. The remaining 10 percent were in programs that would lead to certification by the end of the school year.[144]

COMMUNITY SCHOOL DISTRICT 2. Much earlier, New York City's Community District 2 was an oasis widely heralded as a turnaround story, with a strategic emphasis on professional development for teachers and principals. But student achievement gains clearly relied on both a development and recruitment strategy.[145] In 1996, after a decade of reforms focused on strengthening teaching, this "majority minority" district—which serves large numbers of low-income and immigrant students—realized sharp achievement gains that ranked it second in the city in reading and math.

Sweeping changes instituted by Superintendent Anthony Alvarado stressed strong recruitment of well-qualified individuals and continuing professional development for teachers and principals, coupled with a relentless concentration on instructional improvement. At the same time, Alvarado recognized the need for more talented and committed teachers and principals. Backed by the teachers union, he replaced nearly half the teacher workforce and two-thirds of principals over a period of years through a combination of retirements, pressure, and inducements. Meanwhile, the central office carefully managed the recruitment, hiring, and placement of new teachers and principals. It ended the hiring of unprepared teachers and sought recruits from several leading teacher education programs in the city, forging partnerships for student teaching and professional development with these institutions. Similar programs for developing principals were launched. The district's growing reputation for quality also attracted other teachers. Salary changes were not within the district's purview. Its strategies, rather, involved recruiting aggressively, creating university partnerships to develop a pipeline of well-prepared teachers, and supporting teachers with strong mentoring and professional development.

NEW HAVEN, CALIFORNIA. California success stories are notable because that state in recent years has ranked first in the nation in the number of unqualified teachers. In this high-demand context, with state policies that were, until recently, relatively unsupportive (for example, low expenditures, lack of reciprocity with other states, restricted teacher education options), some districts have nonetheless achieved significant staffing improvements. New Haven Unified School District, just south of Oakland in Union City, which enrolls 14,000 mostly low-income and minority students, is one that succeeded. New Haven combined high salaries, aggressive recruiting, and close mentoring with a high-quality training program worked out with area universities. Although not a top-spending district, it invested resources in salaries and good teaching conditions. In 1998, for example, New Haven's salaries were more than 30 percent higher than nearby Oakland's, where large numbers of unqualified teachers were hired, even though New Haven's per pupil spending was below Oakland's.[146]

Thus, over an extended period the district built a well-prepared, highly committed, and diverse teaching staff. For the 2001–02 school year, ten of its eleven schools had no uncredentialed teachers. The district averaged 0.1 percent uncredentialed teachers—while some neighboring districts averaged more than 20 percent.[147] New Haven uses advanced technology and a wide range of teacher supports to recruit from a national pool of exceptional teachers and to hire them quickly. The district was one of California's first to implement a Beginning Teacher Support and Assessment Program that assists teachers in their first two years in the classroom: all beginning teachers get help from a trained mentor, who is given release time for the purpose. In addition, New Haven collaborated with California State University-Hayward on the right kind of alternative-certification program, combining college coursework and an internship, including student teaching, conducted under the close supervision of university- and school-based educators. As a result of these initiatives, the district has a teacher surplus in the midst of general shortages.[148]

SAN DIEGO, CALIFORNIA. Using similar strategies, San Diego City Schools recently overhauled its teacher recruitment and retention system, aggressively recruiting well-trained teachers, collaborating with universities on new training programs in high-need fields, and creating smooth pathways with local schools of education. It offers contracts to well-prepared teachers as early as possible (sometimes as much as a year in advance of hiring) and reaches out to teachers in other states. The district also streamlined the hiring process, putting the entire system online, improving its capacity to manage hiring data, vacancy postings, and interviews that had slowed the process and caused many candidates to give up and go elsewhere. In the fall of 2001, districts like San Francisco and Los Angeles hired hundreds of uncredentialed teachers, and the state as a whole hired more than 50 percent of novices without full credentials. But San Diego filled almost all of its 1,081 vacancies with credentialed teachers, eliminating all but eleven of the hundreds of previously hired emergency permit teachers who had been assigned largely to high-minority, low-income schools.[149] Student achievement improved dramatically as these reforms were instituted.

What State and Local Successes Tell Us

Taken together, these state and local cases demonstrate that determined, well-focused, and sustained efforts can make a difference in staffing even hard-to-staff schools, which in turn greatly increases the probability of student learning gains. These cases also make clear that schools can be staffed without lowering the bar on teacher standards by counting untrained novices as "highly qualified" or by encouraging states to dilute certification requirements. Although it is important to broaden the sources of supply for teaching, it is also essential to safeguard the quality of that supply if the NCLB goals for children's learning are to be achieved. This can be achieved by clarifying three aspects of the law:

—Teachers should be considered "fully certified" under NCLB's definition of "highly qualified" when they have *completed* a traditional or alternative-route program.

—"Full certification" should continue to include content and pedagogical preparation.

—Standards should be adopted for acceptable alternate-route (and traditional) programs. One careful synthesis of teacher preparation research suggests, for example, that the following components should be included in high-quality, alternate-certification programs (components that could be applied equally to traditional programs):

   —High entrance standards;

   —Intensive training in instruction, management, curriculum, assessment, and how to work with diverse students;

   —Extensive mentoring and supervision by well-prepared teachers;

   —Frequent and substantial evaluation;

   —Guided practice in lesson planning and teaching, with benchmarks for competence before one assumes full responsibility as a teacher; and

   —High exit standards tied to state standards for teaching.[150]

Around such standards states and districts can improve teacher preparation, with the federal government developing incentives to attend such programs, thereby boosting supply while encouraging the elimination of ineffective alternatives.

The Need for a National Teacher Supply Policy

While we can learn a good deal from state and local successes, such cases are the exceptions to the rule. They stand out amid widespread use of underprepared teachers and untrained aides for disadvantaged children in schools that suffer from poor working conditions, inadequate pay, and high teacher turnover. Thus while much that must be done lies at the state, district, and even school level, the federal government has a critical role to play and should focus on three goals: enhancing the supply of qualified teachers targeted to high-need fields and locations; improving retention of qualified teachers, especially in hard-to-staff schools; and creating a national labor market by removing interstate barriers to mobility.

This can be accomplished, we believe, by drawing in part on the federal experience with medical manpower programs. Since 1944, the federal government has subsidized medical training and facilities to meet the needs of underserved populations, fill shortages in certain fields, and increase diversity in the medical profession.[151] The federal government also collects data to monitor and plan for medical manpower needs. This consistent commitment, on which we spend hundreds of millions of dollars annually, has contributed significantly to America's world-renowned system of medical training and care. Although the teacher labor market is also vital to the nation's future, federal efforts in this area have tended to be modest, fragmented, and inconsistent over time.[152] The federal government has periodically adopted programs to enhance the supply of teachers, but these have not continued on the scale and with the targeting needed. There has been little investment in developing a national system to monitor and adjust the teacher labor market.[153] There have been scarce efforts to develop the capacity of training institutions to ensure a supply of teachers in high-demand locales and fields. There has been no serious attempt to establish comprehensive federal-state partnerships like those created to meet shortages in the health field. Thus we recommend measures to create a federal teacher manpower program that substantially addresses the real problems we face.

Increasing Supply in Areas of Shortage

Though surpluses of candidates in elementary education, English, and social studies have long existed in most states, the numbers of teachers trained in high-need areas like mathematics, physical science, special education, bilingual education, and English as a Second Language (ESL) are inadequate. The nation requires targeted incentives to attract qualified teachers to schools and areas that historically have been undersupplied. A two-pronged approach seems warranted. First, the federal government should consolidate all of its fragmented fellowship, scholarship, and loan forgiveness programs into a single, sustained program of service scholarships and forgivable loans that includes the following elements:

—Scholarships allocated on the basis of academic merit and indicators of potential success in teaching, such as perseverance, capacity, and commitment.

—Scholarships targeted in substantial part to areas of teaching short-age, with the federal government allocating half the funds to national priorities while reserving the other half for states to establish their own priorities.

—Scholarships awarded in exchange for teaching in priority schools, defined on the basis of criteria such as poverty rates and the percentage of language minority students.[154]

—Awards available for training at the undergraduate or graduate level, with scholarships forgiven over three to five years in exchange for teaching in high-need areas and fields. Because the chances of staying in teaching increase significantly after three years, calibrating the length of the service required with an inducement of sufficient size will be important to the initiative's success.

The federal government is the appropriate primary source of such programs for two reasons. First, the program can influence the flows of talent across areas of the country. Second, the budgetary implications are extremely modest for the federal government relative to the states. This is an area where a relatively small federal outlay can go a long way—and save the nation sizable sums.

Assume, for example, that the country needs an annual influx of 40,000 new teachers supported by such scholarships and that each candidate would receive up to $20,000 to cover tuition for undergraduate or graduate teacher preparation.[155] Such a program, costing $800 million a year, could meet most of the nation's teacher supply needs in a few years. Given that we currently lose billions of dollars each year because of early attrition from teaching—much of it a result of hiring underprepared teachers—this program would repay itself many times over if it induces recipients to remain in teaching even for several more years.

Such a program alone, however, is insufficient to attack the systemic nature of teacher shortages in urban and isolated rural schools. Recall that teacher labor markets are intensely local and that many young teachers have a strong preference to teach close to home, hurting some districts' efforts to attract qualified applicants. Urban and rural schools must lure applicants from other areas, which is often difficult, or enhance the pool of college graduates who grew up in neighborhoods served by urban schools. This second prospect suggests a recruitment strategy to underwrite the development of "grow your own" programs in urban and rural areas.[156]

Grants are needed to build the capacity of teacher preparation programs within cities where the problems are most severe. These programs need to meet three criteria: ensuring a high-quality teacher preparation experience, attracting local residents to the programs, and ensuring a pipeline from preparation to hiring.

Some cities have many higher education opportunities, but not all are affordable to local residents or have close ties with the district to facilitate an easy pathway from preparation to hiring. The value of many alternate-route programs is that they finance and prepare candidates explicitly for a given district; thus the district reaps the investment's benefits, and candidates know they will have a job. When these are high-quality programs with the components described earlier, the bargain is a good one. Some cities, like New York and San Diego, have created local university partnerships that include underwriting the preparation of candidates, with service in the city's schools required in exchange. Some of these universities enable candidates to engage in practice teaching in professional development schools that are particularly successful with urban and minority students, so that they learn effective practices rather than mere survival. And some programs target local residents and longtime paraprofessionals already knowledgeable about and committed to their communities. The key is a combination of strong training targeted at local talent and strong incentives for hiring and retention in the district.

Such opportunities can be encouraged by a new federal grant program, which could include a state or local matching requirement, directed to urban universities and districts to create or expand programs that meet the standards for program quality that we have described and that support local candidates from preparation through hiring. Some funds can be used for program development or expansion, while others can provide subsidies to enable candidates to attend, with pledges for service in the district. Analogs are available in federal support for urban medical training models (see appendix 7A).

If these institution-building grants operated in the fifty largest cities, with an average of two programs per city (calibrated to size and need), and if each developmental grant allocated $1 million per program for each of five years, the annual cost would be $100 million (with attendant administrative and evaluation costs adding marginally to this sum). This small addition to the previously noted scholarship program keeps total yearly expenses far below the savings gained from reduced attrition. If necessary, the programs can be phased in over time to spread out the costs.

The models that emerge might well include new forms of professional development schools that emulate the teaching hospitals used to develop state-of-the-art medical practices. They might also include new applications of distance technology, new forms of collaboration by the private and public sectors, and new kinds of partnerships among schools, districts, and several universities. The subsequent diffusion of successful models would make the investment worth its weight in gold.

Improving Teacher Retention

Besides incentives for entering teaching, improving teacher retention in high-need areas is an essential goal of a federal teacher supply program. Growing evidence indicates that high turnover, especially in the early years, is a major part of the problem for the system, especially in hard-to-staff schools. The federal government can help stem such attrition by becoming engaged in several areas, starting with helping to ensure that teachers in such schools receive appropriate preparation and mentoring.

PREPARATION AND SUPPORT. While quality local programs to prepare urban teachers will go a long way toward supplying schools, a great unfinished task in American education is to create conditions for better support of new teachers, encompassing hiring procedures, protected initial assignments, provision of mentors and other supports, and improved evaluation to help novices. These matters have been neglected for too long, and they particularly harm hard-to-staff schools that need greater personnel stability if they are to create effective learning communities. The intervention point clearly is induction, beginning with hiring and assignment practices, reduced teaching loads, close fits between qualifications and teaching duties, and the orchestration of support from experienced teachers and administrators. How might more effective induction practices be promoted?

State certification policy is one vehicle. As evidenced by such cases as Connecticut, states can establish conditions for effective induction through certification requirements established for new teachers. Besides encouraging such innovations through the Department of Education's leadership activities, the federal government can create a targeted, matching grant program aimed explicitly at supporting effective induction practices. Since many states and some districts have created induction programs, some resources already are focused on these needs. Relatively few programs, however, ensure that expert mentors in the same teaching field are made available for in-classroom support, the component of induction with the greatest effect on teacher retention and learning.

A federal program could supply grants to state agencies willing to develop statewide induction programs that are integrated with their licensure and certification requirements. States might use such grants to fund universities, districts, and other agencies to develop and test model induction programs, concentrating on support for new teachers in hard-to-staff schools. Another part of the program could distribute grants to high-need districts to support induction practices such as mentor cadres and related supports.

The annual costs would be exceedingly modest. If start-up grants to states averaged $500,000 per state annually for three years running and were phased in ten states at a time, the total direct cost of this initiative would be $75 million, allocated over seven years. The grants to local districts might allocate an average of $250,000 a year for three years of start-up funds, with the requirement that districts, like states, design programs that could be institutionalized. If one hundred district grants were given to twenty districts a year and phased in over time, this initiative would total $75 million, also spread over seven years. If the federal government took on the role of evaluating and disseminating knowledge from these programs, the nation would benefit considerably from new policies and practices that receive hardy tests under a variety of conditions.

PAY AND WORKING CONDITIONS. Incentives clearly are of great importance, as is evident from states and localities that have implemented successful policies directed at salaries, benefits, and working conditions. Too many urban districts are doubly disadvantaged in the competition for teaching talent. They have difficult living and working conditions, and they offer salaries below those of nearby suburban districts. As noted, Connecticut provides an example of how a state dealt with these problems by both raising and equalizing salaries.

While pay and working conditions are centrally the concerns of states and localities, the federal government can encourage more states to address these issues by sponsoring research within and across states on the success of various strategies in different contexts. These might include systemic state strategies like Connecticut's and local experiments with compensation plans. Experiments with extra pay for teaching in hard-to-staff schools (sometimes known as "combat pay") generally have proved ineffective, but some states and districts are exploring further innovation with compensation and working conditions that bear watching. For example, some analysts have advocated advancement on teacher salary schedules based on indicators of performance in teaching, including National Board Certification and other measures of merit or accomplishment. California implemented $10,000 bonuses for National Board–certified teachers, increased to $30,000 for those teachers who teach in low-performing schools. California also implemented its Teachers as a Priority Program, which sent resources to high-need schools to recruit and retain fully certified teachers through improving working conditions, adding mentors, reducing class sizes, and providing hiring bonuses. Moreover, hard-to-staff districts might experiment with pay packages that include, for example, special housing, parking or transportation allowances, additional medical and retirement benefits or summer-based professional development opportunities for travel, workshops, institutes, and other experiences.

Besides sponsoring research, the federal government might help stimulate the development and testing of innovative compensation and support models explicitly designed to retain effective teachers in needy schools and districts. In this case, the Department of Education or other relevant agency can announce a national grant program to support two phases of work, the first to develop innovative compensation plans, the second to evaluate trials of these models to determine their effectiveness. If ten to twelve such grants were let, then studied over a significant period, the knowledge return could be substantial, leading to the adoption of new compensation practices in districts that historically have had difficulty retaining teachers. Once evaluation research validates the worth of such models, there will be a basis for states and districts to invest in these models out of operating funds.

THE PROSPECT OF SUCCESS. Finally, teachers are more likely to stay in schools where they feel they can succeed. Research stresses the importance of professional supports and redesigned schools to build stronger teacher-student relationships that promote trust, motivation, commitment, and collective efficacy.[157] These "soft" features of schools are alterable through more skillful management and organization, which can be supported through development of new administrative leadership programs and continued support of redesigned schools, such as those offered through the New American Schools development program and the Small Schools Act.

Teachers in difficult classrooms, however, may be discouraged from staying by perverse incentives that may be encouraged by NCLB. Under that law, schools are being branded as "in need of improvement" (and will later be labeled as "failing") if all students and such subgroups as poor, minority, and limited-English-proficient students do not all show adequate yearly progress on test scores. Schools stand to be reconstituted and states and districts stand to lose funds based on missing testing targets. The problem is not only that school scores are so volatile as to be useless as indicators of improvement and that the targets adopted are likely to result in more than half the nation's schools being seen as failing over the next few years.[158]

The problem is also that the stigma is likely to make it even harder for such schools to recruit and retain highly qualified teachers. Evidence suggests these labels and the accompanying pressure can chase teachers away from such schools, thus exacerbating their problems.[159]

If evidence mounts that schools face a teacher exodus because they are seen as failing or because of rising dismay at excessive accountability pressures, countervailing measures may be necessary. Besides amending NCLB to develop more sensible measures of progress, the federal government, along with states and localities, may need to create other inducements to teach, and remain teaching, in such schools.[160] Otherwise, even less-qualified individuals may end up instructing these students.

Facilitating a National Labor Market for Teachers

Finally, the federal government can create the foundation of a national labor market for teachers, including the removal of unnecessary interstate barriers to teacher mobility. Because teacher supply and demand vary regionally, the country can only benefit if states with teacher surpluses in certain fields can recruit from states with corresponding shortages. The federal government can work with states to accomplish three goals:

—Develop common licensing exams and interstate agreements about content and pedagogical coursework to facilitate reciprocity and respond to the standard called for by NCLB;
—Create a system of pension portability across the states; and
—Provide labor market data and analyses for federal, state, and local planning.

Several groups already are working on these agendas in ways that could be leveraged toward genuine changes. For example, the Interstate New Teacher Assessment and Support Consortium, sponsored by the Council of Chief State School Officers, has brought together more than thirty states to create licensing standards and new assessments for beginning teachers. The consensus they have forged can be the basis for an eventual national system. The organization of State Higher Education Executive Officers, along with the Education Commission of the States, has examined how to achieve teacher pension portability, and TIAA-CREF has also developed such plans. A public/private partnership to stimulate the next steps in these plans could be extremely productive.

Finally, the long-standing federal role of keeping statistics and managing research is well suited to the job of creating a database and analytic agenda for monitoring teacher supply and demand. Such a system, which would inform all other policies, can document and project shortage areas and fields, determine priorities for federal, state, and local recruitment incentives, and support plans for institutional investments where they are needed.

In making all of these recommendations, we are mindful of the looming federal deficits. However, these initiatives can be accomplished for less than 1 percent of the $350 billion tax cut enacted in May 2003, and, in only a few years, they will build a strong teaching force that can last decades. We stress again, moreover, that these proposals can save far more than they cost. The savings include the several billion dollars now wasted because of high teacher turnover as well as the costs of grade retention, summer schools, and remedial programs required because too many children are poorly taught. This is to say nothing, moreover, of the broken lives and broader societal burdens that can be avoided with strong teachers in the schools that most need them. In the competition for educational investment, the evidence strongly points to the centrality of teacher quality to educational improvement. That should be a centerpiece of the nation's education agenda. The benefits of this strategy for students' school success, employability, and contributions to society will repay the costs many times over.

Appendix 7A. Federal Funding for Health Professionals

Since 1944, the federal government has offered loans to students preparing for health profession careers and has supported the development of medical education programs. These programs were expanded during the 1950s by the Medical Manpower Act and in 1963 by the Health Professions Education Assistance Act, which have been amended and expanded regularly ever since. Over a half century, a strong federal role in managing the medical workforce and strengthening medical training has contributed to America's world-class system of medical training. Title 42 (chapter 6A, subchapter V of the U.S. Code) details the many components of this system, which include the following.

—*Forgivable loans, scholarships, fellowships, and traineeships.* These are designed to increase the numbers of doctors and nurses in fields of high demand, improve the geographic distribution of health professionals in medically underserved and rural areas, and recruit as medical students individuals who are members of minority groups.

—*Investments in health professions schools.* These are designed to underwrite the costs of planning, developing, and operating training programs in high-need fields (currently, for example, family medicine, internal medicine, pediatrics, and general dentistry), often with special consideration for projects that prepare practitioners to work with underserved populations. Federal funds also create "Centers of Excellence" at certain medical schools for increasing the supply of minority medical students and faculty and improving the capacity of professionals to address minority health issues. Programs have developed community-based health facilities and established area health education centers that assess regional health personnel needs and develop training programs to meet such needs, especially in underserved areas (with some costs funded by state and local partners). Training programs for public health workers have been expanded, especially in "severe shortage disciplines" (for example, epidemiology, biostatistics, environmental health, maternal and child health, public health nursing, and behavioral and mental health).

—*Support for analysis of the health professions workforce.* A uniform health professions data reporting system collects, compiles, and analyzes data on health professions personnel and students-in-training. A nonfederal analytic infrastructure conducts research on high-priority workforce questions, including projections of supply and need by specialty and location (through grants to states and other institutions). Federal funds are provided to evaluate and assess these programs.

Over the years, as needs have been identified, Congress has developed innovative strategies to address emerging manpower and service needs. For example, recent amendments to the Public Health Service Act (PL 107-251) added elements to the existing support for health centers and the National Health Service Corps. These included the creation of integrated health care networks in rural areas, grants to expand telehealth resources, and expansion of training grants to mental health professionals and individuals in other training fields experiencing shortages, such as dentists. Using partnership strategies, some grants are directed to states to improve their capacity to recruit and distribute high-need professionals. For example, section 340G (42 USC 256g) provides for grants to states for innovative programs "to address the dental workforce needs of designated dental health professional shortage areas in a manner that is appropriate to the states' individual needs." States may use the funds for loan forgiveness programs for dentists who agree to practice in shortage areas or who agree to provide payments on a sliding scale; for recruitment and retention efforts;

for grants or no-interest loans to help dentists establish or expand practices in shortage areas; and for the establishment or expansion of dental residency programs. Through these evolving strategies and the hundreds of millions of dollars annually allocated to them, the federal government responds to local needs for health professionals and manages the labor market so that these needs can be better met.

Appendix 7B. Federal Funding for Education Professionals

Federal involvement in education manpower issues also emerged in the postwar era in the United States, but it has been more spotty than the government's steady, consistent involvement in the health professions. Rather than developing any overarching rationale or policy, federal efforts were attached to other priorities, such as national defense or civil rights, which supplied justification for a federal role. In addressing teacher recruitment needs and shortages, the national government relied on incentives with limited time horizons.

The earliest legislation offered support for veterans returning from World War II. The Serviceman's Readjustment Act of 1944 contained a provision to help defray tuition and other costs for GIs, with teachers colleges and normal schools on the list of approved institutions. Subsequently, as the nation was drawn into the cold war, national defense emerged as paramount. Among its provisions, the National Defense Education Act of 1958 launched a loan program that became identified with its chief sponsor, Congressman Carl Perkins. Title II, the National Defense Loan Program, supplied student loans for college education, with special consideration for students with a superior academic background who expressed a desire to teach in elementary or secondary school. The program provided that loans are canceled at the rate of 10 percent annually for each year of service in a public school. The Higher Education Act of 1965 increased the rate of cancellation on Perkins loans from 10 percent to 15 percent for teachers who served in schools with high concentrations of students from low-income families. Such teachers are eligible for 100 percent of loan cancellation, based on extended years of service, rather than 50 percent available to other teachers. The 1998 reauthorization provided Perkins loan cancellations at the rate of 15 percent for years one and two of service, 20 percent for years three and four, and 30 percent for year five of service. The amendments added teachers of learning-disabled students to those who teach in high poverty (Title I) schools or in subject-matter shortage areas, including mathematics, science, foreign languages, and bilingual education, among others. These provisions remain in effect. Although they are modestly helpful, these loans are a retroactive support for individuals who find their way into teaching, not a proactive recruitment device to attract college students into training programs that ensure they will be induced into shortage fields and well prepared to teach these disciplines.

A new theme—civil rights—entered the federal mix beginning in the 1960s. In addition to the Perkins loans, the Higher Education Act of 1965 contained provisions aimed at staffing inner-city and rural schools. This act established the National Teacher Corps, which operated for the next fifteen years. That program worked through grants to institutions of higher education, which were authorized to train recruits, who then served in schools attended by poor children. Following a few months of initial training, recruits entered schools as interns on teams made up of an experienced teacher and other recruits. The interns continued their training while working and received starting salaries from the districts where they worked, while experienced teachers received added compensation for team leadership. Over the years, the program was evaluated regularly and improved. For example, the model evolved from isolated placements in individual schools to clusters that included feeder schools to middle and high schools, and the training/program evaluation cycle was lengthened from two to five years. The act also funded fellowships that universities allocated to support full-time graduate study at the master's level in education. A number of master of arts in teaching (MAT) programs evolved out of these fellowships. These programs became, in essence, the first alternatives to traditional undergraduate teacher education. The early MAT efforts, one-year master's degree programs at places like Harvard, Stanford, Columbia's Teachers College, and Duke, later became models for many university-based alternative programs in the 1990s.

The combination of these investments in recruitment and a reduction in teacher demand led to the virtual elimination of emergency hiring of teachers by 1979. Although there were serious questions about the quality of teacher supply at that time,[161] most federal teacher recruitment programs of the 1960s and 1970s were eliminated in 1981. By the late 1980s, however, concern about the quality and supply of teachers began to emerge again. In 1986, the Paul Douglas Teacher Scholarship Program (formerly the Congressional Teacher Scholarship Program) was authorized. Over a ten-year period until its demise in 1996, this program provided scholarships to outstanding high school graduates who planned to pursue careers in pre-K–12 teaching. Applicants had to be ranked in the top 10 percent of their high school graduating class or have GED scores in the top 10 percent of the state or nation. The program operated through the states, which were allowed to add their own selection criteria in response to particular targets and needs. State criteria often included such factors as recruitment from historically underrepresented groups, from low-SES backgrounds, from candidates who wanted to teach in poor schools, and for teaching mathematics and science. The program was modest in size, allocating only $15 million from 1987 through 1994. Loans under the program were forgiven at the rate of two years of teaching service for each year of scholarship award; this provision was modified to one year of teaching for one year of scholarship support for teaching in subject shortage fields. Evaluations indicated that nearly two-thirds of recipients completed teacher certification, and two-thirds of these people taught.

Another program, started in 1986, sought to tap retiring military personnel for teaching. The U.S. Army began a pilot program for servicemen to enroll in teacher certification programs before discharge. The U.S. Navy followed several years later with a program of its own. These programs worked through cooperating colleges and universities to ease the transition from the services into teaching. Some years later, the army also established several alternative teacher certification programs for armed forces personnel, with pilots in Texas and Georgia.

The Troops to Teachers Program (TTT) began as a joint venture between the U.S. departments of Defense and Education. The 1993 National Defense Authorization Act (PL 102-484, section 4441) formally established this program, which offered stipends of up to $5,000 to allow former members of the armed services to obtain teacher certification. School districts received up to $50,000 over five years for every TTT teacher they hired. The stipends and the grants were discontinued after 1995, but in 1999 the TTT program was reauthorized and transferred from the Defense Department to the Education Department. TTT, too, has been a very modest effort, with the 2001 appropriation reaching only $3 million, when it was placed within the Eisenhower Professional Development Program. The program operates through grants to states that submit proposals outlining the services and activities they will undertake. As of 2000, twenty-two states had joined the program, and thirteen more were considering it. Studies that have tracked the program report high rates of participation in math, science, special education, and vocational education at the high school level and in urban teaching. Teachers are more likely to be male (86 percent) and minority (33 percent) than the overall teacher workforce.

Under the No Child Left Behind Act, the TTT Program is a subpart of the Transitions to Teaching initiative but is still a distinct program. Participants can still receive stipends of $5,000 a year (up to $5,000 may be awarded annually in return for a commitment to teach for three years) or bonuses of $10,000 (up to $3,000 annually in return for an agreement to teach for three years in a high-need school). The Transitions to Teaching Program authorizes five-year grants to partnerships and eligible entities to establish programs to recruit and retain highly qualified midcareer professionals and recent college graduates as teachers for high-need schools, including recruitment through alternate-route programs that condense the period of preparation. This is a new authority in the No Child Left Behind law, but Congress provided $31 million for similar activities in 2001. These institutional funds may be used for scholarships, pre- or postinduction activities, placement initiatives, payments to schools to supply incentives for teachers, collaboration with institutions of higher education to develop recruitment programs, and other strategies. Program participants must teach in a high-need school for at least three years following receipt of support.

Besides continued funding for the Perkins loans, another part of the reauthorized Higher Education Act established the Federal Family Education Loan Program, together with a Direct Lending provision. Together, these supplied loan and principal forgiveness of up to $5,000 for Stafford loans for borrowers who agree to teach for five consecutive years in low-income elementary or secondary schools (that is, schools where more than 30 percent of students are eligible for Title I aid). Loan repayment is deferred during the five-year teaching commitment. These provisions were further amended in 2001–02 to include three years of Stafford and Federal Supplemental loans for those who teach in a federally designated teacher-shortage area, including subject matter, grade level, or geographic shortages.

Notes

1. Many recent polls demonstrate that large majorities of parents and members of the general public (90 percent) believe that getting and supporting well-qualified teachers is the strategy most likely to improve schools; that such teachers should have knowledge of content, how children learn, and how to teach; and that salaries—and taxes—should be raised if necessary to get well-qualified teachers in all schools. See, for example, Educational Testing Service, *A National Priority: Americans Speak on Teacher Quality* (Princeton, N.J., 2002); Recruiting New Teachers, *The Essential Profession: A Survey of Public Attitudes toward Teaching, Educational Opportunity, and School Reform* (Belmont, Mass., 1998).

2. Donald Boyd, Hamilton Lankford, and Susanna Loeb, *The Draw of Home: How Teacher Preferences for Proximity Disadvantage Urban Schools,* Working Paper 9953 (Cambridge, Mass.: National Bureau of Economic Research, 2003).

3. Richard M. Ingersoll, "Teacher Turnover and Teacher Shortages: An Organizational Analysis," *American Educational Research Journal*, vol. 38, no. 3 (2001), p. 516.

4. National Commission on Teaching and America's Future, *What Matters Most: Teaching for America's Future* (New York, 1996), p. 93; John W. Miller, Michael C. McKenna, and Beverly A. McKenna, "A Comparison of Alternatively Certified and Traditionally Prepared Teachers," *Journal of Teacher Education*, vol. 49, no. 3 (1998), pp. 165–17; Linda Darling-Hammond, Sheila N. Kirby, and Lisa Hudson, *Redesigning Teacher Education: Opening the Door for New Recruits to Science and Mathematics Teaching* (Santa Monica, Calif.: RAND, 1989).

5. Clarke Fowler, "Fast Track . . . Slow Going?" *Ed Policy*, vol. 2, no. 1 (2002); Margaret Raymond, Stephen H. Fletcher, and Javier Luque, *Teach for America: An Evaluation of Teacher Differences and Student Outcomes in Houston, Texas* (Palo Alto, Calif.: Hoover Institution, Center for Research on Education Outcomes, 2001).

6. Robin R. Henke and others, *Progress through the Teacher Pipeline: 1992–93 College Graduates and Elementary/Secondary School Teaching as of 1997* (National Center for Education Statistics, 2000); National Commission on Teaching and America's Future, *No Dream Denied: A Pledge to America's Children* (New York, 2003).

7. National Commission on Teaching and America's Future, *No Dream Denied: A Pledge to America's Children*, p. 84.

8. Natalia Mehlman, "My Brief Teaching Career," *New York Times*, June 24, 2002, p. A19.

9. U.S. Department of Education, *Meeting the Highly Qualified Teachers Challenge: The Secretary's Annual Report on Teacher Quality* (June 2002).

10. In education, including in the NCLB legislation, "licensure" and "certification" often are used interchangeably. However, in most other professional fields, licensure refers to state requirements governing entry to a field, while certification denotes advanced standing based on standards set by a profession. For example, states grant physicians a license to practice medicine; professional boards grant certification in particular medical specialties. Similarly, the National Board for Professional Teaching Standards certifies teachers who demonstrate "accomplished practice," while states grant licenses to practice. Here, we conform to general usage, using "certification" and "licensure" as equivalent terms for the mandatory state requirements for entry to teaching.

11. U.S. Department of Education, *Meeting the Highly Qualified Teachers Challenge*, p. 19.

12. For a review of the evidence on which the report's recommendations are based, see Linda Darling-Hammond and Peter Youngs, "Defining 'Highly Qualified Teachers': What Does 'Scientifically-Based Research' Actually Tell Us?" *Educational Researcher*, vol. 31, no. 9 (2002), pp. 13–25.

13. No Child Left Behind Act of 2001 (Public Law 107-110), Title IX, Part A, Sec. 9101.

14. 34 CFR Part 200, *Federal Register* 67, no. 231 (December 2, 2002), p. 71712.

15. Ibid., p. 71765.

16. Ibid., p. 71764.

17. Texas Legislature, House Bill 318, 2003 legislative session.

18. Carol Keeton Strayhorn, "ED 4: Alleviate the Texas Teacher Shortage," *E-Texas: Limited Government, Unlimited Opportunity* (Austin: January 2003) (on line).

19. Ronald F. Ferguson, "Paying for Public Education: New Evidence on How and Why Money Matters," *Harvard Journal of Legislation,* vol. 28, no. 2 (1991), pp. 465–98.

20. *Teacher Quality,* Thomas B. Fordham Foundation (www.edexcellence.net/topics/teachers.html [March 2002]).

21. Richard Murnane and others, *Who Will Teach? Policies That Matter* (Harvard University Press, 1991), p. 94.

22. Ibid., p. 95.

23. Henry M. Levin, "Teacher Certification and the Economics of Information," *Educational Evaluation and Policy Analysis,* vol. 2, no. 4 (1980), p. 7.

24. Thomas L. Good and Jere Brophy, *Contemporary Educational Psychology,* 5th ed. (New York: Longman, 1995).

25. For reviews, see Linda Darling-Hammond, "Teacher Quality and Student Achievement: A Review of State Policy Evidence," *Education Policy Analysis Archives,* vol. 8, no. 1 (2000); Suzanne M. Wilson, Robert E. Floden, and Joan Ferrini-Mundy, *Teacher Preparation Research: Current Knowledge, Gaps, and Recommendations* (Seattle: Center for the Study of Teaching and Policy, February 2001).

26. James Coleman and others, *Equality of Educational Opportunity* (Government Printing Office, 1966); Ronald Ferguson and Helen Ladd, "How and Why Money Matters: An Analysis of Alabama Schools," in Helen Ladd, ed., *Holding Schools Accountable* (Brookings, 1996); Eric Hanushek, "The Trade-off between Child Quantity and Quality," *Journal of Political Economy,* vol. 100, no. 1 (1992), pp. 84–117; Eric Hanushek, *School Resources and Achievement in Maryland* (Baltimore: Maryland State Department of Education, 1996).

27. For discussions, see Richard J. Murnane, "Understanding the Sources of Teaching Competence: Choices, Skills, and the Limits of Training," *Teachers College Record,* vol. 84, no. 3 (1983), pp. 564–89; Andrew J. Wayne and Peter Youngs, "Teacher Characteristics and Student Achievement Gains: A Review," *Review of Educational Research,* vol. 73, no. 1 (2003), pp. 89–122.

28. See, for example, Edward Begle, *Critical Variables in Mathematics Education: Findings from a Survey of Empirical Literature* (Washington: National Council for Teachers of Mathematics, 1979); David H. Monk, "Subject Area Preparation of Secondary Mathematics and Science Teachers and Student Achievement," *Economics of Education Review,* vol. 12, no. 2 (1994); Harold Wenglinsky, "How Schools Matter: The Link between Teacher Classroom Practices and Student Academic Performance," *Education Policy Analysis Archives,* vol. 10, no. 12 (2002).

29. Monk, "Subject Area Preparation of Secondary Mathematics and Science Teachers and Student Achievement," pp. 125–42.

30. Ibid., p.142.

31. Ibid.

32. Wenglinsky, "How Schools Matter."

33. Daniel Goldhaber and Dominic Brewer, "Does Teacher Certification Matter? High School Certification Status and Student Achievement," *Educational Evaluation and Policy Analysis*, vol. 22, no. 2 (2000), pp. 129–45; Parmalee P. Hawk, Charles R. Coble, and Melvin Swanson, "Certification: Does It Matter?" *Journal of Teacher Education*, vol. 36, no. 3 (1985), pp. 13–15; Monk, "Subject Area Preparation of Secondary Mathematics and Science Teachers and Student Achievement."

34. Julian R. Betts, Kim S. Rueben, and Anne Danenberg, *Equal Resources, Equal Outcomes? The Distribution of School Resources and Student Achievement in California* (San Francisco: Public Policy Institute of California, 2000); Mark Fetler, "High School Staff Characteristics and Mathematics Test Results," *Education Policy Analysis Archives*, vol. 7, no. 9 (1999); Edward J. Fuller, *Do Properly Certified Teachers Matter? A Comparison of Elementary School Performance on the TAAS in 1997 between Schools with High and Low Percentages of Properly Certified Regular Education Teachers* (Austin: Charles A. Dana Center, University of Texas at Austin, 1998); Edward J. Fuller, *Do Properly Certified Teachers Matter? Properly Certified Algebra Teachers and Algebra I Achievement in Texas*, paper presented at the annual meeting of the American Educational Research Association, New Orleans (2000); Laura Goe, "Legislating Equity: The Distribution of Emergency Permit Teachers in California," *Educational Policy Analysis Archives*, vol. 10, no. 42 (April 2002).

35. Ferguson, "Paying for Public Education: New Evidence on How and Why Money Matters"; Robert P. Strauss and Elizabeth A. Sawyer, "Some New Evidence on Teacher and Student Competencies," *Economics of Education Review*, vol. 5, no. 1 (1986), pp. 41–48.

36. Darling-Hammond, "Teacher Quality and Student Achievement."

37. Goldhaber and Brewer, "Does Teacher Certification Matter? High School Certification Status and Student Achievement," p. 139. Emphasis added.

38. Some opponents of teacher certification have misconstrued one finding of this study to argue against teacher education requirements. Because students of a small number of science teachers with temporary or emergency certification (24 of 3,469 teachers in the sample) did no worse than students of certified teachers, these opponents have termed teacher certification unnecessary (for example, see Strayhorn, "ED 4: Alleviate the Texas Teacher Shortage"). However, these teachers, like those with standard certification, were found to be more effective than uncertified teachers. Another analysis of these data (Linda Darling-Hammond, Barnett Berry, and Amy Thoreson, "Does Teacher Certification Matter? Evaluating the Evidence," *Educational Evaluation and Policy Analysis*, vol. 23, no. 1 [2001], pp. 57–77) showed that most science teachers in the sample with temporary or emergency certificates had many years of experience and subject matter and education training comparable to that of certified teachers. Their backgrounds and teaching contexts suggested that many were previously certified, out-of-state entrants working on a temporary credential while becoming certified in a new state. Others were certified in math or another subfield of science. It is not surprising, then, that their students did about as well as those of certified teachers with similar qualifications. Only a third of the National Education Longitudinal Study sample teachers on temporary/emergency licenses were new entrants to teaching with little education training. The

students of this subsample had smaller achievement gains than those of the more experienced, traditionally trained teachers in an analysis of covariance that controlled for pretest scores, content degrees, and experience.

39. Betts, Rueben, and Danenberg, *Equal Resources, Equal Outcomes? The Distribution of School Resources and Student Achievement in California;* Fetler, "High School Staff Characteristics and Mathematics Test Results"; Goe, "Legislating Equity."

40. Fuller, *Do Properly Certified Teachers Matter? A Comparison of Elementary School Performance on the TAAS in 1997 between Schools with High and Low Percentages of Properly Certified Regular Education Teachers;* Fuller, *Do Properly Certified Teachers Matter? Properly Certified Algebra Teachers and Algebra I Achievement in Texas;* Celeste Alexander and Ed Fuller, "Does Teacher Certification Matter? Teacher Certification and Middle School Mathematics Achievement in Texas," paper presented at the annual meeting of the American Educational Research Association, San Diego, 2004.

41. L. Darling-Hammond, Ruth Chung, and Fred Frelow, "Variation in Teacher Preparation: How Well Do Different Pathways Prepare Teachers to Teach?" *Journal of Teacher Education,* vol. 53, no. 4 (2002), pp. 286–302.

42. James R. Jelmberg, "College-Based Teacher Education versus State-Sponsored Alternative Programs," *Journal of Teacher Education,* vol. 47, no. 1 (1996), p. 61.

43. Traci Bliss, "Alternative Certification in Connecticut: Reshaping the Profession," *Peabody Journal of Education,* vol. 67, no. 3 (1992), p. 52.

44. Trish Stoddart, "An Alternate Route to Teacher Certification: Preliminary Findings from the Los Angeles Unified School District Intern Program," *Peabody Journal of Education,* vol. 67, no. 3 (1992).

45. Michael McKibbin, *Teaching Internship Programs: Alternative Preparation and Licensure in California: Purposes, Procedures, and Performance* (Sacramento: California Commission on Teacher Credentialing, 1998).

46. California State University, Office of the Chancellor, *First System Wide Evaluation of Teacher Education Programs in the California State University: Summary Report* and *Preparing Teachers for Reading Instruction (K–12): An Evaluation Brief by the California State University* (Long Beach, 2002).

47. Patrick M. Shields and others, *The Status of the Teaching Profession 2001* (Santa Cruz, Calif.: Center for the Future of Teaching and Learning, 2001), p. 37.

48. Frank W. Lutz and Jerry B. Hutton, "Alternative Teacher Certification: Its Policy Implications for Classroom and Personnel Practice," *Educational Evaluation and Policy Analysis,* vol. 11, no. 3 (1989), pp. 237–54.

49. N. Mitchell, *Interim Evaluation Report of the Alternative Certification System* (REA87-027-2) (Dallas: Dallas Independent School District Department of Planning, Evaluation, and Testing, 1987).

50. Lutz and Hutton, "Alternative Teacher Certification: Its Policy Implications for Classroom and Personnel Practice," p. 250.

51. D. Gomez and R. Grobe, *Three Years of Alternative Certification in Dallas: Where Are We?* paper presented at the annual meeting of the American Educational Research Association, Boston (1990).

52. Miller, McKenna, and McKenna, "A Comparison of Alternatively Certified and Traditionally Prepared Teachers," pp. 165–76.

53. Ibid., p. 174.

54. Raymond, Fletcher, and Luque, *Teach for America*.

55. Ildiko Laczko-Kerr and David C. Berliner, "The Effectiveness of 'Teach for America' and Other Under-Certified Teachers on Student Academic Achievement: A Case of Harmful Public Policy," *Education Policy Analysis Archives*, vol. 10, no. 37 (2002).

56. Paul T. Decker, Daniel P. Mayer, and Steven Glazerman, *The Effects of Teach for America on Students: Findings from a National Evaluation* (Princeton: Mathematica Policy Research).

57. For one synthesis, see Wilson, Floden, and Ferrini-Mundy, *Teacher Preparation Research: Current Knowledge, Gaps, and Recommendations*. For another, see SRI International, *Alternative Certification: Design for a National Study* (Menlo Park, Calif., 2002).

58. A decade ago, only a quarter to a third of newly hired teachers were "newly minted." This proportion has increased with growing demand, reaching as many as half of new hires in the late 1990s. In a few high-demand states like California, the proportion has reached 60 percent, but this is unusual.

59. Various studies of the teacher supply have found that about 20 percent to 30 percent of teachers who have left the classroom eventually return to teaching in the same state. See Barbara Q. Beaudin, "Teachers Who Interrupt Their Career: Characteristics of Those Who Return to the Classroom," *Educational Evaluation and Policy Analysis*, vol. 15, no. 1 (1993), pp. 51–64; Massachusetts Institute for Social and Economic Research, *Report on the Status of Teacher Supply and Demand in Massachusetts* (Amherst, 1987); Murnane and others, *Who Will Teach?* Some leave to teach in another state, although most studies have not had data sets to track these individuals. The likelihood that those who have left teaching will re-enter depends heavily on salary levels and work conditions. See Beaudin, "Teachers Who Interrupt Their Career: Characteristics of Those Who Return to the Classroom," and Barbara Q. Beaudin, "Former Teachers Who Return to Public Schools: District and Teacher Characteristics of Teachers Who Return to the Districts They Left," *Educational Evaluation and Policy Analysis* vol. 17, no. 4 (1995), pp. 462–75. Also see National Commission on Teaching and America's Future, *No Dream Denied: A Pledge to America's Children*.

60. Erling E. Boe and others, *National Trends in Teacher Supply and Turnover for Special and General Education* (Philadelphia: Center for Research and Evaluation in Social Policy, University of Pennsylvania, 1998), found that, nationally, delayed entrants make up about a third of new entrants to teaching annually, which in this case would be about 50,000.

61. Between 1983 and 1999, annual graduates with a bachelor's or master's degree in education jumped from 134,870 to 234,408. However, this does not translate directly into new teacher supply, since bachelor's degrees in education now represent fewer than half of newly prepared teachers. Most now receive a degree in a disciplinary field and a second major, minor, or master's in education. While a growing share of teachers are trained in master's programs, many master's degrees are gained after teachers have already completed initial preparation.

62. Because a large majority of alternative programs are run by or in collaboration with universities, their graduates are counted in university totals. Estimates of alternative-certification programs vary, depending on classification, but by 1999, 40 states and the District of Columbia had 117 state-authorized programs (Emily Feistritzer and David Chester, *Alternative Teacher Certification: A State-by-State Analysis 2000* [Washington: National Center for Education Information, 2000]). In addition, the American Association of Colleges for Teacher Education cataloged 328 alternative programs run by colleges and universities (American Association of Colleges for Teacher Education, *Alternative Paths to Teaching: A Directory of Post-Baccalaureate Programs,* Washington, 1996).

63. American Association for Employment in Education, *Educator Supply and Demand in the United States: 2000 Research Report* (Columbus, Ohio, 2000).

64. For example, see Michael Gormley, Associated Press, "State: The Teacher Shortage Is Abating," *Boston Globe,* January 2, 2003; Yilu Zhao, "To Find Teachers, Raise Hand High and Yell, 'Me!' " *New York Times,* October 5, 2002, p. A16.

65. Ingersoll, "Teacher Turnover and Teacher Shortages."

66. Ibid.; Henke and others, *Progress through the Teacher Pipeline.*

67. Some researchers using longitudinal data from the 1993–94 Baccalaureate and Beyond survey find a four-year attrition rate of about 20 percent for those who entered teaching directly after college (Henke and others, *Progress through the Teacher Pipeline*). Other researchers extrapolate from cross-sectional data on teacher attrition (from the 1999–2000 Schools and Staffing Surveys) to estimate a five-year attrition rate for beginning teachers, including private school teachers, of 46 percent. However, the five-year attrition rate for public school teachers is only about 38 percent (Ingersoll, "Teacher Turnover and Teacher Shortages: An Organizational Analysis"). Furthermore, some individuals who left teaching for childrearing or further study will have returned to the classroom in the first five years—a proportion that, other estimates suggest, could be about 20 percent of leavers. With this adjustment, the five-year cumulative attrition rate for public school teachers would be just over 30 percent.

68. Ingersoll, "Teacher Turnover and Teacher Shortages: An Organizational Analysis," p. 516; Eric A. Hanushek, John F. Kain, and Steven G. Rivkin, *Do Higher Salaries Buy Better Teachers?* Working Paper 7082 (Cambridge, Mass.: National Bureau of Economic Research, 1999), especially p. 15.

69. Aprile D. Benner, *The Cost of Teacher Turnover* (Austin: Texas Center for Educational Research, 2000), p. 2.

70. Eric Hanushek, John F. Kain, and Steven G. Rivkin, *Teachers, Schools, and Academic Achievement,* Working Paper 6691 (Cambridge, Mass.: National Bureau of Economic Research, 1998); John F. Kain and Kraig Singleton, "Equality of Educational Opportunity Revisited," *New England Economic Review,* May-June 1996, pp. 87–111.

71. Shields and others, *The Status of the Teaching Profession 2001.*

72. Stephen Carroll, Robert Reichardt, Cassandra Guarino, and Andrea Mejia, *The Distribution of Teachers among California's School Districts and Schools* (Santa Monica, Calif.: Rand, 2000).

73. Analysts have long recognized that salary differentials across teaching areas contribute to shortages, based on the sensible proposition that individuals are influenced by available salaries. In response, some have argued for altering the structure of public school salary schedules by allowing differential pay across teaching specialties. Some experiments along these lines have appeared over the years, including recent efforts in Cincinnati, Ohio, and Douglas County and Denver in Colorado, among others. In 2003 the Kentucky State Department of Education awarded grants to ten districts for innovations in salary systems. These experiments are worth careful study, but for the most part salary schedules have remained uniform and fixed. For further discussion of this issue, see Joseph A. Kershaw and Roland N. McKean, *Teacher Shortages and Salary Schedules* (McGraw-Hill, 1962) and Murnane and others, *Who Will Teach?*

74. National Center for Education Statistics (NCES), *America's Teachers: Profile of a Profession, 1993–94* (U.S. Department of Education, 1997).

75. NCES, *Digest of Education Statistics, 1999* (U.S. Department of Education, 2000).

76. Educational Testing Service, *The State of Inequality* (Princeton, N.J., 1991); Jonathan Kozol, *Savage Inequalities* (Crown Publishers, 1991).

77. Education Trust, *The Funding Gap: Low-Income and Minority Students Receive Fewer Dollars* (Washington, 2002).

78. Some researchers point out, however, that while one-third of the inequality in educational spending is within-state, almost two-thirds is between-state. Even accounting for between-state differences in the costs of education, this basic fact points to the need for equity policies at the federal level (Ann Flanagan and David Grissmer, "The Role of Federal Resources in Closing the Achievement Gap," in Tom Loveless and John E. Chubb, eds., *Bridging the Achievement Gap* [Brookings, 2002]).

79. Valerie E. Lee and David T. Burkam, *Inequality at the Starting Gate: Social Background Differences in Achievement as Children Begin School* (Economic Policy Institute, 2002).

80. NCES, *America's Teachers: Profile of a Profession,* table A 8.11.

81. Susan P. Choy and others, *Schools and Staffing in the United States: A Statistical Profile, 1990–91* (NCES, U.S. Department of Education, 1993).

82. Shields and others, *The Status of the Teaching Profession 2001,* pp. 21–23.

83. Richard M. Ingersoll, *Out-of-Field Teaching, Educational Inequality, and the Organization of Schools: An Exploratory Analysis* (R-02-1) (Seattle: Center for the Study of Teaching and Policy, January 2002); Craig D. Jerald, *All Talk, No Action: Putting an End to Out-of-Field Teaching* (Washington: Education Trust, August 2002); Hamilton Lankford, Susanna Loeb, and James Wyckoff, "Teacher Sorting and the Plight of Urban Schools: A Descriptive Analysis," *Educational Evaluation and Policy Analysis,* vol. 24, no. 11 (2002), pp. 37–62.

84. Ingersoll, "Teacher Turnover and Teacher Shortages: An Organizational Analysis"; Lankford, Loeb, and Wyckoff, "Teacher Sorting and the Plight of Urban Schools: A Descriptive Analysis"; Eric Hanushek, John Kain, and Steven Rivkin, *Why Public Schools Lose Teachers,* Working Paper 8599 (Cambridge, Mass.: National Bureau of Economic

Research 2001); Benjamin Scafidi, David L. Sjoquist, and Todd R. Stinebrickner, *The Impact of Wages and School Characteristics on Teacher Mobility and Retention,* unpublished manuscript (Georgia State University, September 2002).

85. Jerald, *All Talk, No Action;* Lankford, Loeb, and Wyckoff, "Teacher Sorting and the Plight of Urban Schools"; National Center for Education Statistics, *Qualifications of the Public School Teacher Workforce: Prevalence of Out-of-Field Teaching 1987–88 to 1999–2000* (Washington, 2002).

86. Lankford, Loeb, and Wyckoff, "Teacher Sorting and the Plight of Urban Schools," pp. 38–39.

87. Dale Ballou, "Do Public Schools Hire the Best Applicants?" *Quarterly Journal of Economics,* vol. 111, no.1 (1996), pp. 97–133. Dale Ballou and Michael Podgursky, *Teacher Pay and Teacher Quality* (Kalamazoo, Mich.: Upjohn Institute for Employment Research, 1997); Arthur E. Wise, Linda Darling-Hammond, and Barnett Berry, *Effective Teacher Selection: From Recruitment to Retention* (Santa Monica, Calif.: RAND, 1987).

88. Boyd, Lankford, and Loeb, *The Draw of Home: How Teacher Preferences for Proximity Disadvantage Urban Schools,* p. 12.

89. Erika Hayasaki, "Teacher Shortage Abates," *Los Angeles Times,* February 10, 2003, p. A1.

90. William H. Baugh and Joe A. Stone, "Mobility and Wage Equilibration in the Educator Labor Market," *Economics of Education Review,* vol. 2, no. 3 (1982), pp. 253–74.

91. Dominic J. Brewer, "Career Paths and Quit Decisions: Evidence from Teaching," *Journal of Labor Economics,* vol. 14, no. 2 (1996), pp. 313–39; Daniel Mont and Daniel I. Rees, "The Influence of Classroom Characteristics on High School Teacher Turnover," *Economic Inquiry,* vol. 34, no. 1 (1996), pp. 152–67; Richard J. Murnane, Judith B. Singer, and John D. Willett, "The Influences of Salaries and 'Opportunity Costs' on Teachers' Career Choices: Evidence from North Carolina," *Harvard Educational Review,* vol. 59, no. 3 (1989), pp. 325–46; Neil D. Theobold, "An Examination of the Influence of Personal, Professional, and School District Characteristics on Public School Teacher Retention," *Economics of Education Review,* vol. 9, no. 3 (1990), pp. 241–50; Neil D. Theobold and R. Mark Gritz, "The Effect of School District Spending Priorities on the Exit Paths of Beginning Teachers Leaving the District," *Economics of Education Review,* vol. 15, no. 1 (1996), pp. 11–22.

92. Hanushek, Kain, and Rivkin, *Do Higher Salaries Buy Better Teachers?;* R. Mark Gritz and Neil D. Theobold, "The Effects of School District Spending Priorities on Length of Stay in Teaching," *Journal of Human Resources,* vol. 31, no. 3 (1996), pp. 477–512. For the effects on math and science teachers, see Richard J. Murnane and Randy Olsen, "The Effects of Salaries and Opportunity Costs on Length of Stay in Teaching: Evidence from North Carolina," *Journal of Human Resources,* vol. 25, no. 1 (1990), pp. 106–24; Murnane and others, *Who Will Teach?*

93. Rob Greenwald, Larry V. Hedges, and Richard D. Laine, "The Effect of School Resources on Student Achievement," *Review of Educational Research,* vol. 66, no. 3 (1996), pp. 361–96.

94. Ferguson, "Paying for Public Education."

95. Joseph Michael Pogodzinski, *The Teacher Shortage: Causes and Recommendations for Change* (Department of Economics, San Jose State University, 2000).

96. Susanna Loeb and Marianne E. Page, "Examining the Link between Teacher Wages and Student Outcomes: The Importance of Alternative Labor Market Opportunities and Non-Pecuniary Variation," *Review of Economics and Statistics,* vol. 82, no. 3 (2000), pp. 393–408.

97. Lankford, Loeb, and Wyckoff, "Teacher Sorting and the Plight of Urban Schools."

98. NCES, *America's Teachers.*

99. Pogodzinski, *The Teacher Shortage.*

100. Loeb and Page, "Examining the Link between Teacher Wages and Student Outcomes."

101. Hanushek, Kain, and Rivkin, *Why Public Schools Lose Teachers.*

102. Lankford, Loeb, and Wyckoff, "Teacher Sorting and the Plight of Urban Schools."

103. Linda Darling-Hammond, *Doing What Matters Most: Investing in Quality Teaching* (New York: National Commission on Teaching and America's Future, 1997); Ingersoll, "Teacher Turnover and Teacher Shortages"; Ingersoll, *Out-of-Field Teaching, Educational Inequality, and the Organization of Schools.*

104. NCES, *America's Teachers,* table A 4.15.

105. Darling-Hammond, *Doing What Matters Most.*

106. Carroll, Reichardt, Guarino, and Mejia, *The Distribution of Teachers among California's School Districts and Schools;* Scafidi, Sjoquist, and Stinebrickner, *The Impact of Wages and School Characteristics on Teacher Mobility and Retention;* Hanushek, Kain, and Rivkin, *Do Higher Salaries Buy Better Teachers?*

107. Peter Harris, *Survey of California Teachers* (Peter Harris Research Group, 2002).

108. Susanna Loeb, Linda Darling-Hammond, and John M. Luczak, *Teacher Turnover: The Role of Working Conditions and Salaries in Recruiting and Retaining Teachers,* Stanford University School of Education, forthcoming.

109. Daniel De Vise, "A+ Plan Prompts Teacher Exodus in Broward County," *Miami Herald,* November 5, 1999, p. 1B.

110. Charles Clotfelter and others, "Do School Accountability Systems Make It More Difficult for Low Performing Schools to Attract and Retain High Quality Teachers?" paper prepared for the annual meeting of the American Economic Association, Washington, February 2003.

111. Loeb, Darling-Hammond, and Luczak, *Teacher Turnover.*

112. Henke and others, *Progress through the Teacher Pipeline.*

113. National Commission on Teaching and America's Future, *No Dream Denied.*

114. Linda Darling-Hammond, "Access to Quality Teaching: An Analysis of Inequality in California's Public Schools," *Santa Clara Law Review,* vol. 43 (2003), pp. 101–239; Suzanne Tyson, Helen Hawley, and Michael McKibbin, *Pre-Internship Teaching Program: A Progress Report to the Legislature.* (Sacramento: California Commission on Teacher Credentialing, 2000), p. 3.

115. Lucinda Grey and others, *New Teachers in the Job Market. 1991 Update* (U.S. Department of Education, Office of Educational Research and Improvement, 1993).

116. Michael D. Andrew and Richard L. Schwab, "Has Reform in Teacher Education Influenced Teacher Performance? An Outcome Assessment of Graduates of Eleven Teacher Education Programs," *Action in Teacher Education,* vol. 17 (1995), pp. 43–53.

117. Linda Darling-Hammond, ed., *Studies of Excellence in Teacher Education* (Washington: American Association of Colleges for Teacher Education, 2000).

118. M. D. Andrew and R. L. Schwab, "Has Reform in Teacher Education Influenced Teacher Performance? An Outcome Assessment of Eleven Teacher Education Programs," *Action in Teacher Education,* vol. 17, no. 3 (1995), pp. 43–53; M. D. Andrew, "The Differences between Graduates of Four-Year and Five-Year Teacher Preparation Programs," *Journal of Teacher Education,* vol. 41 (1990), pp. 45–51; and John J. Denton and W. H. Peters, "Program Assessment Report: Curriculum Evaluation of a Nontraditional Program for Certifying Teachers" (Texas A&M University, 1988).

119. National Commission on Teaching and America's Future, *No Dream Denied.*

120. Darling-Hammond, Chung, and Frelow, "Variation in Teacher Preparation: How Well Do Different Pathways Prepare Teachers to Teach?"

121. National Commission on Teaching and America's Future, *What Matters Most.*

122. Shields and others, *The Status of the Teaching Profession 2001,* p. 101.

123. National Commission on Teaching and America's Future, *No Dream Denied.*

124. For example, one study documented the difficulties out-of-state candidates experienced in seeking teaching positions; California Commission on Teacher Credentialing, *A Report on Issues Involving the Recruitment and Retention of Teachers Prepared in Other States* (Sacramento: California Commission on Teacher Credentialing, June 1998). Problems included costs of courses and exams, confusion about how to complete the many and varied requirements and redundancy with other requirements teachers had already met elsewhere. In a survey of out-of-state teachers who had received an initial permit to teach in California, credential requirements were the leading factor in decisions to leave the state.

125. Wise, Darling-Hammond, and Berry, *Effective Teacher Selection: From Recruitment to Retention.*

126. National Commission on Teaching and America's Future, *What Matters Most.*

127. HGSE News, *New Research Finds School Hiring and Support Practices Fall Short* (Harvard University, April 22, 2003).

128. Patrick M. Shields and others, *The Status of the Teaching Profession: Research Findings and Policy Recommendations. A Report to the Teaching and California's Future Task Force* (Santa Cruz: Center for the Future of Teaching and Learning, 1999).

129. Shields and others, *The Status of the Teaching Profession 2001,* p. 84.

130. Darling-Hammond, "Access to Quality Teaching: An Analysis of Inequality in California's Public Schools."

131. Susanna W. Pflaum and Theodore Abrahamson, "Teacher Assignment, Hiring and Preparation," *Urban Review,* vol. 22, no. 1 (1990), pp. 17–31; Phillip C. Schlechty, *Schools for the 21st Century: Leadership Imperatives for Educational Reform* (San Francisco: Jossey-Bass, 1990); Wise, Darling-Hammond, and Berry, *Effective Teacher Selection.*

132. California Assembly Select Committee on Low Performing Schools, *Testimony for the Select Committee, 2001* (Sacramento, 2001), p. 5.

133. See E. Bridges, "Evaluation for Tenure and Dismissal," in Jason Millman and Linda Darling-Hammond, eds., *Handbook of Teacher Evaluation* (Newbury Park, Calif.: Sage Publications, 1990); Clotfelter and others, "Do School Accountability Systems Make It More Difficult for Low Performing Schools to Attract and Retain High Quality Teachers?"

134. In fall 1999, Connecticut had 30 percent students of color and the twelfth largest Hispanic enrollment in the nation, and in 2002, 36 percent of students attended Title I schools. In the same years, North Carolina had 38 percent students of color, including the eighth largest enrollment of African Americans, and 38 percent of students attended Title I schools. See *Digest of Education Statistics, 2001* (NCES, U.S. Department of Education, 2002), table 42, and National Assessment of Educational Progress State Data, 2002 (www.nces.ed.gov/nationsreportcard/statedata).

135. Paul E. Barton, *Raising Achievement and Reducing Gaps: Reporting Progress toward Goals for Academic Achievement. A Report to the National Education Goals Panel* (Government Printing Office, 2001).

136. Joan Boykoff Baron, *Exploring High and Improving Reading Achievement in Connecticut* (Washington: National Educational Goals Panel, 1999).

137. Darling-Hammond, "Teacher Quality and Student Achievement," 2000; Suzanne M. Wilson, Linda Darling-Hammond, and Barnett Berry, *A Case of Successful Teaching Policy: Connecticut's Long-Term Efforts to Improve Teaching and Learning* (Seattle: Center for the Study of Teaching and Policy, 2001).

138. Carla Asher, *Improving Teaching in North Carolina: How School Design Intersects with School Reform* (Center for the Study of Teaching and Policy, forthcoming).

139. National Commission on Teaching and America's Future, *What Matters Most*.

140. Connecticut State Board of Education, *The Other Side of the Equation: Impact of the Teacher Standards Provisions of the Education Enhancement Act* (Hartford, 1992), p. 3.

141. National Education Goals Panel, *The National Education Goals Report: Building a Nation of Learners* (Government Printing Office, 1998).

142. Connecticut State Department of Education, *Impact of Education Enhancement Act, Research Bulletin, School Year 1990, No. 1* (Hartford, 1990).

143. Baron, *Exploring High and Improving Reading Achievement in Connecticut*, p. 28.

144. Elizabeth Hayes and Alison Gendar, "Pay Hike Lures Better-Qualified Teachers," *New York Daily News*, July 25, 2002, p. 10.

145. Richard F. Elmore and Deanna Burney, "Investing in Teacher Learning: Staff Development and Instructional Improvement," in Linda Darling-Hammond and Gary Sykes, eds., *Teaching as the Learning Profession: Handbook of Policy and Practice* (San Francisco: Jossey-Bass, 1999).

146. Jon Snyder, "New Haven Unified School District: A Teaching Quality System for Excellence and Equity," in Amy M. Hightower and others, eds., *School Districts and Instructional Renewal* (Teachers College Press, 2002).

147. Ken Futernick, "A District-by-District Analysis of the Distribution of Teachers in California and an Overview of the Teacher Qualification Index" (California State University, April 2001).

148. For details, see Snyder, "New Haven Unified School District."

149. Linda Darling-Hammond and others, "Building Instructional Quality: Inside-out, Bottom-up, and Top-down Perspectives on San Diego's School Reform (Center for the Study of Teaching and Policy, University of Washington, April 2002).

150. Wilson, Floden, and Ferrini-Mundy, *Teacher Preparation Research: Current Knowledge, Gaps, and Recommendations*, p. 30.

151. See appendix 7A for a brief history of federal involvement in medical manpower policy.

152. See appendix 7B for a brief history of federal involvement in the teacher labor market.

153. Although the Schools and Staffing Surveys (SASS) provide useful data for monitoring aspects of supply and demand, they have never been fully exploited for this purpose. Modifications to the questionnaires have made the data about training and certification too imprecise for some important analyses. Furthermore, the delay between surveys and the delay in releasing data to the public for outside analysis make them much less useful than they could be for monitoring supply trends. Although the SASS was intended to occur every three years, the delayed 1999–2000 survey came six years after the 1993–94 survey.

154. While Title I status is a key indicator, the Title I program fails to reach a large portion of students from poor families. Thus a national program of teacher scholarships ultimately should be tied to service targeted at the actual distribution of poor children, not to Title I school status alone.

155. Of the 250,000 teachers hired annually, about 50,000 enter without standard certification in their main teaching field. This overestimates the need, since many of these teachers are certified in some field, if not the one in which they are teaching, and some are in transition from one state to another or have been hired without yet taking the state licensing examinations, so they are only temporarily in the "not fully qualified" category.

If each of the 40,000 new teachers needed would receive $20,000, that would be enough to pay full tuition and some stipend in a public college or university for a one-year master's program in teaching for recent graduates or mid-career entrants—or enough for two to three full years of undergraduate tuition in a state university for juniors and seniors preparing to teach.

156. We are indebted to Susanna Loeb for suggesting this point and for elaborating it in several papers she has written with her colleagues.

157. For one example, see Anthony S. Bryk and Barbara L. Schneider, *Trust in Schools: A Core Resource for Improvement* (New York: Russell Sage Foundation, 2002).

158. Robert L. Linn and Carolyn Haug, "Stability of School-Building Accountability Scores and Gains," *Educational Evaluation and Policy Analysis*, vol. 24, no. 1 (2002), pp. 29–36.

159. Clotfelter and others, "Do School Accountability Systems Make It More Difficult for Low Performing Schools to Attract and Retain High Quality Teachers?"; David N. Figlio, *What Might School Accountability Do?* (Cambridge, Mass.: National Bureau of Economic Research, 2001); DeVise, "A-Plus Plan Prompts Teacher Exodus"; Barbara Benham Tye and Lisa O'Brien, "Why Are Experienced Teachers Leaving the Profession?" *Phi Delta Kappan,* vol. 84, no. 1 (2002), pp. 24–32.

160. This might include school improvement measures that rely on aggregated longitudinal scores for individual students, rather than annual cross-sectional estimates that can fluctuate from year to year for a variety of reasons unrelated to school practices; averages of these longitudinal score gains over multiple years; annual targets that are not statistically unreasonable; and multiple measures of school practice and performance that extend beyond test scores.

161. For example, see Phillip C. Schlechty and Victor S. Vance, "Recruitment, Selection, and Retention: The Shape of the Teaching Force," *Elementary School Journal,* vol. 83 (1983): 469–87; Carnegie Forum on Education and the Economy, *A Nation Prepared: Teachers for the Twenty-First Century* (Carnegie Corporation of New York, 1986).

8

Multiple "Choice" Questions: The Road Ahead

HENRY M. LEVIN

American federalism, as embodied in the Tenth Amendment to the Constitution, rests on the principle that the national government has limited powers and relegates all remaining authority to the states. In recent years this principle has raised many issues in education, an area where federal and state interests often overlap and sometimes conflict. Underlying the federalism concept is the idea of placing decisions closest to the social unit affected by them. This suggests that not only legislatures, school boards, and government agencies must be considered in education policymaking but families and children as well. In this respect, school choice is an extension of Tenth Amendment issues, because there is overlap, and potential conflict, between the interests of society and of families. This chapter explores how school choice figures in this complex interplay of educational policymaking.

School choice certainly is not new. Parents have long sought high-quality schools that are compatible with their values and their children's needs, typically as a central part of deciding where to live. Within the limits of financial resources, job opportunities, and other factors, they have chosen communities whose schools most closely match their preferences. Some parents have taken advantage of such public choice opportunities as magnet schools or open enrollment policies, while others have looked outside the public school system. About 10 percent to 15 percent historically have accepted the financial burden of enrolling their children in private schools with religious or educational purposes or more abundant resources. Others have taken on the task of home schooling.

What has distinguished choice in recent years, however, has been the use of newer options as strategies for education reform, especially for the disadvantaged. Charter schools, which are semiautonomous public schools, first emerged in 1992 and in a decade numbered at least 2,000. School vouchers—publicly funded certificates for private school tuition—were limited to a few modest efforts in the 1990s, but a 2002 Supreme Court ruling in their favor has triggered voucher legislation or constitutional initiatives in at least twenty states, and Congress has enacted a federal voucher program for Washington, D.C.[1] The No Child Left Behind Act of 2001 requires public school choice for students who are in schools that fail to meet certain standards for two years in a row, and it funds such things as tutoring and summer classes for those pupils in schools that fail for three consecutive years. This raises the prospect of Washington sometimes financing such services at private schools, a foot in the door for another kind of federal voucher.

The recent surge in demand for choice, not surprisingly, has been concentrated in cities with large populations of poor, minority, and immigrant students, where most of American's education problems reside. Schools serving these students have long suffered from weak academic performance, with little evidence of improvement under traditional governing structures. Some argue that the problem is insufficient funding, the poor quality of teachers, low expectations, or other factors. Others, however, see the trouble as largely bound up with political institutions and forces that will not yield to normal pressures for change.[2] Their main solution is to provide better alternatives for families, especially those who cannot afford existing choice options, and, in the process, to pressure traditional schools to improve.

Among advocates, then, school choice is lauded as promising improved education through competition, matching students to schools that best meet their needs, enhancing possibilities for student diversity, and providing a greater breadth of education offerings and experimentation. Among detractors, it is charged with undermining community and social cohesion, reducing student diversity, skimming off the best students from the most advantaged and motivated families, and leaving the most vulnerable pupils behind in worse circumstances. These are complex claims, and to judge them we need to understand the many dimensions of school choice. These include the long-standing tension between family preferences and society's needs, the striking array of choice mechanisms that most American families already enjoy, and the criteria by which each choice plan might best be analyzed. Then we can look at the future of school choice and possible roles for various levels of government.

A History of Tension

Although our public education system emerged from the nineteenth century "common" school movement, in many respects schools were hardly common. They had to be fashioned, after all, for families from different regions, races, ethnic and linguistic roots, religions, political beliefs, and economic means. In a free society, parents have the right to rear their children as they see fit, which suggests that they should be able to choose schools that best support their family preferences.

A democratic and capitalist society, however, also depends on schools to achieve essential common goals. One is to impart the knowledge, skills, and values required to participate in our political, economic, and social institutions. The other is to provide each generation with more equal opportunity, so that rewards are obtained by individual merit, not passed on, unearned, through parents' economic status or connections or other inherited privileges. Balancing family childrearing preferences with a common educational experience has long been a source of tension for public schools.

The traditional solution was to establish state education systems that permitted considerable local discretion. The political, religious, economic, ethnic, and racial status of the majority, or of powerful elites outside the majority, then determined local school practices and resources. How much was spent on education, for example, depended on local property taxes, which in turn depended on a community's wealth and its willingness to invest in schools.[3] Within communities, local school board decisions were predicated on the practices and beliefs of dominant groups.[4] And within schools students from different social classes often were placed in tracks that reflected their social status more than their educational abilities.[5] Historically, then, school districts and schools within states varied widely in education spending, religious practices, racial and sexual segregation, treatment of the handicapped, and educational opportunity generally. Common schools, supposedly preparing students for common social institutions, actually reflected "democratic localism," permitting the fiction of a common school for all amid a quite different reality.[6]

In the second half of the twentieth century, these practices came under assault. Successful challenges were initiated in state and federal courts on behalf of poor school districts, racial minorities, females, at-risk students, children with disabilities, and pupils with a limited command of English. Congress and state legislatures passed laws protecting these groups' rights and, in some cases, providing additional education resources for them. Religious practices were barred from schools in almost all forms. All of this pushed schools toward more uniform practices and reduced the advantages of families that could no longer get their children into higher tracks with better teachers or into schools with more resources or with religious orientations that supported their beliefs. Moreover, simply moving to other communities, a common practice for middle-class families in search of compatible schools, no longer provided the full range of opportunities that once had been available.[7]

By 1970 the success of legal and legislative strategies to achieve more equal educational opportunity and funding, along with more uniform school practices, led to rising pressures for increased choice and school differentiation, particularly among those who had lost privileges. If local political power and residential choice could no longer be relied on for schools that echoed the racial preferences, values, religious practices, or wealth of local residents, other alternatives would be sought. Initially these alternatives centered on ways to increase choice within the public schools. Thus the 1970s and 1980s were characterized by increased family options among public schools within a district or among districts.[8] Later, however, the persistent failure of inner-city reforms and funding to improve the education of disadvantaged children raised questions about whether existing schools were capable of success. By the 1990s, market-based alternatives emerged to create more school choice in general and to address the needs of poor, minority, and immigrant pupils. The result has been an intricate web of more than a dozen versions of school choice.

Multiple Choice Answers

There are two basic frameworks for these multiple choice plans: public choice approaches and private ones.[9] Public approaches include intradistrict choice, interdistrict choice, and charter schools. Private approaches include educational vouchers, tuition tax incentives, and home schooling. School choice through housing mobility has elements of public and private choice.

Public Choices

Public approaches involve choice plans created within existing arrangements for establishing and operating public schools. In the case of charter schools, there is some modification of these arrangements, though charter schools are still considered public schools.

CHOICE WITHIN DISTRICTS. The most common form of intradistrict choice is open enrollment, under which parents can enroll students in any school in the district that has openings. In another approach known as "controlled choice," parents are limited to options that will not increase racial segregation.[10] Beyond this, many urban districts have established magnet schools, particularly at the middle and high school levels.[11] As the name suggests, magnet schools are expected to attract students on the basis of academic specialization or themes. Many cities have magnet schools specializing in the sciences or arts. Others may focus on occupations, such as health or finance. Although these schools also offer classes in conventional subjects, they provide enriched opportunities in the areas of specialization. They may also apply a thematic focus to conventional subjects. For instance, a magnet school preparing health personnel may embed a study of health issues in social studies or English or tailor math and science courses to problems faced by health professionals, including, say, a course in epidemiology to convey an understanding of statistics and the spread of disease.

Magnet schools are by no means recent inventions; they were created in some school districts a century ago. Their growth in recent decades, however, has been heavily influenced by their use as an instrument for racial desegregation, particularly in large cities, where magnet schools can attract students from many neighborhoods. They have, in fact, shown some success in integrating student bodies as well as in raising student achievement.[12]

Finally, in many urban areas attempts have been made to break down the size of larger schools by creating "mini-schools" within buildings and letting parents and students choose the ones they prefer. Some cities have elementary schools of six to eight grades with 2,000 students, middle schools of two to three grades with 1,500 to 2,000 students, and high schools with 4,000 or more students. It is generally recognized that schools of this size are too large and impersonal and set a bureaucratic rather than an educational tone. By dividing them internally into smaller schools with fewer students, it is possible to create academic themes and provide choices within a given facility.[13] Although the smaller size advantages have been recognized in the literature, the choice possibilities have been less discussed.

CHOICE ACROSS DISTRICTS. A number of states permit students to attend schools in districts other than where they reside, again as long as there are openings. Minnesota has gone farthest in this direction. It allows students not only to enroll in other school districts but also to take courses in public institutions of higher education.[14] Many states have interdistrict choice programs that are somewhat more restricted. These include, among others, South Dakota, Michigan, Vermont, New Jersey, Oklahoma, Iowa, Georgia, and Massachusetts. Typical arrangements require districts to agree to participate by accepting students from other districts, but in some cases parents can enroll children in districts where they work. State funding is shifted from the initial district to the one where the child is enrolled.

CHARTER SCHOOLS. The most dynamic movement of public choice in the early twenty-first century is that of charter schools.[15] Launched in 1992, charter schools by mid-2001 numbered slightly under 2,000, though some charter advocates suggest that there are now nearly 2,700 charter schools teaching more than 650,000 pupils.[16]

The charter laws in thirty-nine states and the District of Columbia establish different criteria and chartering authorities for such schools, but they share a number of common characteristics beyond the fact that they are largely independent. Those wishing to launch charter schools must apply to chartering agencies, explaining their goals and how they intend to achieve them and presenting financing and governance plans. Each sponsoring state provides funds for the schools. Charter schools generally have great leeway in choosing curriculum, staff, and educational goals and are accountable in various ways, such as participating in state testing programs. Since charters, granted for limited periods, usually must be renewed every three to five years, their performance is reviewed periodically by chartering agencies.

Creators of charter schools can vary widely. Parents, community groups, educators, and nonprofit organizations can create them. It is assumed that charter schools' independence, in conjunction with their need to attract and retain students, will spur innovation and high quality. Some suggest that the ultimate result will be improved student achievement, greater parental involvement and satisfaction, and higher teacher empowerment, and that these will carry over to the other public schools that must compete with charter schools. Thus far, however, the evidence is mixed.[17]

Charter schools have been largely responsible for the emergence of a relatively new U.S. education phenomenon that has become an integral part of choice—educational management organizations, or EMOs. In some cases, EMOs have contracted with charter school boards to manage their schools. Establishing a charter school requires, among other things, finding a facility, teachers, equipment and instructional materials, training personnel and implementing a curriculum, and other educational services. Many charter school creators lack the capacity to do these things by themselves. The EMOs agree to operate the school under contract in exchange for a fee, usually based on a per student amount related to state funding.

Contracting between EMOs and charter schools has led to parallel arrangements in some districts to establish EMO contracts with public schools. By contracting directly with EMOs for specific schools, districts are able to expand choice options. Their obvious incentive is to maintain district enrollments to counter the lure of charter schools. Thus EMOs have been used to expand choice within districts as well as to play a role in managing charter schools. However, whether EMOs can be successful and profitable is still very much an open question.[18]

Private Choices

Private choice approaches include such market-based mechanisms as educational vouchers and tuition tax incentives as well as home schooling.

SCHOOL VOUCHERS. Educational vouchers are simply publicly funded certificates that parents can redeem at private schools to offset tuition expenses. The rationale for vouchers is not only that education quality is best promoted through market competition but also that schools should be removed from a system of democratic political control that makes it impossible for them to set and pursue straightforward educational goals. School vouchers were first proposed by conservative economist Milton Friedman almost half a century ago. They attracted little interest, however, until they were advanced as a solution for inner-city school problems. During the past two decades, pro-voucher constitutional initiatives have been proposed in several states, but they have yet to win voter support.[19] In the past decade, however, vouchers have been adopted legislatively in Cleveland, Milwaukee, and Florida and, more recently, in Colorado. In addition, a large number of voucher plans are supported by private funds,[20] and a few voucher experiments have tested whether a modest voucher for private schools would raise student achievement.[21]

Perhaps the most contentious voucher issue has been whether the Establishment Clause of the First Amendment to the Constitution prohibits the use of publicly funded vouchers at religiously affiliated schools. In June 2002 the U.S. Supreme Court, in *Zelman* v. *Simmons-Harris,* ruled that the Cleveland plan, in which almost all voucher students attend religious schools, did not violate the Establishment Clause. But this decision will not diminish the voucher controversy.[22]

As with other market mechanisms, voucher advocates contend that competition will provide incentives for increased educational quality and for schools to innovate. Opponents argue that vouchers will undermine equity and democratic education by balkanizing educational experiences and stratifying the population according to race, religion, political belief, and social class. There is little firm evidence at this time to support either side's views.[23]

TAX INCENTIVES. Tuition tax credits are the main tax incentive for enrolling children in private schools.[24] A tax credit reduces taxes owed by the amount of the credit. Thus a family could receive a tax credit of up to $1,000 for the tuition of each child enrolled at a private school, or a smaller amount if the tuition were less than $1,000. Some six states sponsor tuition tax credits, and advocates have been promoting them in many other states. Some states, such as Minnesota, also provide more modest tax deductions for educational expenses; deductions reduce taxable income, rather than actual taxes, by the amount of the deduction. In some states, such as Arizona, businesses or families can get a tax credit for contributing to a tuition fund rather than underwriting the tuition of an offspring.

Tuition tax credits generally have been set at modest levels, typically about $500 a year per child, a small fraction of tuition costs at even the least expensive independent schools. However, there is political pressure to raise the amount in those states that have adopted them. Tuition tax credits are attractive to political libertarians, who object to government intervention in education and see the tax credit as a simple transaction to reduce taxes for those using private schools. In contrast, they worry (for good reason) that educational vouchers are likely to result in closer government scrutiny and regulation of participating independent schools.[25]

HOME SCHOOLING. As the name suggests, with this approach all or part of a child's education is provided at home rather than at a school.[26] In some cases one or both parents serve as teachers; in others, families join together, with parents sharing teaching responsibilities. Curriculum materials are readily available for home schooling, with Internet sites increasingly providing this service. Many home schooling families have rejected both public and private schools because they find the education these provide incompatible with their religious, philosophical, political, or social values. Because such parents also are often suspicious of government data collection, comprehensive home schooling information is hard to obtain. Nevertheless, it appears that home schooling grew at a rapid rate in the 1990s—from about 300,000 students in 1990 to more than 800,000 in 1999.[27] A significant number of home schooling families also take advantage of public school offerings, including courses and athletic opportunities.

It should be evident from all of this that, contrary to complaints by choice advocates, there is no dearth of school choice. On the contrary, the options are substantial for most of the population. Recent estimates suggest that 60 percent to 70 percent of U.S. students are in situations where their families have a choice of schools.[28] One can see the magnitude of available choice by drawing from recent estimates.[29] Of nearly 54 million students expected to enroll in elementary and secondary schools in the autumn of 2002, about 60 percent were expected to attend schools of choice, as follows:

—36 percent through residential location;

—10 percent through tuition-paid private schools;

—10 percent through intradistrict options (for example, magnet schools, open enrollment);

—2 percent through home schooling;

—About 1 percent through charter schools;

—Less than 1 percent through interdistrict options; and

—Less than 0.1 percent through public or private vouchers.

These choices reflect various constraints, particularly the limited number of charter schools, voucher opportunities, and interdistrict options. Participation in such alternatives would likely expand if they were more widely available. Furthermore, the most important source of choice, residential location, is highly restricted according to income and racial segregation. That is why the poor, minorities, and immigrants have the least access to choice and why they are most often the focus of school reforms based on choice.

Multiple Choice Questions

With school choice encompassing so many designs, the logical question is which ones do or do not work? That depends, however, on what one means by "work," since there are multiple ways of judging. To deal with this challenge, an evaluation framework was developed at the National Center for the Study of Privatization in Education,[30] and it has proved useful in assessing choice arrangements according to the four major goals surrounding them:

Freedom to choose. At the heart of choice alternatives is the ability of families to select schools that emulate their educational philosophies, religious beliefs, political outlooks, or other childrearing preferences.

Productive efficiency. A common claim for school choice is that it will improve school efficiency and effectiveness by producing better educational results for any given outlay of resources. This contention is based on the view that competition for students will create strong incentives not only to meet student needs but also to improve educational productivity.[31]

Equity. A universal goal of American schools is to provide equal educational opportunity. Choice advocates argue that the ability to choose schools will generate better options for students who are locked into inferior neighborhood schools and that a competitive marketplace will provide incentives for all schools to improve. Detractors argue that more advantaged families are the main beneficiaries of school choice because of their superior information resources and access to transportation. They also assert that school choice further segregates the poor and the disenfranchised because those with power and status tend to choose schools with students from similar backgrounds.

Social cohesion. Our republic, as noted, requires citizens to master the skills and knowledge needed for civic and economic participation. This usually is interpreted as requiring a common school experience with regard to curriculum content and teaching of values, language, and knowledge of democratic institutions. Some have argued that it requires mastery of a shared knowledge base.[32] School choice critics worry that increased choice will erode social cohesion by balkanizing schools, their populations, and the content and values imparted to them.

It should be evident from the wide differences among these goals that designing and evaluating choice plans is a complicated chore. Unfortunately, even rigorous evaluations of school choice plans often are limited to a single dimension, such as student achievement (a productive efficiency measure) or racial composition of enrollments (equity and social cohesion measures), while other important goals are ignored. Such evaluations tell us little. A comprehensive evaluation strategy that includes all four goals is essential for policy decisions.[33]

A further cause of complexity in assessing choice plans is that even those in the same category often differ in important respects. Voucher arrangements, for example, range from pure free-market approaches to plans providing vouchers only for children in failing schools to others for all inner-city students—and there are additional differences among them. Similarly, in the thirty-six states and District of Columbia where charter schools operate, financial arrangements for the schools, criteria for approving charters, and monitoring of schools vary widely. The differences in details among such plans can lead to contradictory educational outcomes even within the same type of choice options.

To a large degree, these outcomes can be projected by applying three policy tools to the design or analysis of a school choice plan: finance, regulation, and support services. The applications of these policy tools largely determine the effect of the choice arrangement on freedom of choice, productive efficiency, equity, and social cohesion. Consider some examples:

Finance. All school choice arrangements can be analyzed in terms of their funding levels. Meager financing obviously promises to stimulate fewer meaningful alternatives than generous financing. Funding levels for charter schools and vouchers, for example, will determine how many schools seek to participate and the quality of services they can provide. Magnet schools often get more money than neighborhood schools, allowing them to provide a richer set of options to attract students. Such extra funding must be taken into account when judging productive efficiency. Their academic results, in other words, cannot simply be compared with nonchoice schools funded at lower levels. In some cases, charter schools are funded generously compared with funding of conventional public schools. In other case, they are shortchanged, particularly on funds for facilities. In still other cases, charter schools have access to far greater philanthropic contributions than public schools.

Similarly, voucher plans have different funding levels. Some call for a flat and modest voucher, with parents permitted to put up additional sums. Others call for larger vouchers and extra funding for those with greater education needs. Each plan has different consequences for equity and productive efficiency, and school choice evaluations must consider specific finance provisions in addressing a plan's consequences.[34]

Regulation. All school choice plans have regulations that set out requirements for schools and students. For example, many states permit interdistrict choice only if there is space in a receiving school or district. Other rules affect whether funding from the home district is transferred to the receiving district. More typical choice regulations for schools address admission eligibility, curriculum, information, and testing requirements. Such rules are important, moreover, only to the degree that they are carefully monitored and enforced. Not all states with strong regulations have rigorous monitoring and enforcement regimes. Some lightly regulate charter schools; others set stringent requirements. With vouchers, some plans set extensive regulations on the eligibility of families and schools. For example, the Cleveland and Milwaukee plans focus on students from low-income families. Cleveland requires testing of voucher students; Milwaukee does not. Both, moreover, allow some discretion in admissions, and both permit religious institutions to participate. The strength of a choice plan's regulations and enforcement greatly influences its impact.

Support services. If funding and regulations alter the nature and results of choice plans, support services determine their accessibility. Gaining access to school options requires knowledge of their availability and offerings as well as the transportation to take advantage of a specific choice. If families are unaware of the schools and their features or do not have suitable transportation, they will not consider enrolling their children.

Support services can vary from the elaborate to the nonexistent. For example, schools may be required to make extensive information available to families eligible to choose schools. Counselors may be employed to help parents sift through the information. Parent meetings, with presentations, can be arranged in affected neighborhoods, or fairs can be held, with schools making their own presentations. For parents with access to computers who are familiar with the Internet, websites can be created, searchable according to location, size, curriculum, philosophy, teacher characteristics, test results, and other salient features of choice schools.[35]

Obviously, transportation also is vital. With magnet schools, education authorities usually provide transportation. This is not the case, however, with charter schools; charter families typically must provide their own transportation. In the few urban areas with good public transportation, access to school choices may not require special arrangements, at least for older children. Transportation is rarely provided for interdistrict choice unless it is part of an organized effort to reduce racial segregation. However, to the degree that parents commute to other school districts for work, they may readily provide their own transportation. In the absence of information and transportation, school choice will be relatively uninformed and limited.

An Example: Varied Effects of Vouchers

To understand the consequences of any plan, it is necessary to study the plan's details. Four different educational voucher plans—a free-market approach, a compensatory-market approach, a failing-school approach, and an inner-city plan—illustrate how diverse combinations of features can create large differences in what seems to be the same choice mechanism.

Free-Market Approach

The classic free-market approach to vouchers is that of Milton Friedman.[36] Friedman recommended a modest voucher from public funds for each student. Parents could add private spending at their discretion. Schools could set their own tuition on the basis of the program they wished to provide and the clientele they wished to attract. Students who were limited to the public voucher would receive a minimal education, but those with wealthier parents could purchase a higher-quality education. Regulation would be minimal, and there would be no provision for transportation or information. This would promote a large choice of schools at different tuition levels, with few restrictions on schools that enter the market. Equity would be undermined by the fact that spending on a child's education and on transportation access would be heavily determined by parental income, and social cohesion would be weakened by a lack of common educational content among schools with diverse philosophies and curricula. Of the four educational goals, the free-market approach stresses *freedom of choice* and *productive efficiency* through competition at the expense of equity and social cohesion.

Compensatory-Market Approach

The best example of a compensatory market approach is the design constructed by Christopher Jencks and associates in anticipation of a voucher experiment for the U.S. Office of Economic Opportunity in the early 1970s.[37] That plan stressed *social cohesion* and *equity* at the expense of freedom of choice and productive efficiency by establishing a variety of regulations and support services. It called for regulating admissions and curriculum and requiring standardized testing and reporting of results. It also included larger vouchers for the poor—so-called compensatory vouchers—a system of transportation and information and a prohibition against adding private funds to the voucher. The regulations and the fixed government voucher for each child according to need, with no private augmentation, would reduce freedom of choice relative to the Friedman plan. The high cost of providing transportation and information and monitoring regulations for eligible schools would add considerably to costs and reduce productive efficiency.[38] But larger vouchers for the poor, regulations on admissions and information, and transportation services would increase *equity*. The common curriculum and testing requirements would support *social cohesion*.

Failing-Schools Approach

This strategy provides vouchers for students whose schools have persistently failed to improve academically. For several years, for example, Florida has empowered students in failing schools to attend other public schools or to receive a voucher of about $4,000 to attend a private school. Until this year, few schools met the failure criterion, so there has been little experience with the plan. The Florida provisions, as well as a Pennsylvania tutoring program for struggling students, influenced the federal No Child Left Behind Act of 2001, which provides federal compensatory funds to pay for supplemental services for students in persistently failing schools.[39]

Failing-school vouchers clearly expand *freedom of choice* for students eligible to receive them, and it may stimulate higher *productive efficiency* among public schools that fear the loss of students. To the degree that it provides better options for students who are the worst off educationally, it is likely to improve *equity*. However, the lack of a common experience when students are permitted to select among diverse options does not augur well for social cohesion.

Inner-City Vouchers

Inner-city students are widely viewed as suffering from the worst schools in America. Such students typically are from poorer families who cannot afford private schools. High proportions are from immigrant and minority families, and their schools are heavily segregated by income and race. The underlying motive behind inner-city vouchers is to provide private school choice to students with the fewest options and the poorest educational opportunities. Both the Milwaukee[40] and Cleveland[41] plans provide vouchers to low-income, inner-city students, worth up to $2,250 in Cleveland and almost $6,000 in Milwaukee. Private schools that meet state requirements, including religious schools, are eligible to participate. Regulations are minimal, with no required curriculum. Testing and reporting of the results are required in Cleveland but not in Milwaukee. Schools have great leeway in deciding whom to admit, although they must not discriminate by race, ethnicity, or sex. Transportation is provided at public expense, as are some information resources.

The inner-city voucher plan is designed to increase *freedom of choice* for those who lack it and to increase *equity* by limiting the additional choice to the inner city's low-income and minority families. Because of the high cost of support services, especially small-scale transportation modes, its effects on productive efficiency are more ambiguous. However, public costs are reduced in Cleveland by the lower-value voucher, inducing students to attend low-cost and highly subsidized religious schools. Given the lack of any attempt to create a common experience for students, social cohesion seems to be a low priority in both cities, though Cleveland's testing does provide some commonality in outcomes.

One could just as easily apply these measures to charter schools across the nation, which also have widely different approaches to finance, regulation, and support services. On funding, for example, some states provide meager support, others generous assistance. On admissions, some let charter schools accept any students, while others have selection rules. On curriculum, teacher qualifications, teacher unionization, testing procedures, and reporting of test results, charter school regulations also differ widely, as do their support services. What the analysis would show for charter schools as for vouchers—and, indeed, for all choice plans—is that no strategy can possibly maximize outcomes for all four goals. While some designs would improve results along more than one criterion, almost all would also reduce results on others. Providing information and transportation, for example, would improve choice for all participants and especially for the poor. But it also would raise costs, probably reducing productive efficiency (unless gains from competition resulting from the better information and access were to offset the transportation and information costs). Adoption of regulations that are strenuously monitored and enforced could increase equity and social cohesion, but at the sacrifice of freedom of choice and productive efficiency.

Ultimately, then, much of the debate over details of school choice plans revolves around the political power and preferences of the stakeholders. Those who value freedom of choice above all probably would willingly sacrifice some equity and social cohesion, eschewing regulations and support services and allowing parental add-ons to vouchers. Conversely, those who most value social cohesion probably would willingly sacrifice some freedom of choice by requiring a common core curriculum or other standardized features.

It is an understatement to say that choice advocates may agree on the general case for choice but disagree profoundly on specifics. Strong differences occur even among people in the same general political category. Thus many political liberals who are preoccupied with equity want to see greater freedom of choice for inner-city students through vouchers, even though liberals usually are antagonistic to marketplace solutions for public services. At the same time, cultural conservatives favor a common curriculum and knowledge framework, a substantial commitment to a uniform mandate on school content.[42] Conservatives with libertarian views reject regulatory requirements entirely in favor of market accountability through consumer or client judgments.

How Achievable Is Each Goal?

Besides whatever preferences they may have for some goals over others, policymakers need to understand how achievable each goal might be. Because there are so many approaches to school choice and so many variations within each approach, generalizations about effectiveness are difficult. Nevertheless, we can examine the evidence available so far.

Unsurprising Effects of Freedom of Choice

As would be expected, the most positive evidence of effectiveness for school choice is that, by definition, it increases freedom of choice. Families who take advantage of choice opportunities report greater satisfaction with their schools than comparable nonchoice families.[43] This, too, is unsurprising, since parents who exercise choice generally are those who are unhappy with their children's current schools. The evidence on choice and family satisfaction is consistent. For example, among parent applicants who were randomly assigned to receiving or not receiving vouchers for private schools, those who received and used the vouchers reported higher school satisfaction.[44] Surveys of parents who participated in open enrollment, alternative schools, and charter schools in Minnesota also conclude that satisfaction with these choices was high.[45] Evaluations of satisfaction among charter school parents show similar results.[46]

Cloudy Results on Productive Efficiency

Whether school choice improves productive efficiency is far more controversial. Most studies addressing this question ignore costs, examining only results. Since productive efficiency measures effectiveness relative to cost, those studies do not tell us much. Studies of cost, moreover, are few and examine such factors as private school tuition or public school operating costs based on school accounting procedures, two highly incomplete and misleading cost measures.[47]

The matter is complicated by the common view that all schools should be compared on the basis of the same criteria, particularly student achievement. Those with higher student achievement for a given set of students and school resources are deemed to have higher productive efficiency. But one aim of school choice is to let parents and student choose schools with goals that more closely match their preferences. By definition, then, school choice is meaningful only if there are distinctive choices. This means that productive efficiency cannot be appropriately measured according to a single school objective. Indeed, political libertarians would conclude that schools that prosper are viewed as productively efficient and those that founder are not.

Three Kinds of Achievement Studies

This, however, has not stopped those concerned with evaluating school choice as a reform strategy from being preoccupied with test results. In fact, three different types of studies have been initiated to address whether school choice improves student achievement, with a special focus on children of low-income and minority families.

The first type compares public and private school achievement after attempting to control statistically for differences in student characteristics. A summary of these studies suggests that private schools show slightly better results, perhaps placing students in the fifty-third percentile, compared with similar public school students in the fiftieth percentile.[48] A related type of study examines competition in all forms and its effects on student achievement. The forms of competition include the numbers of school districts, numbers of schools, and private school opportunities available in a given region. One of the studies found a slight achievement advantage associated with competition, in the range previously found for private schools.[49] None of the studies reviewed, however, considers the expense of creating more competition or its cost effectiveness. These studies look indirectly at the effectiveness side of the equation (devoid of cost analysis) to infer the impact of school choice on achievement.

A second type of study compares the academic effectiveness of specific types of choice arrangements, such as magnet schools or charter schools. Typically, such studies attempt to compare the achievement of the choice schools with nonchoice schools with similar enrollments, rarely controlling for differences in school resources. The results have been ambiguous and contentious. For example, a California study found that California charter schools serving low-income students slightly exceeded the achievement of comparable public schools that provided no choice.[50] However, a reanalysis of that study found data and methodological errors, which, when corrected, showed nonchoice schools to be slightly superior to charter schools.[51] A Brookings Institution study of charter schools in six states showed poorer achievement in charter schools, as did a study of Michigan charter schools.[52] The general consensus is that we do not have definitive comparisons of charter schools and nonchoice schools, both for methodological reasons and because charter schools are a relatively recent phenomenon.[53]

Comparisons of educational vouchers in Milwaukee and Cleveland have led to some controversy over their effectiveness. In Milwaukee, the results vary from no effect to an effect for mathematics but not reading to an effect for both mathematics and reading.[54] In Cleveland the most recent results appear to show little or no advantage for voucher students.[55] A study of the national system of vouchers in Chile, where school vouchers have been employed for more than two decades, also shows little effect on student achievement.[56]

The third approach to measuring achievement in choice schools is the randomized field trial. Harvard University professor Paul Peterson and his colleagues randomly assigned educational vouchers among a group of voucher applicants, forming a group of voucher recipients and a similar control group.[57] A voucher of about $1,400 a year was applied mainly to tuition at low-cost Catholic schools for up to three years. While this methodology was a big step forward in evaluating effectiveness, it was beset with many challenges.[58] Among the three settings studied, New York, Washington, D.C., and Dayton, Ohio, no overall achievement advantages were found for educational vouchers after three years.[59] However, an achievement advantage was found for African Americans in New York, though not for the overall voucher group in that city or for other subgroups such as Hispanics. The advantage for African Americans was shaky, however, when methodological errors were corrected in a reanalysis.[60]

In sum, the data on productive efficiency are ambiguous at best and suggest more questions than answers. By omitting costs of school choice systems compared with those of existing systems and limiting measures to student achievement, the studies are seriously incomplete.[61] Beyond this are other problems: the studies' methodologies are not necessarily adequate to resolve the issues at hand, and all are limited to small-scale choice programs and thus cannot tell us what might happen if the approaches were greatly expanded.[62]

Equity Can Go Both Ways

Equity, or fairness in access to any school choice benefits, is commonly raised in advocating or questioning school choice. As previously noted, however, evidence on equity is hard to address without details of the choice scheme contemplated. Which part of the population is eligible for the plan? What types of information and transportation are available to eligible choosers? Which portion of the eligible population takes advantage of choice? What happens to those who do not?

Without such information, little can be said about equity effects. In general, it is known that persons with lower education and income are less likely to take advantage of school choice, in part because of a lack of information and transportation. Those with greater economic and educational resources are most likely to choose among available options.[63] Hence universal choice schemes tend to skim more advantaged students from underperforming schools, leaving behind those who are less advantaged. There is substantial evidence that the quality of student peers affects the achievement of other students.[64]

Choice programs without restrictions also tend to increase racial segregation among both public schools and through private school enrollments.[65] Though potential choosers indicate that they select other schools solely for their academic records and teachers, it appears that race and social class are important indicators of choice for magnet schools[66] and charter schools.[67] For this reason, some school districts have established systems of controlled choice, limiting families to selecting open-enrollment schools or magnet schools where their choices do not contribute to segregation.[68]

In summary, according to a variety of measures and studies, unfettered choice promises to have negative consequences for equity. As a result, many choice strategies limit eligibility to students from failing schools or poverty backgrounds or restrict choices that would increase racial segregation. Choice plans may also restrict the ability of schools to reject applicants or require a lottery for choosing students among applicants.

Little Evidence on Social Cohesion

Among the four criteria for judging school choice plans, social cohesion is the one with the least evidence. In part, this is because there is no agreement on how to measure the integration of students into democratic institutions and their commitment to civic participation. The usual approach is to survey student attitudes, but, as widely recognized, respondents often give "socially desirable" answers to such politically sensitive questions. For example, one study found that while potential choosers say that they stress school and teacher quality in picking a school, student race and social class seem to be the leading criteria actually used for selecting schools.[69]

Recent studies on civic education and behavior that might reflect on social cohesion also are inconclusive. One study, for example, found that some private schools are as effective as or superior to public schools in teaching democratic norms and political tolerance but that others are less effective.[70] Understandably, some observers fear that unfettered choice would largely eliminate the common experience sought in public schools as ideology, religion, politics, and educational philosophy become the dominant determinants of teaching and curriculum. Of course, regulation of curriculum, testing, and admissions could reduce these differences, but they also would reduce choice.

What Might Lie Ahead

At least two school choice developments on the horizon bear watching. One is what happens under the No Child Left Behind Act (NCLB), the other the consequences of the Supreme Court ruling in the Cleveland voucher case. Both promise to create additional rhetoric and pressure for public and private choice—but other factors are likely to limit the actual effects.

NCLB Choice: No Powerful Lever

NCLB, of course, requires states to monitor progress on both math and reading (and then science) tests in grades 3–8 and narrow the gap between advantaged and disadvantaged students. All students are expected to reach proficiency in core subjects by the 2013–14 school year. One of the principal mechanisms for reaching these goals is supposed to be school choice. If a school fails to meet requirements for "adequate yearly progress" for two consecutive years, the district must offer students in the school the option of transferring to a higher-performing school, and the district is required to provide transportation to the new school. If a school fails to meet requirements for "adequate yearly progress" for three consecutive years, the district must allow students in the school to use Title I funds to obtain supplemental education services from public or private providers.

Thus NCLB represents the first significant use of federal funds to pro-mote choice among public schools, including charter schools, and private alternatives. To the degree that students in persistently failing schools use the Title I allocation (the allocation varies according to state distribution, but it generally comes to about $1,000 per student), the act effectively will provide federally funded vouchers for private educational services as well as public choice.

In the fall of 2002 the choice implications had yet to be felt much, because to shift students from failing schools to better public schools requires space in receiving schools. Because of recent enrollment increases in many parts of the nation and widespread budget strains, most school sys-tems do not have excess space, especially in their best schools. In New York City, for example, students in 331 failing schools (of about 1,100 overall) were eligible to transfer in the fall of 2002. The district sent letters with this information to 280,000 households. But only 3,600 students applied, and 1,500 were placed in other schools. The meager initial response by fami-lies, the relatively small number of available spaces, and the distance between failing schools and available places substantially limited the school choice option and its use as a sanction for failing schools. Although it is likely that more families will apply over time and that more spaces will open up, it seems that school choice may not be the powerful level for reform anticipated by the act's authors.

Vouchers: No Rapid Spread

In *Zelman*, the Supreme Court handed down a relatively narrow ruling, holding that the Cleveland Voucher Program, or CVP, did not violate the Establishment Clause of the First Amendment to the Constitution. In that program, public school students receive vouchers of up to $2,250, usable at any private school that will accept them. In fact, however, almost the only private schools with tuition levels that low are religious schools, which usually are highly subsidized by parent churches. Consequently, almost all of the students in the state-sponsored program were attending religious schools. By a slim 5-to-4 majority, the High Court held that the CVP "is a program of true private choice . . . neutral in all respects towards religion. It is part of a general and multifaceted undertaking by the State of Ohio to provide educational opportunities to the children of a failed school district," where charter schools and magnet schools also are available.

The decision, of course, does not require states to take any action. Indeed, many state constitutions forbid state aid to religious institutions, with a number containing considerably stronger prohibitions than the First Amendment's. According to one study, only nineteen state constitutions could accommodate the Supreme Court ruling; fifteen state constitutions place heavy restrictions on voucher programs, with the others in between.[71] Accordingly, if advocates seek to establish voucher systems that include religious schools (which account for about 75 percent of all private schools nationally), they will have to confront the constitutions of many states. In some cases the adoption of vouchers will first require constitutional changes entailing popular referendums or constitutional conventions—major obstacles to constitutional modification. Indeed, constitutional initiatives to adopt vouchers failed—by margins of more than 2 to 1—in both California and Michigan in 2000. In other states there promise to be direct legal challenges to state constitutions, as in Colorado, where state leaders recently enacted a voucher law for low-income students that has been rejected by the court. In light of the difficulty of mustering political support in many states, of constitutional opposition, and of the availability of other choice alternatives, rapid adoption of voucher plans should not be expected in the near future.

Who Is Responsible?

The entanglement of federal, state, and local responsibility should be eminently clear. Washington's NCLB choice provisions, for example, essentially are modeled on Florida's "failing-schools" versions of choice and are mainly intended to help expand educational choice in weak urban school systems. A local voucher program for Cleveland, sponsored by the state, led to a U.S. Supreme Court decision that advocates are using in their efforts to modify state constitutions and laws and spread more state and local voucher programs. It is impossible in such circumstances to say that any one level of government is "in charge" of school choice. It might be useful, however, to examine, at least briefly, federal, state, and local roles according to our four criteria. Freedom of choice, productive efficiency, equity, and social cohesion are important to all levels of society and their governing institutions, implying a shared responsibility. However, some would seem more central at higher levels and others at lower levels.

Freedom of choice seems particularly important at the state and local levels. Providing adequate funding for choice schools and regulatory provisions that permit diversity are necessary to ensure a healthy supply of school options at these levels. Provision of information, transportation, and nonrestrictive admission policies are important prerequisites for obtaining access to the available supply.

Productive efficiency is also mainly a responsibility of states and local educational entities. Market rivalries would be greater if they produce more competitors and a larger supply of schools. Information and transportation would increase competition too by making families aware of options and raising access and demand for choice schools. State and local governments need to monitor the market to ensure that schools meet at least minimal requirements for fiscal stability and capable management. This type of due diligence is necessary to ensure that schools are capable of providing educational programs and that they do not disrupt learning by closing in the middle of a school year.

Equity is important for national and state governments. Both need to enforce laws on racial, gender, and economic equity in education and to contribute financially to help state and local governments to make that objective a reality. The equity goal also requires federal and state governments to monitor choice schools that receive public monies to ensure equity.

Social cohesion is also associated more fully with national and state governments because of its implications for citizen preparation and participation, though local civic behavior is also at stake. Curriculum, testing, and desegregation are typical responses to ensuring that students are prepared for their civic responsibilities. In our current education system, the states will need to address these domains and determine the regulation and monitoring required, without treading too heavily on freedom of choice.

Of the four criteria, however, the nation's principal focus now is on productive efficiency and equity, especially as measured by test scores and reducing achievement gaps among different ethnic and income groups. These may be worthy goals, but they may also undermine meaningful choice as all schools are judged on the basis of a limited set of official performance measures. Centralizing the governance and monitoring of schools and imposing curriculum and testing standards and sanctions are at the heart of state and federal policies being pressed on local school systems today. While lip service is given to choice, centralized standards are designed to limit choice, not enhance it. If all schools are evaluated on narrow performance measures and subject to sanctions for not meeting such standards, schools will become more and more compliant with those restrictions, even within a framework that ostensibly promotes the virtues of choice. Surely the chief objectives of No Child Left Behind and state regulations that reward or punish schools and students according to test scores result in pressure for uniformity among all schools. The greater the pressure to get all schools to conform to the standards criteria, the less salient will be the promise of meaningful choice among schools. Thus despite the expansive political rhetoric of school choice movements, the underlying momentum is in the opposite direction.

Notes

1. Spencer S. Hsu and Justin Blum, "D.C. School Vouchers Win Final Approval," *Washington Post,* January 23, 2004, p. A1.

2. John E. Chubb and Terry M. Moe, *Politics, Markets, and America's Schools* (Brookings, 1990).

3. John E. Coons, William H. Clune III, and Stephen D. Sugarman, *Private Wealth and Public Education* (Harvard University Press, 1970).

4. Michael B. Katz, *Class, Bureaucracy and Schools: The Illusion of Educational Change in America* (Praeger, 1971).

5. Jennie Oakes, *Keeping Track: How Schools Structure Inequality* (Yale University Press, 1985).

6. Katz, *Class, Bureaucracy and Schools.*

7. Charles M. Tiebout, "A Pure Theory of Local Expenditures," *Journal of Political Economy,* vol. 64 (1956), pp. 416–24.

8. William H. Clune and John F. Witte, eds., *Choice and Control in American Education* (Falmer Press, 1990).

9. Henry M. Levin, "The Economics of Educational Choice," *Economics of Education Review,* vol. 10, no. 2 (1991), pp. 137–58.

10. Amy Stuart Wells and Robert Crain, "Controlled Choice and Racial Diversity," presented at the conference on School Choice and Racial Diversity, National Center for the Study of Privatization in Education, Teachers College, Columbia University, May 22, 2000 (to be published in Janelle T. Scott, ed., *School Choice and Student Diversity: Examining the Evidence* [Teachers College Press, forthcoming]).

11. Claire Smrekar and Ellen Goldring, "Social Class Isolation and Racial Diversity in Magnet Schools," presented at the conference on School Choice and Racial Diversity, National Center for the Study of Privatization in Education, Teachers College, Columbia University, May 22, 2000 (to be published in Janelle T. Scott, ed., *School Choice and Student Diversity: Examining the Evidence* [Teachers College Press, forthcoming]).

12. Adam Gamoran, "Student Achievement in Public Magnet, Public Comprehensive, and Private City High Schools," *Educational Evaluation and Policy Analysis,* vol. 18, no. 1 (Spring 1996), pp. 1–18.

13. Michelle Fine, ed., *Chartering Urban School Reform* (Teachers College Press, 1994).

14. William Lowe Boyd, Debra Hare, and Joe Nathan, *What Really Happened? Minnesota's Experience with Statewide Public School Choice Programs* (Center for School Change, Hubert H. Humphrey Institute of Public Affairs, University of Minnesota, May 2002).

15. Peter Cookson Jr. and Kristina Berger, *Expect Miracles: Charter Schools and the Politics of Hope and Despair* (Boulder, Colo.: Westview Press, 2002); Chester E. Finn, Bruno V. Manno, and Gregg Vanourek, *Charter Schools in Action: Renewing Public Education* (Princeton University Press, 2000); Gary Miron and Christopher Nelson, *What's Public about Charter Schools?* (Thousand Oaks, Calif.: Corwin Press, 2002); Joseph Murphy and Catherine Dunn Shiffman, *Understanding and Assessing the Charter School Movement* (Teachers College Press, 2002); RPP International, *A National Study of Charter Schools: Third-Year Report* (Office of Educational Research and Improvement, U.S. Department of Education, 1999).

16. A national evaluation carried out for the U.S. Department of Education in the summer of 2001 found fewer than 2,000 charter schools in operation. See Lee Anderson and others, *A Decade of Public Charter Schools: Evaluation of the Public Charter Schools Program, 2000–2001 Evaluation Report,* report prepared for the U.S. Department of Education under contract no. EA 98-CO-0074 (Menlo Park, Calif.: SRI International, 2002). The Center for Education Reform, which strongly supports charter schools, suggested the higher numbers for the 2002–03 school year.

17. For example, compare Finn, Manno, and Vanourek (*Charter Schools in Action*) with Miron and Nelson (*What's Public about Charter Schools?*).

18. Henry M. Levin, "The Potential of For-Profit Schools for Educational Reform," Paper 47 (National Center for the Study of Privatization in Education, Teachers College, Columbia University, 2002).

19. Terry M. Moe, *Schools, Vouchers, and the American Public* (Brookings, 2001).

20. Terry M. Moe, *Private Vouchers* (Hoover Institution Press, 1995).

21. William G. Howell and Paul Peterson, with Patrick Wolf and David Campbell, *The Education Gap: Vouchers and Urban Schools* (Brookings, 2002).

22. Henry M. Levin, "A Comprehensive Framework for Evaluating Educational Vouchers," *Educational Evaluation and Policy Analysis,* vol. 24, no. 3 (Fall 2002), pp. 159–74; R. Kenneth Godwin and Frank R. Kemerer, *School Choice Tradeoffs: Liberty, Equity, and Diversity* (University of Texas Press, 2002).

23. Brian Gill and others, *Rhetoric versus Reality: What We Know and What We Need to Know about Vouchers and Charter Schools* (Santa Monica, Calif.: RAND, 2001).

24. Clive Belfield, "Tuition Tax Credits: What Do We Know So Far?" Occasional Paper 33 (National Center for the Study of Privatization in Education, Teachers College, Columbia University, 2001).

25. Dennis J. Encarnation, "Public Finance and Regulation of Nonpublic Education: Retrospect and Prospect," in Thomas James and Henry M. Levin, eds., *Public Dollars for Private Schools* (Temple University Press, 1983), pp. 175–95.

26. Patricia Lines, "Home Schooling Comes of Age," *Public Interest,* no. 140 (2000), pp. 74–85.

27. Patricia Lines, *Support for Home-Based Study* (ERIC Clearinghouse on Educational Management, University of Oregon, 2003).

28. Jeffrey R. Henig and Stephen D. Sugarman, "The Nature and Extent of School Choice," in Stephen D. Sugarman and Frank R. Kemerer, eds., *School Choice and Social Controversy: Politics, Policy, and Law* (Brookings, 1999), pp. 13–35; Caroline M. Hoxby, "How School Choice Affects the Achievement of Public School Students," in Paul T. Hill, ed., *Choice with Equity* (Hoover Institution Press, 2002), pp. 141–78.

29. Henig and Sugarman, "The Nature and Extent of School Choice."

30. Levin, "A Comprehensive Framework for Evaluating Educational Vouchers."

31. Hoxby, "How School Choice Affects the Achievement of Public School Students."

32. E. D. Hirsch Jr., *Cultural Literacy: What Every American Needs to Know* (Houghton-Mifflin, 1987).

33. Levin, "A Comprehensive Framework for Evaluating Educational Vouchers."

34. Center for the Study of Public Policy, *Educational Vouchers: Report Prepared for the U.S. Office of Economic Opportunity* (Cambridge, Mass., 1970). This report recommends larger vouchers for the poor to provide them with better educational resources and to make such students more attractive to competing schools. But if the reputation and attractiveness of a school is positively related to the socioeconomic backgrounds of its students, even an additional amount for a lower socioeconomic student may not compensate for a loss of school prestige and attractiveness by taking such students.

35. Mark Schneider and Jack Buckley, "What Do Parents Want from Schools? Evidence from the Internet," *Educational Evaluation and Policy Analysis*, vol. 24, no. 2 (2002), pp. 133–43.

36. Milton Friedman, "The Role of Government in Education," in *Capitalism and Freedom* (University of Chicago Press, 1962).

37. Center for the Study of Public Policy, 1970.

38. Henry M. Levin and Cyrus E. Driver, "Costs of an Educational Voucher System," *Educational Economics*, vol. 5, no. 3 (1997), pp. 265–83.

39. Bess Keller, "Pa. OKs Private-Tutoring Grants to Parents," *Education Week*, May 16, 2001, pp. 1, 25.

40. John F. Witte, *The Market Approach to Education* (Princeton University Press, 2000).

41. Kim K. Metcalf, *Evaluation of the Cleveland Scholarship Program: Summary Report, 1998–2000* (Bloomington: Indiana Center for Evaluation, Indiana University, 2001).

42. William J. Bennett, *James Madison High School: A Curriculum for American Students* (U.S. Department of Education, 1987); Hirsch, *Cultural Literacy*; Diane Ravitch, "Education after the Culture Wars," *Daedalus* (Summer 2002), pp. 5–21.

43. Gill and others, *Rhetoric versus Reality*, pp. 128–37.

44. Howell and Peterson, with Wolf and Campbell, *The Education Gap*.

45. Boyd, Hare, and Nathan, *What Really Happened?* pp. 35–39.

46. Miron and Nelson, *What's Public about Charter Schools?* pp. 148–69.

47. Henry M. Levin and Patrick J. McEwan, *Cost-Effectiveness Analysis*, 2nd ed. (Thousand Oaks, Calif.: Sage Publications, 2000); Levin, "The Potential of For-Profit Schools for Educational Reform."

48. Patrick J. McEwan, "Comparing the Effectiveness of Public and Private Schools: A Review of Evidence and Interpretations," Occasional Paper 3 (National Center for the Study of Privatization in Education, Teachers College, Columbia University, 2000).

49. Clive Belfield and Henry M. Levin, "The Effects of Competition between Schools on Educational Outcomes: A Review for the United States," *Review of Educational Research,* vol. 72, no. 2 (2002), pp. 279–341.

50. Simeon P. Slovacek, Antony J. Kunnan, and Hae-Jin Kim, *California Charter Schools Serving Low SES Students: An Analysis of the Academic Performance Index* (Los Angeles: School of Education, California State University, 2002).

51. David Ragosa, *A Further Examination of Student Progress in Charter Schools Using the California API* (Los Angeles: Center for Research on Evaluation, Standards, and Student Testing, University of California, 2002).

52. Tom Loveless, *How Well Are American Students Learning?* (Brown Center on Educational Policy, Brookings, 2002); Miron and Nelson, *What's Public about Charter Schools?*

53. Gill and others, *Rhetoric versus Reality.*

54. Witte, *The Market Approach to Education;* Cecilia Elena Rouse, "Private School Vouchers and Student Achievement: An Evaluation of the Milwaukee Parental Choice Program," *Quarterly Journal of Economics,* vol. 113, no. 2 (May 1998), pp. 555–602; Jay Greene, Paul E. Peterson, and Jiangtao Du, "School Choice in Milwaukee: A Randomized Experiment," in Paul E. Peterson and Bryan C. Hassel, *Learning from School Choice* (Brookings, 1998), pp. 335–56.

55. Metcalf, *Evaluation of the Cleveland Scholarship Program;* Kim K. Metcalf and others, *Evaluation of the Cleveland Scholarship and Tutoring Program: Summary Report 1998–2001* (Bloomington: Indiana Center for Evaluation, Indiana University, 2003).

56. Patrick J. McEwan and Martin Carnoy, "The Effectiveness and Efficiency of Private Schools in Chile's Voucher System," *Educational Evaluation and Policy Analysis,* vol. 33, no. 3 (2000), pp. 213–39.

57. Howell and Peterson, *The Education Gap.*

58. Ibid.; Alan B. Krueger and Pei Zhu, *Another Look at the New York City School Voucher Experiment* (Industrial Relations Section, Princeton University, 2003).

59. Howell and Peterson, *The Education Gap.*

60. Krueger and Zhu, *Another Look at the New York City School Voucher Experiment.*

61. Levin and Driver, "Costs of an Educational Voucher System."

62. Patrick J. McEwan, "The Potential Impact of Large-Scale Voucher Programs," *Review of Educational Research,* vol. 70, no. 2 (2000), pp. 103–49.

63. Henry M Levin, "Educational Vouchers: Effectiveness, Choice, and Costs," *Journal of Policy Analysis and Management,* vol. 17 (1998), pp. 373–92.

64. Ron Zimmer and Eugenia Toma, "Peer Effects in Private and Public Schools across Countries," *Journal of Policy Analysis and Management,* vol. 19, no. 1 (2000), pp. 75–92; Eric Hanushek and others, "Does Peer Ability Affect Student Achievement?" Working Paper 8502 (Cambridge, Mass.: National Bureau of Economic Research, 2001).

65. Hamilton Lankford and James Wyckoff, "Why Are Schools Racially Segregated? Implications for School Choice Policies," in Janelle T. Scott, ed., *School Choice and Stu-*

dent Diversity: Examining the Evidence (Teachers College Press, forthcoming); Charles T. Clotfelter, "Private Schools, Segregation, and the Southern States," paper prepared for the Conference on the Resegregation of Southern Schools, University of North Carolina, Chapel Hill, August 30, 2002; Robert Fairlie, "Racial Segregation and the Private/Public School Choice," presented at the Conference on School Choice and Racial Diversity, National Center for the Study of Privatization in Education, Teachers College, Columbia University, May 22, 2000 (to be published in Janelle T. Scott, ed., *School Choice and Student Diversity: Examining the Evidence* [Teachers College Press, forthcoming]).

66. Jeffrey R. Henig, "Choice in Public Schools: An Analysis of Transfer Requests among Magnet Schools," *Social Science Quarterly,* vol. 71, no. 1 (1990).

67. Schneider and Buckley, "What Do Parents Want from Schools?"; Gregory R. Weiher and Kent L. Tedin, "Does Choice Lead to Racially Distinctive Schools? Charter Schools and Household Preferences," *Journal of Policy Analysis and Management,* vol. 212, no. 1 (2002), pp. 79–92; Carol Ascher and Nathalis Wamba, "Charter Schools: An Emerging Market for a New Model of Equity," presented at the Conference on School Choice and Racial Diversity, National Center for the Study of Privatization in Education, Teachers College, Columbia University, May 22, 2000 (to be published in Janelle T. Scott, ed., *School Choice and Student Diversity: Examining the Evidence* [Teachers College Press, forthcoming]).

68. Wells and Crain, "Controlled Choice and Racial Diversity"; Smrekar and Goldring, "Social Class Isolation and Racial Diversity in Magnet Schools."

69. Schneider and Buckley, "What Do Parents Want from Schools?"

70. Kenneth Godwin and others, "Comparing Tolerance in Public, Private, and Evangelical Schools" (Denton: Department of Political Science, North Texas State University, 2001).

71. Frank R. Kemerer, "The U.S. Supreme Court's Decision in the Cleveland Voucher Case: Where to from Here?" Occasional Paper 51 (National Center for the Study of Privatization in Education, Teachers College, 2002).

9

The American Kibbutz?
Managing the School's Family Role

NOEL EPSTEIN

More than thirty years ago, when he was a middle school principal in Philadelphia, Paul Vance was intrigued by Bruno Bettelheim's *The Children of the Dream,* a study of communal child rearing on an Israeli kibbutz and its implications for U.S. education. So Vance joined colleagues in discussions about whether some of the commune's methods might be applied to Philadelphia schools. "In those days," he recalls, "it was evident to some of us . . . that the schools were replacing the family as primary care provider for kids, particularly for poor kids."[1]

Today, as former superintendent of schools in Washington, D.C., and Montgomery County, Maryland, Vance is well aware of how America's school-as-family phenomenon has flourished. It is not only that educators provide children with before-school programs, breakfasts, lunches, after-school programs, after-school snacks, and sometimes dinners. It is not only the familiar school role of teaching the basics of sex. It is not only the growth of prekindergarten programs, the pressure for more public schools to begin taking children at age three or four, or that until recently elementary school students in one program occasionally slept overnight at school. It is also that educators have become responsible for keeping students off drugs, ensuring that they do not bring weapons to school, instilling ethical behavior through character education, curbing AIDS and other sexually transmitted diseases through instruction or condom distribution, battling drunk driving, preventing student suicides, fighting tobacco use, providing a refuge for homeless children, tackling child obesity, making sure students are inoculated and receive other health services, tending to children of teenage parents, and otherwise acting in loco parentis. Indeed, at one Washington high school he visited after taking that district's reins in mid-2000, Vance says, "They had 38 different projects" that were not directly related to or aligned with academic instruction, many of them addressing health and social concerns. "One was for the young women on saying no to sex—abstinence. One was for the young men. One was for the young mothers." Others were for "values education, drugs, alcohol, tobacco—you name it."[2]

In light of such developments, it is not unreasonable to ask if the American school's child-rearing role has indeed begun to resemble that of the kibbutz. This is not to suggest, of course, that our public schools will ever be similar to the kind of kibbutz that Bettelheim visited for his study in 1964, when commune children were raised together from birth, living and sleeping apart from parents in children's houses.[3] (Those collective sleeping arrangements have since disappeared from Israel, just as much else about the kibbutz movement has changed. The children's houses now are essentially day care centers, with infants typically sent there at four months old.)[4] The point is that our public schools, as David Tyack has observed, "have become major agencies of broad social welfare, not just academic institutions," and that this parental role of schools has been expanding significantly in recent years.[5] Many other public and private agencies, of course, tend to children and youth, but schools are where the most extensive set of family-like responsibilities have come to reside, a phenomenon that raises important questions:

—*How is today's movement similar to, or different from, its U.S. predecessors?* Early childhood care and education surely were not invented for today's working parents. Schools in early America enrolled children as young as two years old, relieving rural mothers who toiled on farms.[6] U.S. "infant schools" of the 1820s and 1830s, established to help working mothers and to teach morality to poor children, accepted toddlers as young as eighteen months old.[7] The day nurseries that spread during the Progressive

Era, running roughly from 1890 to World War I, similarly were designed for children of poor working women.[8] During World War II, when young mothers were needed to help turn out airplanes, ammunition, and other military goods, federally subsidized day care centers tended to about 600,000 of their children, some as young as a year and a half.[9] This, moreover, is to say nothing of the landmark school health and social programs of the Progressive Era that are the predecessors of many of today's efforts.

—*Where is today's movement headed?* Some critics see "noninstructional services not as a virtue, but as a diversion from the main task of schools," as Tyack has remarked, while "others would like to see still more school-linked health and social services."[10] Although near-term budget pressures may restrain the growth of these services, longer-term prospects appear more in their favor, for several reasons. First, health, social service, and related programs address the public's strongest concerns about schools, from drug use to gangs and much else. Second, while these programs still are needed mainly by the poor, many have spread to the wider population, creating larger constituencies. Third, students' personal needs and classroom achievement obviously are not antithetical. That hungry, frightened, depressed, sick, and otherwise hampered children cannot learn well has been stated by so many people, so many times, over so many eras that it has become part of American school lore.

The logical question, then, is not whether to shrink or expand such programs but which ones work poorly and might be cut (politics permitting) and which ones promise notable benefits. For example, a report by the U.S. General Accounting Office (GAO, now the Government Accountability Office) has raised doubts about the long-term effectiveness of the most widely used student substance-abuse program, which has largely been dropped by the school district that created it.[11] However, optometrists, for example, contend that millions of students suffer from undetected vision impairments that restrict their lives and their learning. Obviously, new texts or tests for reading, math, or science will be of little use to students with impaired vision. Will we carefully examine an issue like this and, if the evidence warrants, do something about it?

—*Who should be in charge?* A long-standing question of the school-as-family phenomenon has been how best to manage its various elements, a goal complicated by several factors. For one, programs are widely viewed as discrete entities with separate constituencies—one for school health and one for school meals, one for pregnancy prevention and one for violence prevention, one to battle substance abuse and one to fight obesity. For another, many agencies beyond the schools—health groups, community-based organizations, Head Start centers, social workers, law enforcement officials, and others—often are involved, making for difficult coordinating challenges. For a third, funding comes from many sources and, when it is public, is controlled by various legislative committees. At the federal level, for example, the Department of Education funds some initiatives, and the departments of Health and Human Services, Agriculture, or Justice support others.

Along with private foundations, states have been helping to fund and coordinate programs for several years. Those roles were strengthened, moreover, by the federal No Child Left Behind Act of 2001 (NCLB), at least for the after-school initiatives of NCLB's 21st Century Community Learning Centers program, whose power to distribute new grants was transferred to the states.[12] Perhaps the largest coordinating challenges, however, are at the local level, where needs and resources are often unique and decisions must be made on such questions as whether educators or other agencies should have the ultimate say over noninstructional services provided at schools. Specifically, the central question is whether mayors and county officials, whose authority extends across all agencies (as gubernatorial power does at the state level) should be in charge.

The Road Ahead: Satisfying Demand

The extent to which schools are acting in loco parentis will no doubt distress some Americans. That would be nothing new. Early advocates of sex education, for example, encountered such sentiments. As Jeffrey P. Moran notes, "Traditionalists were disturbed in general by what a Minnesota educator called 'the downward tendency of the home for throwing off its duties and the equally downward tendency of outside agencies to take from the home its privileges.' "[13] Similarly, some saw the introduction of school meals as government intrusion into private affairs. Michael W. Sedlak notes that during an intense 1946 debate in Congress over creating a permanent school lunch program, opponents assailed the idea as a step toward making children "wards of the state." If Washington were to feed students, said Republican senator Robert Taft of Ohio, "we might as well give every school child a pair of shoes."[14] Nonetheless, even if there are still lively debates about what should be included in (or omitted from) sex education or school lunches, such responsibilities now are widely accepted as school functions.

In modern times, the school as family has stirred occasional opposition from cultural conservatives. In 1995, for example, Eagle Forum founder Phyllis Schlafly assailed the trend, declaring:

> The public schools' new mission is to serve as a government nanny, i.e., to be a provider of round-the-clock, round-the-year, cradle-to-grave social welfare services of all kinds, including treatment and counseling for infant care, drug abuse, domestic violence, sex practices, medical care, and job placement. Americans did not vote for this radical change in mission. We didn't even get the chance to debate it.[15]

Such criticism, however, has been voiced only sporadically. More tellingly, it has done little to stem the growth of the schools' parental role. The question is why. Why does resistance to the school-as-family phenomenon appear to have waned? At bottom, the answer seems simple: most Americans want schools to provide these nonacademic services.

In part, this acceptance presumably occurs because the services involve many of the issues that most disturb the nation. Elites in the political, business, and education communities may worry chiefly about test scores, and that concern may still be driving U.S. education policy, as it has for several decades. But student achievement is not what has mainly been troubling the wider citizenry. According to Public Agenda, the public in 1999 ranked the top three problems facing public schools as lack of parental involvement, drug use, and undisciplined students. Inadequate academic standards came in seventh.[16] Similarly, that year's Gallup poll found far more concern about students' behavior than about academics. Among the biggest problems confronting their local schools, respondents said, were lack of discipline, violence and gangs, use of drugs, and crime and vandalism. Concern about academic standards and quality came in ninth.[17] By the 2003 Gallup poll, not a great deal had changed. Among the top five problems facing schools, the public included lack of discipline, overcrowding, and use of drugs. Concern about academic basics, standards, and quality ranked sixth.[18] It is not surprising, then, that there would be demand for programs designed to attack problems that most worry Americans.[19]

It is even less surprising in light of the fact that many of the problems cited are no longer the exclusive property of poor urban communities. Although the need clearly remains greatest there, broader constituencies have emerged for schools to take on roles formerly expected of families. This is commonly ascribed to today's large numbers of employed parents and to welfare reforms that have required single mothers to work. Among married couples with children six to seventeen years old, for example, both parents work in nearly 70 percent of the families, while 79 percent of single mothers with children of school age hold jobs.[20] Parental employment may be the largest single factor behind the growing constituencies for the school-as-family phenomenon, but it is not the sole one. Many forces are at work.

Student Shooting Rampages

School violence once was believed confined to disadvantaged youths in city slums, as popularly portrayed in the 1950s by Evan Hunter's *The Blackboard Jungle*. However, deadly big-city outbreaks of student violence peaked in 1993. What followed in the 1990s were shooting rampages by students in Arkansas and Oregon, Kentucky and Pennsylvania, Georgia and, most dramatically, Columbine High School in Littleton, Colorado. The nation was stunned, and not just by the seemingly indiscriminate nature of the tragedies and their numerous victims. It also was shocked that murder had come to Norman Rockwell families in schools in suburban and rural America. As a study by the Institute of Medicine and the National Research Council put it:

> Between 1992 and 2001, 35 incidents occurred in which students showed up at their school or at a school-sponsored event and started firing at their schoolmates and teachers. These incidents . . . left 53 dead and 144 injured. . . . In most of these new cases, communities that had previously thought of themselves as insulated from lethal youth violence discovered that they, too, were vulnerable.[21]

The shooting sprees were part of a broader pattern of school-related deaths that included such other violent acts as stabbings, beatings, hangings, and strangulation. From mid-1992 to mid-1999, according to the Bureau of Justice Statistics and the National Center for Education Statistics, "There were 358 school-associated violent deaths in the United States, including 255 deaths of school-aged children."[22]

As demand has grown for educators to do something about this carnage as well as about nonlethal student violence—in 2000, children, twelve to eighteen years of age, were victims of about 1.9 million crimes of violence or theft at school, including about 128,000 serious violent crimes such as rape, sexual assault, robbery, and aggravated assault—schools everywhere have taken a variety of steps.[23] For one example, most elementary schools now provide instruction on gun safety. For another, nearly 95 percent of elementary schools, almost 86 percent of middle and junior high schools, and more than 88 percent of high schools teach about anger management. For a third, more than 95 percent of elementary schools, 88 percent of middle and junior high schools, and almost 73 percent of high schools include instruction on bullying, and most middle and junior high schools impart knowledge about sexual assaults.[24] These and other steps are in addition to the virtually universal ban on weapons at school, the uniformed police or security guards at most high schools, and the routine checks of student lockers, desks, or bags at 45 percent of high schools.[25] In short, the overwhelming majority of schools now are responsible for violence prevention as well as for comforting students when classmates, teachers, or school administrators are killed.

Communicable Disease Epidemics

School health programs against infectious diseases have traveled well beyond the immigrant slum children who were their principal targets during the Progressive Era. Today schools far and wide, for example, seek to curb the deadly HIV/AIDS epidemic and other sexually transmitted diseases (STDs), and little wonder. We are experiencing what the Centers for Disease Control and Prevention (CDC) calls "hidden epidemics" in STDs, with 15 million people from all backgrounds and economic levels infected each year—and roughly a quarter of them, or about 3,750,000, in their teens.[26] There is nothing hidden, however, about AIDS. At last count, more than 4,000 U.S. teenagers were suffering from that tragic affliction, and far higher numbers were carrying the HIV virus that typically develops into AIDS over ten years.[27] Not surprisingly, then, more than 85 percent of high schools and more than 75 percent of middle and junior high schools now require instruction in HIV prevention, as do a majority of elementary schools.[28] More than 15 percent of local districts require schools to provide HIV testing and counseling.[29]

Feeding the Children

School meals are another example of an initiative begun for the poor that has spread widely. In the most recent turn of events, for example, Washington is testing whether all U.S. elementary school students should be eligible for free school breakfasts, regardless of their families' incomes. This is a far cry from when school meals were introduced in cities like Philadelphia, Boston, New York, and Chicago at the turn of the twentieth century, prompted in part by muckraking books about the suffering of the poor and their children. As with many other social reforms, public-spirited women took the lead in arranging for the free or low-cost lunches and breakfasts, often serving the meals themselves, before a number of school districts assumed the function.

During the Great Depression, various states and cities adopted school lunch measures to aid malnourished pupils, but what mainly made the meals commonplace were federal programs. The New Deal, for example, gave school-lunch-related jobs to a small army of women and contributed surplus farm commodities to schools, creating what was to become a lucrative market for food producers (in early 1941, the Works Progress Administration's school lunch program employed nearly 65,000 workers). The federal school milk program then began as test efforts in Chicago and New York in 1940. After World War II and the vigorous congressional debate, the lunch program was made permanent with enactment of the National School Lunch Act.[30] That was followed by federally funded breakfast programs for children who arrived early at school, after-school snacks for those remaining after classes, and dinners for students in a seven-state pilot project.[31]

All of these programs are still aimed mainly at the poor, but more privileged families also take advantage of them. Of 28 million students in the school lunch program in the 2002–03 school year, for example, fewer than half received free or reduced-price lunches, while 58 percent were from more affluent homes, buying "full price" meals. (Washington contributes twenty cents toward the cost of each full-paid lunch, twenty-two cents for full-paid breakfasts, and five cents for full-paid snacks.) Arriving early at schools for the School Breakfast Program (SBP) are about 7 million students, chiefly from needy families but, again, including students from more comfortable homes. Indeed, as one study notes, "Between 1997–1998 and 1998–1999, higher income children—that is, those not certified for free or reduced-price meals—accounted for two-thirds of the *growth* in SBP participation."[32]

Antihunger advocates have long been troubled by the relatively low participation of poor students in the school breakfast program. The Food Research Action Center (FRAC), for example, notes, "In the 2001–02 school year, almost 43 children received free or reduced-price school breakfast for every 100 who received free or reduced-price school lunch."[33] The advocates are convinced that this low rate is caused by a stigma attached to subsidized breakfasts and that providing free breakfasts to all students would raise participation by the needy and yield improvements in their dietary intake, attendance, behavior, and learning. The evidence to date, however, is

mixed. For example, an early study of universal free breakfasts at three elementary schools, in Philadelphia and Baltimore, reported positive results,
showing that "higher rates of participation in school breakfast programs are
associated in the short-term with improved student functioning on a
broad range of psychosocial and academic measures."[34] Similarly, an initial three-year study of a half dozen Minnesota elementary schools in a
state-sponsored, universal free breakfast program called "Fast Break to
Learning" was glowing. The program, it found, was warmly embraced by
teachers and parents and "appears to play a role in improving student achievement."[35] However, later findings from a much larger universe of Minnesota's
Fastbreak elementary schools—more than 400 of them—were not encouraging. As a University of Minnesota study issued in April 2003 stated:

> In instituting universal free breakfast programs, the assumption was that
> such programs would lead to improved student participation, which in turn
> would lead to improved academic outcomes such as higher achievement. . . .
> However, we found little evidence to support the conclusion that achieve-
> ment was improving more rapidly in Fastbreak schools than in other schools
> with similar demographic composition.[36]

More important, the three-year national pilot project that is providing
universal free breakfasts to elementary schools in six school districts also
yielded disappointing first-year results, finding neither nutritional nor academic benefits. Evidently, however, this was because few participating students had been skipping breakfast before the pilot program began. That
makes one wonder whether there were problems with the sample or with
advocates' beliefs about how many students go without breakfast in the
first place. This initial evaluation for the U.S. Department of Agriculture,
issued in October 2002, observed:

> Since most elementary school students in this study were consuming
> breakfast, the availability of free breakfast seems to have primarily shifted
> the source of breakfast from home to school. Given the low rate (less than
> 4 percent) of breakfast skipping, it is not surprising that the availability of
> universal-free school breakfast did not have a significant impact on mea-
> sures of dietary intake or school performance.[37]

Those discouraging results, however, have not dampened enthusiasm for
universal free breakfasts among advocates like FRAC, which notes that the
study showed, among other things, that the program was "popular with students, parents, and staff."[38] Pressures to provide free breakfasts for all
students, at least in elementary schools, should be expected to persist.

Enrolling the Very Young

As noted, U.S. schools have enrolled children as young as two since the early days of the republic, and for reasons that are familiar today. As Carl Kaestle has observed, "Parents who sent very young children to school seem to have done so through a desire to have them out from under foot as much as from eagerness to get them started on the three Rs early. . . . One can understand the desire of rural mothers with busy work schedules to be freed from the care of toddlers." He adds that among these "abecedarians," as the beginners were called, were some later prominent figures, including Horace Greeley, *New York Tribune* editor and presidential candidate, who began school when he was two.[39]

Preschool care and education expanded in the 1820s with the advent of infant schools, institutions imported from England. They had originated with the Welsh utopian socialist Robert Owen, who created such a school at his cotton mill in New Lanark, Scotland, intending his workers' young children to "be more influenced by the social pressures of a school environment than by their families."[40] He also promoted infant schools on U.S. shores, delivering speeches to Congress and building an infant school at an Indiana community that he purchased and developed.[41] The schools became popular for a brief period and not only with the downtrodden. While children from disadvantaged families were the central targets, more affluent women soon wanted their little ones in infant schools. Maris Vinovskis, for example, quotes the Infant School Society of the City of Boston as stating that while the infant school system there was begun for the poor, "the discovery has been made, that it is equally adapted to the rich. There is hardly a neighborhood which has not its private infant school." The care and education of the very young spread outside Boston. By 1839–40, infant schools and regular schools in Massachusetts enrolled an estimated 40 percent of the state's three-year-olds.[42]

The obvious question is why infant schools vanished. In part, Vinovskis and others answer this question with the tale of Amariah Brigham, an eminent physician who was to head two insane asylums, help found the American Psychiatric Society, and create and edit what is now its *Journal of Psychiatry*. In 1833 Brigham wrote an influential work arguing that developing young children's minds carried great peril, that in trying to "cultivate the intellectual faculties of children before they are 6 or 7 years of age, serious and lasting injury has been done to both the body and the mind."[43] In other words, Brigham thought that infant schools would likely lead to insanity. The argument had considerable effect. It contributed not only to the demise of infant schools but also to the shaping of the kindergarten movement and the virtual disappearance of three-year-olds and four-year-olds from public schools for more than a century.

That was not the only reason that infant schools disappeared. A growing domestic ethic, for example, generated increased pressures for young children to be raised at home. Such sentiments, however, did not halt the need to provide care for children of immigrant and other mothers who had to work outside the house. As a result, day nurseries for such children expanded from three in 1878 to an estimated 700 in 1916, "explicit responses to . . . the competing demands of maternal employment and child care for the children of poor, working women."[44]

It does not take much to see that various aspects of this history are being repeated today in the tangle of U.S. programs for early childhood care and learning, down to the contemporary debate over whether it is wise to give academic instruction to preschoolers. Nobody argues anymore, of course, that such teaching leads to deranged minds. But in the summer of 2001, for example, David Elkind, professor of child development at Tufts University, squared off on the question with Grover Whitehurst, U.S. assistant secretary of education for research and development. Elkind argued that children of three or four are too young for such instruction, that studies show that children "who have been enrolled in early childhood academic programs eventually lose whatever gains they made vis-à-vis control groups." He added that, in fact, no solid research proves which approach to early childhood learning is superior or inferior. Whitehurst agreed with that. Nonetheless, he made an inferential case for greater preschool emphasis on academics and particularly for teaching such preliteracy skills as letter identification.[45]

If the evidence on that issue is unsettled, federal policy at the moment is not. This is perhaps clearest in President George W. Bush's long-standing emphasis on academics for the more than 900,000 children in the Head Start program for the disadvantaged. Indeed, in the fall of 2003, amid much criticism, the Bush administration began implementing preliteracy and math tests for Head Start children under a new National Reporting System.[46]

History also is repeating itself in the tendency of early childhood initiatives to migrate to children from more comfortable families. While most of the 800,000-plus youngsters in public school prekindergarten programs are poor, disabled, or English language learners, for example, some states—Georgia, New York, Oklahoma, Louisiana, New Jersey, Connecticut, West Virginia—have adopted various versions of universal prekindergarten blueprints. Moreover, despite budget constraints, the extent and nature of the support for universal pre-K programs augurs well for their expansion in the years ahead. Among those supporting universal preschools in a variety of settings, for example, are the American business and financial establishments, as represented by the Committee for Economic Development. In its 2002 publication *Preschool for All: Investing in a Productive and Just Society,* the committee declared that it would be well worth the investment to make publicly funded pre-K programs available to all who want them. The executives estimated that a half-day, school-year version of such a program (as opposed to the full-day, year-round variety required by most employed parents) would cost "*at least* $25 billion to $35 billion."[47]

Not everyone, of course, looks kindly on proposals like that. In the summer of 2003, at an Education Commission of the States panel on "Universal vs. Targeted Prekindergarten," for instance, Krista Kafer, a senior policy analyst at the Heritage Foundation, argued for limiting preschool programs to the disadvantaged. She did not appear hopeful, however, that her view would prevail, stating that "the politicians are just going to grab it."[48] It should come as no surprise if they do, particularly by adding more universal pre-K programs to public school systems. A good number of politicians, after all, have been calling for universal preschool education for some time, as Vice President Al Gore did in the 2000 presidential campaign and as others are doing in their 2004 political campaigns. Support for public preschool programs, moreover, runs well beyond public figures, beyond the business and financial communities, beyond teachers unions and the 71.5 percent of mothers of three- to five-year-olds who work outside the home.[49] As the 2002 Gallup poll found, Americans broadly support the idea: 82 percent favor "making prekindergarten available as part of the public school system."[50]

When School Is Not in Session

If pre-K programs have been expanding, the increase has been modest compared with the school's task of tending to students who are dropped off early or stay late. According to a 2001 survey for the National Association of Elementary School Principals (NAESP), growth has been striking in after-school programs, which most often run until six o'clock in the evening. More than two-thirds of elementary school and middle school principals reported offering such programs—just three years after an informal NAESP survey found that only 22 percent of the principals were providing them. Nearly 60 percent of the programs were no more than five years old, the survey found, and nearly 30 percent were less than three years old.

Moreover, 27 percent of the principals reported that they had before-school programs as well.[51]

After-school programs come in varied forms and have equally varied origins, ranging from nineteenth-century boys' clubs and settlement houses to World War II extended-care programs in which educators tended to 100,000 children of school age of mothers working in the war effort. The main force behind the creation of after-school efforts was a desire to provide a safe haven for children on city streets. As Robert Halpern notes, "The first after-school programs were developed by individual men and women intent on rescuing children from the physical and moral hazards posed by growing up in the immigrant neighborhoods of major cities."[52] Today, with about 8 million "latchkey" children of five to fourteen years of age lacking adult supervision on a regular basis, similar concerns are still very much with us.[53] One law-enforcement group analysis notes, for example, that when school lets out, violent juvenile crime "suddenly triples," that murders, rapes, and robberies increase, as do the risks of juveniles becoming victims of crimes and car crashes (the leading cause of death for youths ten to twenty-four years old).[54] After-school programs, the study suggests, can reduce not only crime and violence but also student smoking, substance abuse, and teen pregnancies.[55]

Americans in general—and especially those with children in after-school programs—evidently hold similar views. According to a 2002 advocacy poll for the Afterschool Alliance, 95 percent of parents with children in after-school programs say that their offspring are "safer and less likely to be involved in juvenile crime" than nonparticipating children. The survey also found that 70 percent of voters favor a universal after-school approach—and that most (58 percent) want after-school programs to be at public schools, rather than at boys' or girls' clubs, YMCAs or YWCAs, churches or synagogues, 4-H clubs, or other community sites.[56]

That broad support helped prevent President Bush from cutting $400 million for fiscal 2004 from the $1 billion federal program for after-school drug prevention, counseling, tutoring, athletics, character education, and other efforts, particularly for disadvantaged students in poor-performing schools and their families. The funding for 21st Century Community Learning Centers,[57] which has grown rapidly from just $40 million in fiscal 1998, was saved despite a first-year evaluation that found the program had little effect on students' academic achievement.[58] It did not hurt that Arnold Schwarzenegger, a leading light of the after-school movement, vigorously defended the program (in 2002 he had won passage of California's Proposition 49 for universal after-school programs there). Making his case for universal after-school programs in prepared congressional testimony, Schwarzenneger stated, "As Columbine and other school shootings across the nation have shown us, troubled children come from all socio-economic backgrounds. Every public school that chooses should have the resources to offer their unsupervised students a safe, educationally enriching place to go after school."[59]

Exceptions That Bear Watching

All this is not intended to suggest that every aspect of the school-as-family phenomenon has spread broadly. Two important exceptions thus far—and both bear watching closely in the years ahead—are school-based health centers and what have variously been called community schools or full-service schools or settlement-houses-in-schools. Both of these movements have been expanding rapidly in recent years. The question is whether they will reach much beyond the disadvantaged communities that they usually serve today.

School-Based Health Centers

As concern grew in the 1980s and 1990s about infectious diseases, student depression and suicide (at last count, nearly 20 percent of high school students had seriously contemplated suicide), teen pregnancy (42 percent of sexually active students used no condom during their last sexual intercourse), uninsured children and other issues, so, too, did school-based health centers.[60] These clinics, which provide primary medical care, mental health counseling, and other services and usually are affiliated with hospitals or other health groups, climbed by about 650 percent in a dozen years, from an estimated 200 in 1990 to nearly 1,500 in 2002. The centers, moreover, are no longer confined chiefly to urban high schools, as they were when they began dotting the landscape in the 1970s. Nearly 40 percent now are in rural areas and suburbs, and most are in elementary schools (37 percent) and middle schools and junior high schools (18 percent).[61]

The growth of the health centers has been part of a wider return of medical treatment to schools. While some Progressive Era physicians had been in the forefront of school health reforms, doctors as a group soon afterward began blocking schools from providing medical treatment, as opposed to first aid, referrals, health education, and other limited services. This opposition did not begin to change until the 1970s, when federal laws—

from section 504 of the 1973 Rehabilitation Act through the current Individuals with Disabilities Education Act—required schools to provide medical and other assistance to disabled pupils. Other developments also helped expand the school's role in health care, including the emergence of affordable nurse practitioners who could diagnose and prescribe (and who staff many centers, along with doctors, mental health professionals, and others) and health coverage for disadvantaged children under Medicaid and the State Child Health Insurance Plan.[62]

The increase in school health clinics, however, generally has not extended to more comfortable communities. This is not because of opposition from traditionalists. As Julia Graham Lear, director of George Washington University's Center for Health and Health Care in Schools, remarks, "Despite a perception that school-based health centers are tracked and targeted by grassroots conservative groups, their opposition has been episodic, infrequent, and, primarily, local."[63] Rather, she worries about severe budget pressures on states, the leading funders of school health centers, ballooning federal deficits, and other problems—including that school health clinics have a much narrower political base than, say, after-school programs. "Although I don't have the numbers," she remarks, "there's little doubt that a significant part of the growth in after-school programs has been for children of middle-class and upper-class professionals," providing the "political support necessary to help after-school programs for poor kids grow." This has not been the case with health centers, "even though problems of mental health, drugs and the like are not class-bound."[64]

Her group released an advocacy poll in August 2003 seeking to show wide backing among parents of school-aged children for school-based health care. It found support on grounds of treating uninsured children, tending to students with chronic diseases like asthma, helping parents get care without missing work, and other benefits.[65] Nonetheless, while Julia Graham Lear can envision school-based health centers making some inroads into more comfortable communities in the future, "I don't think it will follow the universal access of after-school programs."[66]

"Community Schools"

The fullest expression of the schools' expanding role has been occurring in what are most often called "community schools." Generally open year-round (often including weekends and holidays) until well into the evenings, these schools collect under one roof—in various combinations—an array of community services, commonly managed by such outside partners as health agencies, social workers, community-based organizations, and others. They trace their roots to several sources—including Progressive Era settlement houses and Great Depression after-school efforts—and go by many names: Communities in Schools, Children's Aid Society Schools, Bridges to Success, Beacon Schools, and the West Philadelphia Improvement Corps, among others. In truth most are not schools but something closer to one-stop academic-medical care-mental health-home visits-drug education-homework help-pregnancy prevention-crisis intervention-tutoring-parenting class-violence reduction-adult education-and-anything-else-required centers. In other words, they are a way to reorganize many community services, using school facilities as hubs.

What is offered at the centers varies by community and is often designed to engage families in the school and, in the settlement house tradition, to provide education, housing, or other help for parents as well as children. For about half a dozen years, for example, a St. Louis program provided respite care for parents, with their young children staying overnight at school twice a month. "The idea," says Khatib Waheed, an architect of the program at Walbridge Elementary Community Education Center, "was to try to make sure kids would be safe when parents were out. There had been instances of kids left alone, of house fires, of kids who died. Second, parents could have an outlet, to reduce stress and the possibility of violence. . . . Some were foster parents, some grandparents, some young parents."

Waheed, the founding director of the multischool Caring Communities of St. Louis that originated at Walbridge, explains how the program worked: "The kids came at 6 on Friday and stayed until 8 the next morning and had breakfast. There were activities in the evening—storytelling, games, movies, arts, and crafts. Sleeping bags and cots were set up in the gym, but typically most of the kids stayed up the whole night. They were revved up. Some would go to bed and get up at 4 or 5 in morning. . . . There were usually about 75 kids a night. That was the maximum we could handle."

Why did the respite program end? Among other things, "in Missouri, as in other states, there were serious budget issues. Caring Communities was eliminated, and respite care went with it," says Khatib, who now is a senior fellow with the Center for the Study of Social Policy.[67]

If community schools often are unique, they also have much in common. For one, they make up a modest minority of U.S. schools. Estimates by Joy Dryfoos, whose writings have been influential in the growth of such schools, and Martin Blank, director of the Coalition for Community Schools, put community school ranks at 3,000 to 5,000, depending on how broadly the schools are defined.[68] There is no question that community schools have grown at a rapid rate from a tiny base in recent decades, but they still represent no more than 5 percent of U.S. public schools and have been confronting the same severe budget strains as other schools. Some, like Caring Communities schools in St. Louis, have been victims of cutbacks. Others are holding their own and will benefit from the defeat of cuts to federal programs like the 21st Century Community Learning Centers, from which they get substantial help. Still others, like Oregon's Schools Uniting Neighborhoods (SUN) program, are expanding. Spearheaded jointly by Multnomah County and Portland, SUN schools totaled nineteen in the 2002–03 school year. "We are going to 46 schools in January," Diana Hall of the county's Department of School and Community Partnerships said in September 2003. The city already had aligned twelve more schools with the SUN model, and an additional fifteen were to be added in January 2004.[69] The SUN program ultimately hopes to have more than one hundred such schools.[70]

Most community schools are for the disadvantaged. This is not to say such schools do not exist for more comfortable families. Some do. For example, the School of the 21st Century program states, "One of the unique strengths of the 21C model is that it does *not* target at-risk children"[71] This child care and family support program for elementary schools, employed in more than twenty states, was the brainchild of Edward Zigler, director of Yale University's Bush Center in Child Development and Social Policy, who also helped found the Head Start program. The 21C schools (called Family Resource Centers in Kentucky and Connecticut) add all-day child care, after-school and summer programs, home visits for new parents, and various other services to elementary school agendas. While 21C schools are financed in good part by state, local, federal, foundation, and corporate sources, their central child care efforts rely mainly on a sliding scale of parent fees, based on family income.

As noted by Zigler and Matia Finn-Stevenson, associate director of the Bush center and 21C director, 21C outlays are held down by the fact that rent, custodial services, utilities, insurance, and some administrative expenses are absorbed by school districts, as are costs for the time of coordinators, principals, or superintendents. This is a key advantage, they say, of linking child care with public schools.[72] Finn-Stevenson remarks that their schools would like to lower parent fees and increase staff pay but that these issues are complicated by "turf wars" with other child care providers when 21C schools are established. "The schools have to say that they won't charge any less than what others charge and won't pay staff more," she states.[73]

Poor families are, of course, subsidized, often through federal programs like Title I of the Elementary and Secondary Education Act and Head Start.

Indeed, "in 40 percent of the schools, they integrate Head Start and 21C, and you don't know who is paying and who is not," remarks Finn-Stevenson. The schools can be liberal in providing subsidies. "They tell me that a lot of times they don't charge parents who aren't eligible for subsidies but who still don't have the means to pay," Finn-Stevenson says.[74] Nonetheless, 21C schools remain the exception to the rule in reaching beyond the disadvantaged. Most community schools still target the poor, and it remains to be seen when they will develop sufficient support to expand much more widely.

How Far Should the Family Roles Extend?

Whether all public schools' family roles shrink or expand logically should depend on whether a program accomplishes its aims. That raises the question, however, of how to measure whether a program "works." The Bush administration judges mainly by academic effects, whether resulting from the universal free breakfast pilot, the 21st Century Community Learning Centers, or the entire No Child Left Behind Act. That view can be legitimately challenged when it comes to early childhood programs, as David Elkind has done. However, since advocates for the poor have claimed endlessly that health and social programs are needed if disadvantaged students are to learn well, they are in no position to complain when the programs are scrutinized for academic effects. The problems arise when academic questions become too dominant.

Take the 21st Century Community Learning Centers program. Like after-school programs historically, it was created chiefly to help keep millions of unsupervised children out of harm's way. A requirement that some academic activities be included was added in 1998. Yet the primary finding of the first-year evaluation was that the program had little effect on reading tests or grades, with less emphasis on other more troubling conclusions. The study found, for example, that the program "did not reduce the proportion of students in self-care" and "did not increase students' feeling of safety after school." It also showed that participants "were more likely to report that they had sold drugs 'some' or 'a lot' and somewhat more likely to report that they smoked marijuana 'some' or 'a lot' (although the incidence was low)."[75] Creating drug-free refuges and providing adult supervision and a safe environment for latchkey children were driving forces behind after-school programs. These and related issues—especially whether the programs cut juvenile crime and victimization, as law enforcement officials have suggested—should drive evaluations as well. Then policymakers can worry about whether students have received effective tutoring or homework help or other aspects of student achievement.

The need clearly is to support programs that work well on their own terms, alter those that do not, and explore any promising new approaches. If it were shown that school-based programs contributed significantly to the nation's twelve-year decline in teenage pregnancy rates, that would be a self-evident success, regardless of what happened to test scores. If schools provide not only lessons but meals, clothing, shots, and other services to more than 600,000 homeless children, as they do, that is a good in itself.[76] If school-based health centers reduce hospitalizations and school absences for students with asthma, as one study has found, that should be deemed a striking gain.[77] After all, asthma is childhood's leading chronic disease, with the 5 million students who suffer from it losing 14 million school days a year.[78] Health workers are responsible for students' health, not their academic learning, just as mental health programs are responsible for reducing student depression or suicide and after-school programs are supposed to cut juvenile crime and victimization. If they are not effective on those terms, those are the reasons for changing or cutting them, as would be the case if the services still were provided at outside agencies.

Unfortunately, some programs are so popular as to be immune to unfavorable news. The 21st Century Community Learning Centers' funding success in the face of a disheartening initial evaluation is just one example of this political reality. Some view Washington's Safe and Drug-Free Schools program as bulletproof. As Lawrence Sherman has remarked:

> No evidence shows that this half-billion-dollar-per-year program has made schools any safer or more drug-free. However, much of the money has been wasted on performing magicians, fishing trips, and school concerts—and on methods (such as counseling) that research shows to be ineffective. Both the Office of Management and Budget and the Congressional Budget Office have tried to kill this program. Yet both Republican and Democratic presidents have joined with opposition parties in Congress to keep the program alive.[79]

Other initiatives also seem impervious to negative analyses. The authors of a Secret Service report on school shootings cautioned that adding school video cameras, metal detectors and security officers, or developing shooting-response plans and programs on conflict resolution and legal education, "are not likely to be effective in preventing planned school-based attacks."[80] But such approaches are still commonplace. Similarly, the first large-scale study of student drug testing—which the U.S. Supreme Court in 2002 upheld as constitutional as a condition for participating in extracurricular activities[81] and for playing on school athletic teams—found that it does not deter student drug use.[82] It remains to be seen whether this conclusion will have any effect on school drug-testing policies or on claims by the White House Office of National Drug Control Policy. In a guide issued in August 2002, for example, that office contended that drug testing "has been shown to be extremely effective at reducing drug use in schools and businesses all over the country."[83]

Not all elements of popular strategies, however, are entirely immune to cuts or changes. Take the most popular substance-abuse prevention program, called Drug Abuse Resistance Education, or DARE, which was born in Los Angeles in the early 1980s and at last report was being used in about 80 percent of U.S. school districts. It consists of antidrug lessons taught by uniformed, DARE-trained police officers, with the largest efforts aimed at fifth and sixth graders, and it has been found more than once to be ineffective. The GAO, Congress's watchdog agency, reviewed six long-term evaluations of DARE elementary school programs and detected "no significant differences" in illicit drug use—or in attitudes toward or resistance to illicit drug use—between those who received DARE in the fifth and sixth grades and others.[84] Some school districts have cut or dropped DARE. Most notably, the elementary school DARE program in Los Angeles has shrunk to a handful of schools (about thirty DARE officers have returned to the streets), and the district is trying other approaches to discouraging student substance abuse.[85]

Just as important as cutting weak programs, however, is exploring new initiatives that might yield valuable benefits. Consider the issue of students across the nation with undiagnosed vision problems and whether these conditions make it difficult, if not impossible, for them to learn. In 1999, for example, 47 percent of about 1,000 students given comprehensive eye exams at three Los Angeles elementary schools were found to have impaired vision.[86] In 2001, Massachusetts optometrist Antonia Orfield, who had established a pilot vision clinic at Boston's Mather Elementary School, found that more than half of the 800 children tested failed one or more parts of a vision exam.[87] A modest number of the impairments detected were standard distance-vision problems that required eyeglasses. They were a reminder that some children still suffer from the kind of problem that afflicted Ben Carson, the noted pediatric neurosurgeon who had been the worst student in his fifth grade class until he received a pair of glasses and could see the blackboard.[88] Simple school eye chart exams can pick up that kind of problem, but they cannot detect the difficulties many other children have seeing close up, whether or not they have 20/20 eyesight. The charts cannot measure whether children suffer from poor teaming of the eyes (which can result in blurred or jumping images), whether they can track a line of print without losing their place, or whether they find it hard to focus for long on close-up images. Although few realize it, Orfield says, "Stress also interferes with focusing, and there is much more stress on kids than there used to be. So when a kid is under stress, it doesn't matter if he isn't far-sighted. He still might need reading glasses to focus on his work at school."[89]

While nobody has reliable numbers on how many pediatric vision disorders go undiagnosed, Prevent Blindness America puts the ranks of school-children with some form of vision impairment at more than 12 million.[90] Concern about the extent of the problem prompted one state, Kentucky, to require comprehensive eye exams by an optometrist or ophthalmologist before children enter kindergarten or preschool, an effort that began in mid-2000. In its first nine months of operation, according to a sampling of more than 5,000 children who were examined by optometrists, more than 18 percent were found to have eye and vision problems.[91]

In broad terms, comprehensive eye exams are something about which optometrists, who hold Doctor of Optometry (OD) degrees, and ophthalmologists, who have Doctor of Medicine (MD) pedigrees, can agree. Beyond that, however, they see the issue quite differently, so to speak. Optometrists view vision disorders as causing many student learning deficiencies and as treatable not just with glasses but also with eye exercises and other procedures that constitute what is known as vision therapy. Ophthalmologists generally reject such claims, pointing to the brain, not the eye and perception, as the principal source of learning disabilities. Thus Mary Louise Collins, a pediatric ophthalmologist in suburban Baltimore, says, "If you were to take a population of children in a school who never had vision screening, you would find some percentage with vision problems and another percentage who have reading or learning problems. I would argue that the two don't necessarily overlap."[92]

As Collins notes, arguments for vision therapy are filled with anecdotal evidence. Luci Baines Johnson, daughter of President Lyndon Baines Johnson, has recalled of her childhood, "No matter how hard I tried, I didn't succeed at school. . . . Tests said my eyesight was '20/20,' but my eyes weren't functioning together to help me read, write, learn or comprehend what I was seeing. Fortunately my parents found an optometrist who turned my life around. He discovered my visually related learning problem and provided me with the simple but effective vision exercises necessary to train my eyes to work as a team. My grades went from D's to B's to A's."[93]

One cannot, of course, base judgments or policies on anecdotes, as Collins states. In her own work, she says, "I can count two patients in whom vision therapy 'worked' in ten years of practice—cases in which parents, at least, said that their children went through vision training and their grades improved. That's two out of many cases in which patients have gone through vision therapy." She says that she worries about parents ending up with false hopes, sizable bills, and wasted time.[94]

Optometrists, though, do not simply rely on anecdotes. In a "longitudinal, single-masked, random sample study" conducted at a Baltimore elementary school, for example, Paul Harris found that a vision therapy program "made a significant difference in . . . math achievement on standardized testing, and in reading scores on standardized testing."[95] The American Optometry Association has, in fact, put out a compilation of studies on the value of vision therapy.[96] The American Academy of Ophthalmology, however, has its own papers suggesting that there is "no consistent scientific evidence" supporting vision therapy for learning disabilities.[97] "There has never been a randomized, controlled, clinical trial that satisfies both ophthalmologists and optometrists," Collins says.[98]

That is correct in the sense that there has never been a definitive study in this country that both groups accept. Such research clearly is needed, and it is encouraging to hear Collins add that "there may be a study coming along."[99] There has, however, been research, conducted in Israel and published in 1993 in a U.S. ophthalmologic journal, that was favorable to the optometrists' position and that received an ophthalmologist's praise.[100] Firmon E. Hardenbergh, chief of ophthalmology at the Harvard University Health Services at the time, said that the study supported orthoptics [eye exercises that are part of vision therapy] as "the first line of therapy" for children with reading disabilities or deficiencies who have "convergence insufficiency" [eye-teaming] problems.[101] In other words, the optometrists' approach was preferred to the special reading tutoring often recommended by ophthalmologists. Hardenbergh is an exception among ophthalmologists, as is the Harvard health service. Hardenbergh hired Orfield to apply vision therapy there one day a week with Harvard students and the children of Harvard faculty and staff. "He referred hundred of patients to me" over nine years, Orfield says, adding that the health service's current ophthalmologist, and some of its pediatricians, continue referring some patients for vision therapy.[102]

None of this, of course, settles the issue of whether comprehensive school eye exams would lead to therapies that can correct learning problems. It does suggest, though, that reasonable members of both professional groups might be able to work together on settling the matter for the sake of large numbers of affected children and their families.

Who Should Be in Charge?

Given the tangled web of issues, constituencies, funding sources, and public and private agencies involved in the schools' growing family role (and this limited analysis obviously cannot touch on them all), deciding who should be in charge is no easy matter. The standard education governance question is, of course, whether responsibility and accountability should reside mainly with federal, state, or local officials. But in this case there are other questions, particularly whether educators or others should be responsible for noninstructional services provided at school sites. Both questions seem to lead logically to the need for those with cross-agency responsibilities—mayors and county officials as well as governors—to have chief responsibility for these services.

I begin with the traditional level-of-government question, starting with Washington. The Bush administration, not surprisingly, has been pressing traditionalist approaches to various issues, from abstinence-only in sex education to drug testing in schools to academics in early childhood development. However, as noted, the No Child Left Behind Act transferred power over new after-school grants to the states, meaning, as the National Governors Association has observed, "The state role in ELOs [extra learning opportunities] is increasing dramatically."[103] While Washington might strive for greater coordination of its many programs that support noninstructional school services, it would be wise to follow its own after-school example in this area generally and let state and local preferences rule, avoiding one-size-fits-all strategies. The states, after all, have long been vital supporters of many aspects of the movement. Starting in the 1980s, as Joy Dryfoos notes, "New initiatives sprang up all over the country with state governments and state administrators using state grants to initiate school-based health and social services in various forms."[104] They know the territory a lot better, and local officials know it best of all, having long tailored school-based, noninstructional programs to unique local needs. That is where the main responsibility and accountability for such programs should reside.

This, however, raises the question of whether educators or others should be in charge of those programs locally. At present, it is done both ways. The NAESP survey of after-school initiatives, for example, found that the responding principals or one of their teachers directed nearly half of the five-day-a-week programs and that other directors hired by the school or district ran another 25 percent. Private providers were in charge in only 18 percent of the cases. Of the average ten-person after-school staff, moreover, five members were teachers.[105] This situation was generally consistent with the findings of the 21st Century Community Learning Centers evaluation's finding that a third of program coordinators and 60 percent of staff members were school-day teachers.[106] One aim of the federal program is for schools to develop close collaborations with community organizations, but the evaluation found that not much of that was happening. "The tensions and challenges of collaborating," it said, "were evident in some programs, where several school staff members considered the staff of other organizations as inexperienced in school settings and expressed concern about their lack of reliability." Some centers decided "that they could easily function with little to no involvement of outside organizations."[107]

Among the federally funded centers, however, are the more comprehensive, seven-day-a-week, open-until-10 p.m., year-round "community schools" in which outside agencies partner all the time with schools to bring in an array of services. In its fourth year, one SUN elementary school in Oregon, for example, housed about 130 before-school and after-school activities and classes.[108] It certainly can be tricky and time consuming at first to create such collaborations, as was the case for, among others, New York City's Beacon Schools, which had to overcome "battles over control, turf and ideology."[109] In the end, though, according to the Coalition for Community Schools, relocating community services at schools is a major benefit, not a burden. The group says that "community partnerships lessen, rather than increase, the demands made on school staff," that "Teachers in community schools teach. They are not expected to be social workers, mental health counselors and police officers."[110]

Not surprisingly, since community schools are mainly a way of reorganizing existing community services by centralizing them at school facilities, forces outside the school system often initiate the programs. For example, Beacon Schools, which grew out of a desire for a drug-free refuge after the school bell rings, were created and funded by the New York City Department of Youth and Community Development. The original impetus for Oregon's SUN Schools came from political leaders in Portland and Multnomah County, and at the top of their organization chart today is the Multnomah County Board of Commissioners. The election campaign of Mayor David Cicilline in Providence, Rhode Island, was based in part on bringing community schools to that city. Since mayors and county officials are the ones with local cross-agency authority, it is only logical for them to be pivotal to such efforts, just as it is only logical for governors to be the pivotal players at the state level. These are also the visible officials who can be held accountable for results, which is all too rarely the case with education. For example, if one asks Ted Sanders, president of the Education Commission of the States, how many people knew who he was when he was the chief state school officer in Nevada, Illinois, and Ohio, he will reply, "Do you mean other than my wife and children?"[111]

None of this is meant to underestimate the central importance of educators. Indeed, it obviously is vital that mayors and school systems work together on such projects, just as it is essential for both to develop strong relationships with other community partners. These connections are planned, for example, in Washington, D.C. In September 2003, Mayor Anthony Williams and then-school superintendent Paul Vance jointly announced a collaboration in which underperforming schools will provide space for health workers, mental health counselors, and other services provided by city agencies. "We have worked for quite a while to make this option a reality for these students," Vance said.[112] Indeed, in a way he has been working on it for more than thirty years, since first reading about communal child rearing on an Israeli kibbutz in Bruno Bettelheim's *The Children of the Dream*.

Notes

1. Interview with Paul Vance, June 12, 2002.

2. Ibid.

3. Bruno Bettelheim, *The Children of the Dream: Communal Child-Rearing and American Education* (Toronto: Collier-Macmillan Canada, 1969).

4. David Oppenheim, "Perspectives on Infant Mental Health from Israel: The Case of Changes in Collective Sleeping on the Kibbutz," *Infant Mental Health Journal*, vol. 19 (1998), pp. 76–86. For an account of the broader changes affecting the kibbutzim, see Daniel Gavron, *The Kibbutz: Awakening from Utopia* (Lanham, Md.: Rowman and Littlefield, 2000).

5. David B. Tyack, "Health and Social Services in Public Schools: Historical Perspectives," *Future of Children*, vol. 2, no. 1 (Spring 1992), p. 28.

6. Carl F. Kaestle, *Pillars of the Republic: Common Schools and American Society, 1780–1860* (Hill and Wang, 1983), pp. 15–16.

7. Emily D. Cahan, "Past Caring: A History of U.S. Preschool Care and Education for the Poor," 1820–1965 (New York: National Center for Children, January 1989) (www.nccp.org/pub_pch02.html [February 2004]); Barbara Beatty, *Preschool Education in America: The Culture of Young Children from the Colonial Era to the Present* (Yale University Press, 1995), p. 27.

8. Cahan, "Past Caring," p. 14.

9. Cahan, "Past Caring," pp. 27–30; Anna Smith, "The Drama Is Complex, the Cast of Characters Long: Federally Funded Day Care during World War II," abstract of paper submitted for 1999 annual meeting of Social Science History Association (www.ssha. org/gender/smith.html [February 2004]).

10. Tyack, "Health and Social Services in Public Schools," p. 28.

11. U.S. General Accounting Office (GAO), *Youth Illicit Drug Use Prevention: DARE Long-Term Evaluations and Federal Efforts to Identify Effective Programs,* GAO-03-172R, January 15, 2003; Stephanie Stassel, "Schools Seek a New Message to Steer Children Past Drugs: With the Police DARE Program Shrinking, L.A. Unified Is Testing Several Grade-School Curricula," *Los Angeles Times,* February 25, 2003, p. B3.

12. No Child Left Behind Act of 2001 (Public Law 107-110), Title IV, part B; for an explanation of the transferred powers and other aspects of the 21st Century Community Learning Centers program, see www.ed.gov/21stcclc/21qa98.html.

13. Jeffrey P. Moran, *Teaching Sex: The Shaping of Adolescence in the 20th Century* (Harvard University Press, 2000), p. 64.

14. Michael W. Sedlak, "School Delivery of Health and Social Services," in Diane Ravitch and Maris A. Vinovskis, eds., *Learning from the Past: What History Teaches Us about School Reform* (Johns Hopkins University Press, 1995), p. 78.

15. Phyllis Schlafly, "Schools Are Trying to Be a Nanny," *Schlafly Report,* vol. 29, no. 3 (October 1995) (www.eagleforum.org/psr/1995/psroct95.html [February 2004]).

16. Public Agenda, based on survey for National Public Radio, Henry J. Kaiser Family Foundation, and Harvard, June–July 1999 (www.publicagenda.org/issues/pcc_detail. cfm?issue_type=education&list=4 [February 2004]).

17. Lowell C. Rose and Alec M. Gallup, "The 31st Annual Phi Delta Kappa/Gallup Poll of the Public's Attitudes toward the Public Schools," *Phi Delta Kappan,* vol. 81 (September 1999), p. 47.

18. Lowell C. Rose and Alec M. Gallup, "The 35th Annual Phi Delta Kappa/Gallup Poll of the Public's Attitudes toward the Public Schools," *Phi Delta Kappan,* vol. 85 (September 2003), p. 50.

19. In fairness, it should be noted that the 2002 Gallup poll included a miscellaneous question about whether schools have taken on too many responsibilities, in academic and nonacademic areas, "beyond their original role." A majority (54 percent) said that they had. Moreover, 69 percent favored reducing nonacademic responsibilities, while 25 percent favored reductions in both academic and nonacademic areas. There were no indications, however, of what reductions the pollsters or respondents had in mind (Were they thinking of all extracurricular activities? Shop or home economics classes? Other activities?) or of what they considered the school's original role. See Lowell C. Rose and Alec M. Gallup, "The 34th Annual Phi Delta Kappa/Gallup Poll of the Public's Attitudes toward the Public Schools," *Phi Delta Kappan,* vol. 84 (September 2002), pp. 54–55.

20. Bureau of Labor Statistics, Current Population Survey, March 2002, table 4, "Families with Own Children: Employment Status of Parents by Age of Youngest Child and Family Type, 2000–2001, Annual Average."

21. Mark H. Moore and others, eds., *Deadly Lessons: Understanding Lethal School Violence* (National Academy Press, 2002), p. 1.

22. Jill F. DeVoe and others, *Indicators of School Crime and Safety 2002,* NCES 2003–009/NCJ 196753 (U.S. Departments of Education and Justice, 2002).

23. Ibid., p. 5. Observers commonly note that students are more likely to be victims of serious violent crimes away from school than at school, which is certainly true. That, however, does not reduce concerns of parents, educators, and others about keeping the school environment safe.

24. Centers for Disease Control and Prevention (CDC), "School Health Policies and Programs Study 2000" ("SHPPS 2000"), *Journal of School Health,* vol. 71, no. 7 (September 2001), table, "Percentage of Schools at Each Level Teaching Topics and Skills Related to Violence and Suicide Prevention in at Least One Required Class or Course, by Topic and Skill," p. 277.

25. Ibid., table, "Percentage of Districts and Schools at Each Level with Policies to Keep the Environment Safe, Secure, and Productive, by Type of Policy," p. 327.

26. CDC, *Tracking the Hidden Epidemics 2000: Trends in STDs in the United States* (Atlanta, 2000), p. 2.

27. National Institute of Allergies and Infectious Diseases, "HIV Infection in Adolescents: Overview" (National Institutes of Health, May 2003). As this compilation notes, the thirty-six states that conduct HIV case surveillance report that 42 percent of adolescent HIV victims are female.

28. CDC, "SHPPS 2000," table, "Percentage of State, Districts, and Schools Requiring Health Education Topics to Be Taught at Each School Level, by Topic," p. 268.

29. Ibid., table, "Percentage of States and Districts Requiring the Provision of Health and Prevention Services, by Type of Service," p. 295.

30. Gordon W. Gunderson, *The National School Lunch Program: Background and Development,* Food and Nutrition Service, U.S. Department of Agriculture 0-429-783 (Government Printing Office, 1971).

31. The school breakfast program began as a pilot project in 1966 and was made permanent in 1975. After-school snacks are provided under both the National School Lunch Program (snacks were added in 1998) and the Child and Adult Care Food Program (CACFP), which was created in 1966 for preschool children and the elderly in day care and later expanded to include after-school snacks for school-age children. The CACFP pilot project now also provides after-school dinners in Delaware, Illinois, Michigan, Missouri, New York, Oregon, and Pennsylvania.

32. Food Research and Action Center (FRAC), *School Breakfast Scorecard: 1999,* cited in Jonathan Jacobson and others, *Designs for Measuring How the School Breakfast Program Affects Learning,* abstract (Economic Research Service, Food and Nutrition Service, U.S. Department of Agriculture, Alexandria, Va., 2001), p. 1, emphasis in original (www.ers.usda.gov/publications/efan01013/efan01013.pdf [February 2004]).

33. FRAC, "School Breakfast Program" (www.frac.org/html/federal_food_ programs/programs/sbp.html [February 2004]).

34. J. Michael Murphy and others, "The Relationship of School Breakfast to Psychosocial and Academic Functioning: Cross-Sectional and Longitudinal Observations in

an Inner-City School Sample," *Archives of Pediatric and Adolescent Medicine,* vol. 152, no. 9 (September 1998), pp. 899–907.

35. Center for Applied Research and Educational Improvement, University of Minnesota, *School Breakfast Programs: Energizing the Classroom, A Summary of the Three-Year Study of the Universal School Breakfast Pilot Program in Minnesota Elementary Schools* (Minnesota Department of Children, Families and Learning, Minneapolis) (www.nal.usda.gov/fnic/schoolmeals/States/energize.pdf [February 2004]).

36. Kristin Peterson and others, *Fast Break to Learning School Breakfast Program: A Report of the Third-Year Results, 2001–2002* (Office of Educational Accountability, University of Minnesota, 2003), pp. 31–32 (www.education.umn.edu/oea/II/Reports/BreakfastStudy/ThirdYearReport/2003BreakfastStudy.pdf [February 2004]).

37. Lawrence S. Bernstein and others, *Evaluation of the School Breakfast Program Pilot Project: Summary of Findings from the First Year of Implementation,* Nutrition Assistance Program Report Series CN-02-SBP (Office of Analysis, Nutrition, and Evaluation, U.S. Department of Agriculture, Alexandria, Va., 2002), p. ii.

38. FRAC, "Evaluation of the Universal School Breakfast Program Pilot Project: Key Interim Report Findings from the First Year of Implementation" (www.frac.org/html/news/112702bfastSummary.htm [February 2004]).

39. Kaestle, *Pillars of the Republic,* pp. 15–16.

40. Beatty, *Preschool Education in America,* p. 17.

41. Ibid., p. 24.

42. Maris A. Vinovskis, "School Readiness and Early Childhood Education," in Diane Ravitch and Maris A. Vinovskis, eds., *Learning from the Past: What History Teaches Us about School Reform* (Johns Hopkins University Press, 1995), pp. 244–45.

43. Amariah Brigham, *Remarks on the Influence of Mental Cultivation and Mental Excitement upon Health,* 2nd ed. (Boston: Marsh, Capen and Lyon, 1833), p. 5.

44. Cahan, "Past Caring," pp. 13–14.

45. David Elkind, "Much Too Early," and Grover W. Whitehurst, "Much Too Late," the two together making up "Young Einstein," *Education Matters,* vol. 1 (Summer 2001), pp. 9–21.

46. Linda Jacobson, "Criticism over New Head Start Program Mounts," *Education Week,* January 14, 2004, p. 10.

47. Committee for Economic Development, *Preschool for All: Investing in a Productive and Just Society* (New York, 2002), p. 3. Emphasis in the original.

48. Krista Kafer, at ECS panel on *Universal vs. Targeted Prekindergarten,* Denver, July 14, 2003.

49. Elaine L. Chao, *Report on the American Workforce* (U.S. Department of Labor, 2001), table 6, "Labor Participation Rates of Women by Presence and Age of Children, March 1980–2000."

50. Rose and Gallup, *Phi Delta Kappan,* 2003, p. 55.

51. National Association of Elementary School Principals, "After-School Programs Aid Academic Success, Provide Safe Havens for Children: Number of Programs in U.S. More than Doubles during 1990s, Survey of Principals Suggests," press release (Alexandria, Va., September 24, 2001). For full survey, see Belden Russonello and Stewart, *Prin-*

cipals and After-School Programs: A Survey of PreK–8 Principals (August 2001). Both are available at www.naesp.org/afterschool/survey.htm.

52. Robert Halpern, "A Different Kind of Child Development Institution: The History of After-School Programs for Low-Income Children," *Teachers College Record,* vol. 104, no. 2 (March 2002), p. 182; Joy G. Dryfoos, "The Role of School in Children's Out-of-School Time," *Future of Children,* vol. 9, no. 2 (Fall 1999), p. 118.

53. National Institute on Out-of-School Time, "Making the Case: A Fact Sheet on Children and Youth in Out-of-School Time" (Center for Research on Women, Wellesley College, January 2003).

54. CDC, "Youth Risk Behavior Survey, Summary Results" (Atlanta, 2001).

55. Sanford A. Newman and others, *America's After-School Choice: The Prime Time for Juvenile Crime, or Youth Enrichment and Achievement* (Washington: Fight Crime: Invest in Kids, 2002), p. 3. For the leading causes of death among youths, see CDC, "Youth Risk Behavior Survey."

56. Afterschool Alliance, *American Voters: Afterschool Must Remain a Priority,* Poll Alert, Report 5 (Washington, November 2002); Lake, Snell, Perry & Associates and the Tarrance Group, *Nationwide Poll—Afterschool Alliance: Final Weighted Frequencies* (August 2002). Both are available at www.afterschoolalliance.org/poll_reports.cfm.

57. One of the idiosyncrasies of the school-as-family phenomenon—perhaps a reflection of the fact that it is still in the process of defining itself—is its difficulty with labels. Thus "after-school" programs frequently include before-school and summer programs as well. To cover all nonschool hours, some use "out-of-school time," as with Wellesley College's National Institute on Out-of-School Time, while the National Governors' Association prefers "extra learning opportunities," or ELOs. It will be noted that the main federal after-school effort (which does indeed cover before-school and summer programs as well) funds "centers," not schools. Further complicating matters are the multiple names—community schools, full-service schools, settlement-houses-in-schools—given to an important branch of the movement.

58. Mark Dynarski and others, *When Schools Stay Open Late: The National Evaluation of the 21st Century Community Learning Centers Program, First Year Findings* (U.S. Department of Education, 2003), p. xii.

59. Arnold Schwarzenegger, statement before a hearing of the Senate Labor, Health and Human Services Appropriations Subcommittee, May 13, 2003.

60. CDC, "Trends in the Prevalence of Suicide Ideation and Attempts" and "Trends in the Prevalence of Sexual Behavior," National Youth Risk Behavior Survey, Fact Sheets (Atlanta, 2002) (www.cdc.gov/nccdphp/dash/yrbs/pdf-factsheets/suicide.pdf [February 2004] and www.cdc.gov/nccdphp/dash/yrbs/pdf-factsheets/sex.pdf [February 2004]).

61. Center for Health and Health Care in Schools, *2002 State Survey of School-Based Health Centers Initiatives* (George Washington University, 2003); a press release, fact sheet, narrative, and other material from the survey are available at www.healthinschools.org/sbhcs/2002rpt.asp [February 2004]).

62. Julia Graham Lear, *Children's Health and Children's Schools: A Collaborative Approach to Strengthening Children's Well-Being,* in press.

63. Julia Graham Lear, "School-Based Health Centers: A Long Road to Travel," *Archives of Pediatrics and Adolescent Medicine*, vol. 157 (February 2003), pp. 118–19.

64. Interviews with Julia Graham Lear, June 30, 2002, and August 20, 2003.

65. Between 1999 and 2002, the number of uninsured children under age nineteen fell 2.6 percent, from 9.6 million to 7.8 million. See Genevieve M. Kenney, Jennifer M. Haley, and Alexandra Tebay, "Children's Insurance and Service Use Improve," *Snapshots of America's Families*, no. 1 (Washington: Urban Institute, July 31, 2003). See Lake Snell Perry and Associates, *Parents Speak Out: Health and Health Care in Schools* (Center for Health and Health Care in Schools, George Washington University, August 2003).

66. Julia Graham Lear interviews.

67. Telephone interview with Khatib Waheed, August 27, 2003.

68. Estimates provided in e-mail exchanges with Joy Dryfoos, August 19–20, 2003, and in telephone interview with Martin Blank, August 1, 2003; Dryfoos sees about 7,500 additional schools as having a "foot in the door to community schools, on the way but not there yet."

69. Telephone interview with Diana Hall, September 2, 2003.

70. SUN Initiative, *Schools Uniting Neighborhoods: Successful Collaboration in an Environment of Constant Change*, Report to the Annie E. Casey Foundation (Multnomah County, Ore., 2003), p. 19.

71. School of the 21st Century, "Frequently Asked Questions about 21C" (Yale University, 2002), p. 2 (www.yale.edu/bushcenter/21C/pdf/Frequently%20Asked%20Questions.pdf [February 2004]). Emphasis in original.

72. E. F. Zigler, M. Finn-Stevenson, "Funding Child Care and Public Education," *Future of Children*, vol. 6, no. 2 (Summer/Fall 1996), pp. 110–11.

73. Telephone interview with Matia Finn-Stevenson, August 28, 2003.

74. Ibid.

75. Dynarski and others, *When Schools Stay Open Late*, pp. xii–xiii.

76. Sam Dillon, "School Is Haven When Children Have No Home," *New York Times*, November 27, 2003, p. A1.

77. Mayris P. Webber and others, "Burden of Asthma in Inner-City Elementary Schoolchildren: Do School-Based Health Centers Make a Difference?" *Archives of Pediatrics and Adolescent Medicine*, vol. 157 (February 2003), pp. 125–29, abstract (http://archpedi.ama-assn.org/cgi/content/abstract/157/2/125 [February 2004]).

78. CDC, National Center for Environmental Health, *Asthma's Impact on Children and Adolescents* (www.cdc.gov/nceh/airpollution/asthma/children.htm [February 2004]).

79. Lawrence W. Sherman, "The Safe and Drug-Free Schools Program," in Diane Ravitch, ed., *Brookings Papers on Education Policy 2000* (Brookings 2000), p. 126.

80. Marisa Reddy and others, "Evaluating Risk for Targeted Violence in Schools: Comparing Risk Assessment, Threat Assessment, and Other Approaches," *Psychology in the Schools*, vol. 38, no. 2 (2001), pp. 157–72.

81. *Board of Education of Independent School District No. 92 of Pottawatomie County et al v. Earls*, 536 U.S. 822 (2002).

82. Ryoko Yamaguchi, Lloyd D. Johnston, and Patrick M. O'Malley, "Relationship between Student Illicit Drug Use and School Drug-Testing Policies," *Journal of School Health,* vol. 73, no. 4 (April 2003), pp. 159–65.

83. Office of National Drug Control Policy, *What You Need to Know about Drug Testing in Schools* (The White House, 2002), p. i (www.whitehousedrugpolicy.gov/pdf/drug_testing.pdf [February 2004]).

84. GAO, *Youth Illicit Drug Use Prevention,* p. 2.

85. Stassel, *Schools Seek a New Message to Steer Children Past Drugs.*

86. Cory Fisher, "Results of Eye Tests Alarm Educators: Half of Students Examined at Three L.A. Schools Had Vision Problem," *Los Angeles Times,* March 26, 1999, p. A3.

87. Antonia Orfield, "Vision Problems of Children in Poverty in an Urban School Clinic: Their Epidemic Numbers, Impact on Learning and Approaches to Remediation," *Journal of Optometric Vision Development,* vol. 32 (Fall 2001), pp. 114–41.

88. Ben Carson with Cecil Murphy, *Gifted Hands: The Ben Carson Story* (Grand Rapids, Mich.: Zondervan, 1990).

89. Telephone interview with Antonia Orfield, September 9, 2003.

90. Prevent Blindness America, "Help Give Children a Good Start to Learning: Send Them Off to School with Healthy Eyes," news release, August 2003 (www.preventblindness.org/news/releases/childrenseyes2003.htm [September 2003]).

91. Joel N. Zaba and others, "Vision Examinations for All Children Entering Public School—The New Kentucky Law," *Optometry,* vol. 74, no. 3 (March 3, 2003), pp. 149–58.

92. Telephone interview with Mary Louise Collins, July 29, 2003.

93. Message from Luci Baines Johnson, Honorary Chair, 1999 Children's Vision and Learning Campaign, American Foundation for Vision Awareness.

94. Collins interview.

95. Paul Harris, "Learning-Related Visual Problems in Baltimore City: A Long Term Program," *Journal of Optometric Vision Development,* vol. 33 (Summer 2002), pp. 75–115.

96. American Optometric Association, "The Efficacy of Optometric Vision Therapy" (Children's Vision Information Network, www.childrensvision.com/efficacy.htm [February 2004]).

97. American Academy of Ophthalmology, *Complementary Therapy Assessment: Vision Therapy for Learning Disabilities* (Complementary Therapy Task Force, Quality of Care Secretariat, September 1, 2001). This and other papers by the ophthalmologic academy were issued before the 2002 Baltimore study by Harris.

98. Collins interview.

99. Ibid.

100. D. Atzmon and others, "A Randomized Prospective Masked and Matched Comparative Study of Orthoptic Treatment versus Conventional Reading Tutoring Treatment for Reading Disabilities in 62 Children," *Binocular Vision and Muscle Surgery Quarterly,* vol. 8, no. 2 (Spring 1993), pp. 91–106, abstract (viewed at www.vision-therapy.com/vt_research_studies.htm [February 2004]).

101. Firmon E. Hardenbergh, letter dated March 29, 1991, and published together with D. Atzmon and others, abstract, *Binocular Vision and Muscle Surgery Quarterly,* vol. 8, no. 2 (Spring 1993) (viewed at www.vision-therapy.com/vt_research_studies.htm [February 2004]).

102. Orfield interview.

103. National Governors Association, *Extra Learning Opportunities: Vital Components of Student Achievement* (Center for Best Practices, March 25, 2002), p. 1.

104. Joy G. Dryfoos, *Full-Service Schools: A Revolution in Health and Social Services for Children, Youth, and Families* (San Francisco: Jossey-Bass, 1994), p. 179.

105. Belden Russonello and Stewart, *Principals and After-School Programs,* pp. 50, 60. It is worth noting that in addition to government funding, after-school programs generally have instituted fees or tuition, with half charging $25 or less a week and nearly 70 percent providing some form of subsidy for needy families. These fees or tuition were reported to be the main source of funding in wealthier schools. See p. 47 of *Principals and After-School Programs.*

106. Dynarski and others, *When Schools Stay Open Late,* p. 36.

107. Ibid., pp. 43–44.

108. SUN Initiative, *Schools Uniting Neighborhoods,* p. 21.

109. Deborah L. Cohen, "Live and Learn," *Education Week,* June 7, 1995, pp. 27–30.

110. Martin J. Blank, Atelia Melaville, and Bella P. Shah, *Making the Difference: Research and Practice in Community Schools* (Washington: Coalition for Community Schools, 2003), pp. 7–8.

111. Interview with Ted Sanders, April 18, 2001.

112. District of Columbia Public Schools, "DC Public Schools Superintendent Paul L. Vance and Mayor Anthony A. Williams Merge Their Visions to Create Transformation Schools as Neighborhood Places for Children and Families," news release (September 10, 2003).

Contributors

Larry Cuban is emeritus professor at Stanford University's School of Education as well as a former school superintendent and teacher.

Linda Darling-Hammond is Charles E. Ducommun Professor at Stanford University's School of Education and former executive director of the National Commission on Teaching and America's Future.

Noel Epstein is a former education editor of the *Washington Post*.

Susan H. Fuhrman, dean of the University of Pennsylvania's Graduate School of Education, is George and Diane Weiss Professor of Education there. She also chairs the Consortium for Policy Research in Education.

Paul T. Hill, a nonresident senior fellow of Brookings, is a research professor at the University of Washington's Daniel J. Evans School of Public Affairs and director of the Center on Reinventing Public Education.

Michael W. Kirst is a professor of education, business administration, and political science at Stanford University and a senior research investigator with the Consortium for Policy Research in Education.

Henry M. Levin is William Heard Kilpatrick Professor of Economics and Education at Teachers College, Columbia University, and director of the National Center for the Study of Privatization in Education.

James E. Ryan is a professor at the University of Virginia Law School and a former vice chairman of the American Bar Association's Committee on Public Schools.

Gary Sykes is a professor of educational administration and teacher education at Michigan State University's College of Education.

Index

ABOUT THE EDUCATION COMMISSION OF THE STATES

The Education Commission of the States is an interstate compact created in 1965 to improve public education by facilitating the exchange of information, ideas, and experiences among state policymakers and education leaders. As a nonprofit, non-partisan organization involving key leaders from all levels of the education system, ECS creates unique opportunities to build partnerships, share information and promote the development of policy based on available research and strategies. Forty-nine states, three territories, and the District of Columbia constitute the commission's current membership. Each member state or territory is represented by seven commissioners—the governor and six other individuals, typically legislators, chief state school officers, state and local school board members, superintendents, higher education officials and business leaders.